The Social Sciences and
New Testament
Interpretation

The Social Sciences and New Testament Interpretation

Edited by Richard L. Rohrbaugh

HENDRICKSON
PUBLISHERS

© 1996 by Hendrickson Publishers, Inc.
P. O. Box 3473
Peabody, Massachusetts 01961–3473
Printed in the United States of America

ISBN 1–56563–239–7

First Printing — November 1996

Figure 3.2, *Typology of Marriage Strategies in the Bible,* is adapted from
Bruce J. Malina, *The New Testament World: Insights from Cultural An-
thropology* (rev. ed., Louisville: Westminster/John Knox, 1993) 144.
Used with permission.

Figure 4.1, *Maps of Places, Persons, and Things,* is adapted from Jerome
H. Neyrey, ed., *The Social World of Luke–Acts: Models for Interpretation*
(Peabody, Mass.: Hendrickson, 1991) 278–80. Used with permission.

Chapter 4, pages 80–84, 91–95, is adapted from Jerome H. Neyrey,
ed., *The Social World of Luke–Acts: Models for Interpretation* (Peabody,
Mass.: Hendrickson, 1991) 282. Used with permission.

Chapter 5, pages 107–12, is adapted from Jerome H. Neyrey, ed., *The
Social World of Luke–Acts: Models for Interpretation* (Peabody, Mass.:
Hendrickson, 1991) 126–29. Used with permission.

Library of Congress Cataloging-in-Publication Data

The social sciences and New Testament interpretation   /   edited by
    Richard L. Rohrbaugh.
        Includes bibliographical references and indexes.
        ISBN 1–56563–239–7 (paper)
        1. Bible.   N.T.—Social scientific criticism.   2. Sociology, Biblical.
    I. Rohrbaugh, Richard L., 1936–   .
    BS2545.S55S62   1996
    225.6′7—dc20   96–41646
                                                               CIP

Table of Contents

Part III: Social Dynamics

     Jerome H. Neyrey

9 Millennialism   183
     Dennis C. Duling

10 Ancient Reading   206
      Lucretia B. Yaghjian

     Index of Modern Authors   231

     Index of Ancient Sources   235

Abbreviations

AB	Anchor Bible
ABD	*Anchor Bible Dictionary*
AJAH	*American Journal of Anthropological History*
AJS	*American Journal of Sociology*
ANF	Ante-Nicene Fathers
ARA	*Annual Review of Anthropology*
ASR	*American Sociological Review*
ATR	*Anglican Theological Review*
AUSS	*Andrews University Seminary Studies*
BA	*Biblical Archaeologist*
BAR	*Biblical Archaeology Review*
Bib	*Biblica*
BTB	*Biblical Theology Bulletin*
CBQ	*Catholic Biblical Quarterly*
CJ	*Classical Journal*
CRINT	Compendia rerum iudaicarum ad Novum Testamentum
EDCC	*Economic Development and Cultural Change*
EvQ	*Evangelical Quarterly*
GRBS	*Greek, Roman, and Byzantine Studies*
HR	*History of Religions*
HTR	*Harvard Theological Review*
IDB	*Interpreter's Dictionary of the Bible*
ILS	*Inscriptiones latinae selectae*
Int	*Interpretation*
JAAR	*Journal of the American Academy of Religion*
JBL	*Journal of Biblical Literature*
JJS	*Journal of Jewish Studies*
JRelS	*Journal of Religious Studies*
JRS	*Journal of Roman Studies*
JSNT	*Journal for the Study of the New Testament*
JSNTSup	JSNT Supplement Series
JTS	*Journal of Theological Studies*

KJV	King James (Authorized) Version
LCL	Loeb Classical Library
NRSV	New Revised Standard Version
NTS	*New Testament Studies*
OBT	Overtures to Biblical Theology
RSV	Revised Standard Version
SBLDS	SBL Dissertation Series
SBLSP	SBL Seminar Papers
SEÅ	*Svensk Exegetisk Årsbok*
TBT	*The Bible Today*
ZAW	*Zeitschrift für die alttestamentliche Wissenschaft*
ZPE	*Zeitschrift für Papyrologie und Epigraphik*

List of Figures

Introduction

Richard L. Rohrbaugh
Lewis and Clark College

Cross-cultural reading of the Bible is not a matter of choice. Since the Bible is a Mediterranean document written for Mediterranean readers, it presumes the cultural resources and worldview available to a reader socialized in the Mediterranean world. This means that for all non-Mediterraneans, including all Americans, reading the Bible is *always* an exercise in cross-cultural communication. It is only a question of doing it poorly or doing it well.

Although this fact may seem obvious, the full implications of it have yet to dawn on the vast majority of either modern scholars or ordinary readers of the Bible. Because we inevitably read this Mediterranean document through lenses shaped by our own culture, the potential for misunderstanding is both enormous and pervasive. Only with the advent of social-scientific criticism over the last decade, especially with its conscious use of Mediterranean ethnography, have the real implications of our Western, ethnocentric readings of the Bible begun to appear. (For a full discussion of the need for cross-cultural study of the Bible, including methods and results of social-scientific criticism, see Elliott 1993.)

1.0 The Bible in a Strange Land

Over a century ago, Friedrich Schleiermacher asserted that any theory of biblical interpretation must encompass *all* the conditions that affect the reading of a text. That judgment remains fundamentally sound. We must begin, therefore, with a plain fact we have rarely allowed ourselves to acknowledge: no biblical writer had modern Americans in mind when he wrote. The converse is likewise true: all too few Americans have ancient Palestinian peasants in mind when they read the Bible. As the psalmist (137:4) noted long ago, trying to sing the Lord's song in a strange land can be exceedingly difficult. Although our circumstances may be less traumatic than those of the psalmist, the Bible is now being subjected to conditions its authors not only did not anticipate, but probably could not have understood had they tried. Reading the Bible in this strange land to which it was never addressed can be difficult indeed.

What these comments bring into view is the long-understood problem that the Bible was conditioned by the time and place in which it was written. The variety of critical methods that have been developed over the last century for analyzing this conditioning have concentrated primarily on historical, linguistic, and, more recently, literary issues. All these methods are necessary and helpful; yet in spite of what they have taught us, it turns out they are not enough. Now social-science critics, working on the anthropology of the ancient Mediterranean world, have begun to realize the magnitude of the *social* distance between the NT and ourselves. A Mediterranean Bible and the Western world have less in common than we have heretofore perceived.

2.0 Developing Cross-Cultural Understanding

Understanding another culture is never easy. Not only does one have much new to learn, but also one frequently grows uneasy when one finally realizes that one's own familiar and much-loved culture is not the standard for all humanity. As anxiety over societal difference mounts, a profoundly unpleasant culture shock often sets in.

As experts in that phenomenon know, the deep disquietude of culture shock comes from the fact that one is cut off from things familiar. Loss of things we take for granted at home is especially upsetting. For example, something as simple as using the telephone in a foreign country can be a major frustration. Ordering a meal can be no less difficult. Not knowing which gestures are appropriate, what the normal patterns of conversation are, what values people hold, or how to carry out the commonplace tasks of everyday living can be profoundly disturbing. At such moments the unexpected sight of something familiar can bring a huge sigh of relief—as every American suffering from culture shock in a foreign country who has finally turned a corner and seen a pair of golden arches can readily testify.

Culturally sensitive reading of the Bible carries a similar risk. Many of the commonplace theological understandings of Western Christian belief and practice derive from our peculiar cultural adaptations of the Bible. They are familiar to us and therefore comfortable. For most of us they even seem fundamental to basic Christianity. Thus when Western Christians find themselves cut loose from these familiar cultural and theological moorings it is not surprising that they feel somewhat uneasy.

We must point out, then, that by immersing ourselves in strange Mediterranean readings of the Bible we risk theological culture shock. Old certitudes will threaten to disappear. Our comfort level is likely to go down. But as those who have learned to know another culture well can also testify, there is a richness in human experience that a single culture cannot monopolize. The rewards of seeing afresh, of seeing through the eyes of someone socialized in a culture far different from one's own, are thus substantial. It is the promise of that reward which makes the effort of learning to understand the Mediterranean culture of the Bible worthwhile.

3.0 The Problem of Social Distance

A few simple examples will serve to get us started thinking about the implications of saying that the Bible was not written for Western readers. First, we can safely say that few Westerners know anything about, much less believe in, the evil eye. We are unlikely to know anyone who possesses it or anyone who has suffered from it. Yet it was a nearly universal belief in the Mediterranean world of antiquity, just as it is in that region in the present day (Elliott 1988). Everyone in the Mediterranean area knows that people with the evil eye are dangerous and must be avoided. They all know possessors and victims personally. Amulets to ward off the evil eye are commonplace and understood by everyone. Yet when this phenomenon is talked about in the Bible, as it often is (Prov 23:6; 28:22; Deut 15:7–9; 28:54–57; Sir 14:3–10; 18:18; 31:12–13; 37:7–12; Tob 4:15–17; 4 Macc 1:16; 2:15; Matt 6:22–23; 20:1–15; Mark 7:22; Luke 11:33–36; Gal 3:1), we Westerners know neither how to interpret it nor even how to translate the terms for it.

For example, the NRSV translates Matt 6:22–23a as follows:

> The eye is the lamp of the body. So, if your eye is healthy, your whole body will be full of light; but if your eye is unhealthy, your whole body will be full of darkness.

Western commentary on these verses typically suggests that the problem being addressed is an eye that is not open to the clear light of God. For example, Eduard Schweizer argues that the passage is saying that a "simple" or generous eye "admits God's light into the entire body; an evil eye causes terrible darkness of heart" (1975:163). In the same way, W. F. Albright and C. S. Mann suggest that the basic idea is that just as the body is illuminated by the physical eye (as though that organ were a window), so the whole spirit of a person is either illuminated or in darkness through the spiritual eye (1971:81). The point seems to be that an unhealthy eye is bad for the one possessing it.

But in the Middle East, an evil eye is bad for the person being looked at. The ancient Middle Eastern belief was that light is literally generated in the heart and is transmitted out through the eye onto whatever objects are in one's gaze. Because heart and eye are closely bound together, the good or evil light that originates in the heart is always revealed by what comes forth from the eye. The eye thus reveals the character of a person. Good-hearted people possess good eyes and throw off good light; evil-hearted persons possess evil eyes and throw off evil light. Moreover, since this light actually falls on whatever a person looks at, it also brings into being what the heart producing it intends. In this way generous persons can look on others and do actual good, while envious persons can look on others and do real damage. A culturally sensitive translation would therefore read differently:

> The eye is the lamp of the body. So, if your heart is generous (ἁπλοῦς, *haplous*), your whole body will be full of light. But if your eye is evil (πονηρός, *ponēros*), your whole body will be full of darkness.

Our commentary on this passage would have to recognize that genuine fear of the evil eye was a constant concern to Jesus' hearers. They regularly practiced strategies to avoid being looked at by anyone possessing it (*m. ʾAbot* 2.12–13). They would have quickly recognized that Jesus was talking about light that originates in the heart, shines outward onto another, and could do them either good or evil with a mere glance. Jesus' comment therefore addresses a commonplace of everyday life for ancient Mediterranean people even though it requires considerable cross-cultural interpretation in order for readers in the modern West to understand it.

A few additional examples may be useful in clarifying how easily we project the commonplaces of our own culture back onto the NT. If studies of the age structure of populations in the preindustrial cities of the Roman period are correct, about one-third of those who survived the first year of life (hence not counted as victims of infant mortality) were dead by age 6. Nearly 60 percent of these survivors had died by age 16. By age 26, 75 percent were dead; and by age 46, 90 percent were gone. Less than 3 percent of the population made it to age 60 (Carney 1975:88).

Death rates were not evenly spread across all elements of the population but fell disproportionately on the lower-class populations of both city and village. A poor person born in the city of Rome in the year one had a life expectancy of only twenty years. Moreover, for most lower-class people who did make it to adulthood, health would have been atrocious. Studies by paleopathologists indicate that infectious disease and malnutrition were widespread. By age thirty the majority suffered from internal parasites, their teeth were rotted, their eyesight gone. Most had lived with the debilitating results of protein deficiency since childhood. Fifty percent of the hair combs found in archaeological excavations have lice eggs in them. Given poor housing, nonexistent sanitation, economically inaccessible medical care, and bad diet—one-fourth of a Palestinian peasant's 1,800 calories per day came from alcohol—one begins to revise the romanticized picture many twentieth-century Americans have of Jesus' audience. At 32 or 33 years of age, if indeed he lived that long, Jesus would have been older than perhaps 80 percent of his hearers, who would have been ridden with disease, malnourished, and looking at a decade or less of life expectancy. Since few poor people lived out their thirties, we may also have to revise our picture of Jesus. He was hardly one who died in the prime of life.

Add to this picture the fact that infant mortality rates often reached above 30 percent in peasant communities, and then reflect on Jesus' statement about allowing the little children to come to him for of such was the kingdom of God. Childhood in antiquity was a time of extreme vulnerability. Among the population, children suffered first from disease, first from malnutrition, first from poverty. Many never made it to puberty before their parents were sick or dead. In Luke's account (18:15–17) the children brought to Jesus are infants. They are probably being brought by frightened mothers seeking healing or protection for their babies, many of whom will likely die. Thus twentieth-century comment about imaginative and carefree, delightful and spontaneously joyful children cavorting at Jesus' knee simply does not make it. The story is about the vulnerable, the frightened, and the terror-stricken who make up the implausible kingdom of God.

Perhaps by now the point is clear: we tend to imagine the social realities of the twentieth century when confronted with the stories of the Bible. One more brief example might serve to underscore the culture shock we spoke of earlier. This particular example requires looking at one of the most familiar parts of the NT in a most unfamiliar way. Since culture shock is usually a reaction to the familiar becoming unfamiliar, perhaps this example will clarify some of the risks of entering the strange world of the Bible. But if it does, it may also suggest the hidden riches lurking in an overly familiar part of the story.

As Douglas Oakman's study of village life in ancient Palestine has shown, violence was a regular part of village experience (Oakman 1991:168). Fraud, robbery, forced imprisonment or labor, beatings, inheritance disputes, and forcible collection of rents were commonplace. Widows, aged parents without children or parents of abnormal children, the very young, the very old, those with diseases or deformities, and those without land—including artisans in tiny villages like Nazareth—were the most frequent victims. Moreover, one type of violence from which peasants suffered in especially large numbers was the loss of land through manipulated debt. Foreclosure on land became an epidemic. By late in the first century, nearly half the arable land in the entire region of Galilee had been accumulated in this way by just three families. In fact, the entire population of a whole village (Bene Hassan) had become indebted tenants of one of these absentee landlords.

Over against this environment Oakman's studies of the Lord's Prayer are stunning (Oakman 1985, 1987, 1991). He suggests that the petition that we be "forgiven our debts" (Matt 6:12) refers to the actual processes by which peasants lost their land to the urban creditors who systematically exploited the precarious economic conditions of Palestinian peasantry. Moreover, Oakman argues, the prayer's final petition (6:13), that we not be "put to the test"—usually translated with the hopelessly anachronistic idea of not being led into temptation—is the plaintive cry of a peasant that he not be hauled into a debt court in front of a corrupt judge (the Evil One) whose verdicts would give land expropriation the force of law.

When read this way, over against the social realities of first-century Mediterranean peasant life, the Lord's Prayer looks a bit different than it does in our familiar Western worship settings. The irony, however, is that our modern way of reading it, as familiar as it may be to us, is really a case of strangers singing the Lord's song in a foreign land. We have transposed it into the familiar chords of our own culture and thereby set it at considerable social distance from its original readers. Thinking about how Jesus' prayer might have read to Mediterranean peasants frightened by the potential loss of land and livelihood may cause us a bit of theological culture shock, but it may also teach us how authentically the prayer once spoke to the life experience of real people. There is rich meaning here that emerges only when we take the trouble to learn the social setting out of which the text originally came.

4.0 Using the Social Sciences in
New Testament Interpretation

Before reviewing the contributions made by the various authors of this book, we must describe or clarify several theoretical matters. The first is the notion that the Mediterranean world, the world of the NT, can be thought of as a discrete social sphere—what modern anthropologists have come to call a "diffusion sphere" or "culture-continent." This terminology simply means a region sharing a common set of cultural institutions that has persisted over a long period. The case for the Mediterranean as such a culture-continent has been argued elsewhere and cannot be repeated here, but the concept is important. (To review the details of the concept and the case for it, see Gilmore 1982, 1987; Pitt-Rivers 1963; Peristiany 1968; Malina and Rohrbaugh 1992.) It has been adopted by Mediterranean ethnographers and is used by a number of the contributors to this book. It is essential to the cross-cultural study of the Bible to recognize that Mediterranean society is the NT's original social location and therefore the ethnography of that region is critical to all that follows in this book.

Second, if we acknowledge the historical fact that the persons depicted in the Bible once lived in this Mediterranean culture-continent, it is plausible to argue that the circum-Mediterranean area today offers a compelling alternative to Western society as the cultural location in which to ground our reading of the Bible. An important qualification, however, is necessary: the ancient Mediterranean culture-continent and the modern Mediterranean culture-continent are not exact equivalents. In two thousand years things have changed. But two comments might be offered in this regard. The first is that given the persistence of many of the characteristics of culture-continents over long periods, the modern Mediterranean is far closer to the world of the Bible than North America has ever been. The societies of the present-day circum-Mediterranean area thus offer the closest living analog we possess to the value sets and social structures that characterized daily human interaction in the Bible. Our second comment, however, is that exactly how close the match of ancient and modern might really be can never be taken for granted. It must be tested anew in every case—something we can do by comparing models drawn from actual Mediterranean area studies with the social data and dynamics we can extract from biblical texts. Such comparisons are the stuff of which social-scientific criticism is made, yet the difficulties in comparing ancient and modern Mediterranean societies are never far from the surface. (For full discussion of these and other theoretical difficulties in the use of the social sciences in NT interpretation, see Rohrbaugh 1987; Elliott 1993:87–100.)

A third theoretical matter we wish to highlight has to do with the use of cross-cultural models, something every essay in this volume proposes. It is not difficult to state the reasons why models are necessary. Human perception is selective, limited, culture-bound, and prone to be unaware that it is any or all of the above. The cognitive maps with which we select, sort, and categorize complex data interpose themselves between events and our interpretation of them whether we like it or not. The only real question, therefore, may be whether we choose to raise this process to a conscious level and examine it or prefer to leave our biases alone. Cross-cultural models of various aspects of human society are the best tool we have to select, organize, and interpret our data in a culturally sensitive way. Yet this is not to say that model building is itself without severe limitations. Before jumping into an examination of the difficulties that using models presents, therefore, we may need to remind ourselves of the fundamental character of what we are doing.

It has become common to say that the social sciences are generalizing disciplines while history searches out the unique and particular. As Peter Burke has defined them, the social sciences inquire after "the study of human society, with the emphasis on generalising about its structure"; by contrast, history is "the study of human societies, with the emphasis on the differences between them and on the changes which have taken place in each one over time" (Burke 1980:13). Though the two disciplines are obviously complementary, dialogue between them has often been what Burke calls a "dialogue of the deaf." Moreover, since most NT scholars have been trained primarily as historians, they are usually more comfortable with the particular and unique rather than with generalizations about the societies we examine.

These generalizations are, of course, what cross-cultural models are designed to provide. They offer a systematic way of organizing information in order to focus attention on social structure and the dynamics of social process. As such, the task they undertake is something other than the one historians usually address. The two disciplines are designed to answer different sorts of questions, and therefore may complement each other so long as we appreciate each for what it is and do not ask either to do the service of the other.

Of paramount importance is the relationship between generic models and historical particularity. Models are intrinsically generalizations and as such they tend to blur the contours of particular historical situations. Models are abstractions rather than analogies. They select rather than replicate, choosing to eliminate some characteristics of a situation with the intent of isolating selected others in order to highlight them. Their tendency is thus to generalize in such a way that the historical details of social situations fall out of focus. As with reading a page through a magnifying glass, what one sees depends on the focal length of the glass one uses.

The problem may be illustrated by thinking about the use of a *generic* model of honor-shame as a guide to reading texts in the NT. That honor and shame were core values throughout the Mediterranean region in antiquity is beyond dispute. Honor was as much an issue in Egypt as it was in Rome (see ch. 1 below). Yet *what* was honorable could vary from region to region and even from village to village. It also varied considerably among elite and nonelite portions of the population. For example, peasants associated honor with self-sufficiency—being able to provide a subsistence living for one's family without recourse to others to meet basic needs. They saw accumulation of surplus as shameful thievery. City elites, however, associated honor with having large numbers of friends upon whom one could rely for favors and with accumulating sufficient surplus to be able to dole out favors in a display of wealth. Both groups understood the importance of honor, but each had its own perception of how honor should be obtained or preserved.

Thinking about change over time represents something of the same problem. New Testament scholars rightly worry about the appropriateness of applying mishnaic or talmudic law to the earlier situation at the time of Jesus. Later law does not necessarily illustrate conditions in his day. But at the generalizing level at which the social sciences work, such precise dating is less critical. For example, when the claim is made that honor functions as the core social value of Mediterranean societies, we are talking about a value set that has persisted over very long periods. Honor functioned as the core social value throughout the entire biblical period, the mishnaic and talmudic periods, and well beyond. In fact, the Mediterranean region is an honor-shame society yet today. That point can be demonstrated in both ancient texts and modern ethnographies. *What* is honorable may have changed from century to century, but the value placed on honor itself has not. Thus we cannot ignore the particularities of honor systems in various regions and at various points in history, even while we assert that the Mediterranean culture is an honor-shame culture now and has been for centuries.

The use of models is thus not without some dangers. They are not mere templates one can place over any and all data. They must be chosen to fit the level of abstraction appropriate to the data and adapted to regional and historical variations. If they are far from perfect, however, they remain essential. If we simply follow scholarly intuition and fail to examine the implicit, Western models we inevitably use to organize whatever data we encounter, we risk blindly imposing our modern perceptions and categories on every biblical text we read.

5.0 Our Purpose and Approach

The authors of this volume are primarily interested in interpreting biblical texts. We want to know what the NT means. Thus we have not been motivated to study cultural anthropology for the sake of doing historical ethnography. Nor do we use cross-cultural models for the purpose of doing social *history,* though that is an important task for others to undertake. Our concern is primarily to understand the NT by placing it more nearly in the social world out of which it came. While we readily acknowledge that our literary and historical training as NT scholars has stood us in good stead in the past, nonetheless we believe it is necessary to go further. We believe a new vantage point is needed that attempts to break out of the ethnocentric legacy of Western biblical scholarship.

All the authors in the volume are members of The Context Group, an association of scholars interested in using the social sciences as a heuristic aid in NT interpretation. We have worked together in collaborative style for more than a decade now, trying to learn what for all of us has been a new field: the anthropology of the Mediterranean world. We recognize that doing interdisciplinary work of this sort is an intellectual fad, but that does not make doing it well an easy task. We have taught and learned much with and from each other. We have likewise offered our work to both cultural anthropologists and our NT colleagues for criticism. Mistakes have been made along the way. But gradually there has emerged not only a method, social-scientific criticism (Elliott 1993), but also a body of literature in which fresh readings of the NT have demonstrated both the risks and the rewards of using cultural anthropology to aid our task.

One problem we have constantly encountered along the way is that the volume of literature in the field of cross-cultural studies is enormous. No one of us knows it all, nor could we hope to do so. When asked for reading recommendations by colleagues or students who want to engage in this kind of study, therefore, we have had to make constant recourse to each other for help. The idea gradually emerged of putting together bibliographical essays in the several areas of study in which group members had immersed themselves that would be helpful to both students and other scholars.

Since the thickets of anthropological theory are particularly dense, and often deeply controversial, we have learned that some sophistication in the use of this literature is required. The pitfalls are many. Having begun sorting our way through these, however, we believe our experience may be of benefit to others whose primary interest is the NT. In the essays that follow, therefore, each author has endeavored to walk through what is likely unfamiliar territory to most NT scholars with an eye to two important matters.

The first is the usefulness of the material for NT interpretation. Since interpretation is our ultimate interest, relevance for that task has been the basic criterion for what is included in our essays. We have tried to weed out less useful items in order to save time for those who do not intend to become anthropological specialists. Where appropriate, our second concern has been to warn the reader about critical debates and issues in each area and to choose literature that is well respected in the field of anthropology. Anyone perusing the *Annual Review of Anthropology* (a fine source for works in the field) knows how tangled the theoretical debates among anthropologists have recently become. Less theoretical agreement is the trend rather than the reverse. Caveats have thus been entered where necessary.

More traditional sources in NT studies are occasionally cited because of their importance or relevance, but we have tried to concentrate on the anthropological literature that students of the NT are less likely to have encountered in traditional work. While new items are constantly being added in each of the subject areas we have addressed, the resources included will remain the starting place for a considerable time. It is important to recognize that the essays herein are not the traditional bibliographical surveys that go out of date in a year or two. They are points of entry into a field not typically traversed by NT scholars.

Not all the topics currently being explored by social-science critics have been included. Limitations of space simply do not make that possible. The topics chosen, however, are all relevant to those interested in knowing what the NT means. Additional work can perhaps be made available in this format in the future. For the present, however, our intent is simply to provide students and colleagues a secure entry into each of the chosen subject areas that can be pursued further as interest motivates.

Finally, we note that each essay includes at least one example of using the respective anthropological models or studies in working with a biblical text. These examples are offered not only to demonstrate the relevance of cross-cultural studies, but also to illustrate the fresh ways they allow us to look at the NT. After all, the final reward for studying this material, indeed this foreign culture, is that at least in some small measure we can begin reading the NT as it might have been read by the Mediterranean persons for whom it was first intended.

6.0 Authors and Contents

Each of the ten chapters in this book takes on anthropological literature in an area of fundamental importance for NT interpretation. The first series of essays all deal with Mediterranean persons: their values, their sense of self, their symbolic universe, and their family patterns. Honor is the core social value of the Mediterranean world and plays a large role in the NT writings; the first chapter, by Halvor Moxnes, leads the reader into the basic resources on that topic. Closely related is the psychology of the Mediterranean person. Bruce Malina's essay thus provides the reader with a review of sources for the study of the first-century Mediterranean personality that moves far beyond the usual individualistic assumptions of the modern West. It will immediately raise questions about the patterns of social interaction in Mediterranean cultures.

Understanding these patterns of social interaction, what we may call social relations, is obviously basic to reading Mediterranean literature. In the Mediterranean world, social relations begin with the family. Thus K. C. Hanson's chapter on kinship offers a critical review of literature for the study of the family as the center of Mediterranean life. Finally, in every culture social relations are closely linked to the collective sense of what is clean and unclean, pure and impure. Cultural maps that specify the purity or impurity of times, places, persons, or things are all-important. Jerome Neyrey's essay on Mediterranean purity practices provides extensive resources in that area of study.

While the vast majority of the population in antiquity lived in the rural areas, cities often set the terms for the society at large. As a result, city and countryside were often in bitter conflict that worked to the detriment of the villages. The dynamics of this conflict play a large role in the stories of Jesus. Richard Rohrbaugh's essay on the literature about preindustrial cities and Douglas Oakman's on the ancient economy give the reader resources for understanding this conflict more fully. Filling out this second section of the volume is John Elliott's survey of the social-science literature on patronage. The ancient patronage system, controlled by the urban elite, was the means by which resources were mediated to those in dependent positions.

Finally, another series of chapters reviews resources for a variety of items that are prevalent in the pages of the NT. Jerome

Neyrey's survey of the extensive literature on meals and table fellowship complements the studies of city and economy. The chapter
by Dennis Duling reviews important cross-cultural studies of millennialism and apocalypticism. These studies are intended to aid the
reader in understanding these important NT phenomena as a response to social realities in the first century. Finally, Lucretia Yaghjian discusses consequences of the observation that picking up a
book and reading silently to oneself—the way most of us are able to
do with the Bible—is a relatively recent development in human
history. Literacy was not widespread in antiquity and most writing
was intended to be read aloud. Yaghjian's survey of the burgeoning
literature on ancient orality and literacy, and especially the cultural
meaning of reading, provides a foundation for thinking about how
the NT might have been read by its initial recipients and how it is
read today.

7.0 How to Use This Book

This is intended as a book to be used rather than simply read. It
offers students and scholars of the NT who are not familiar with
cultural anthropology or the use of cross-cultural models a set of
sifted resources with which to begin. In that respect it is meant to
save the reader the effort of that first difficult look through unfamiliar territory in order to find the basic materials.

While there is no particular order in which the chapters of this
book should be used, the topics in them not only cohere and complement each other but also reinforce each other. Reading about ancient
Mediterranean families will make little sense unless one understands
the fundamental values of honor and shame. Likewise, trying to
understand preindustrial cities without some knowledge of the ancient economy will be difficult. The sequence of the essays is thus
designed to lead the reader one step at a time into related areas of
inquiry. Yet we also recognize that one cannot learn everything or
everything at once. So it is probable that some topics will interest the
reader more than others and that not all readers will wish to dive in at
the same point. The book should lend itself to that variety of interests.

The essays are also intended as a companion piece to an earlier
collaborative effort of The Context Group: our series of studies on
Luke–Acts (Neyrey 1991). In that volume we used the materials
described in this book to develop social-science studies of particular
Lukan texts. For detailed examples of what can be done with the
literature we survey herein, therefore, the reader might want to
consult that volume.

Finally, each chapter in the book is designed to do several things. The first is to explain the topic and to illustrate its relevance to NT study. To this end textual examples are included in each chapter. The second—the heart of the matter—is to survey the anthropological literature with which most NT scholars and students are not familiar. A third is to flag the highest-priority sources among those surveyed, sometimes including the sequence in which items should be read. A fourth, where appropriate, is to warn the reader about some of the theoretical quagmires with which the field of anthropology is well supplied.

In sum, our intent is to provide a handbook for both students and colleagues wishing to know where to begin in a field in which they were not trained. If this book engenders interest in exploring the strange cultural world of the Bible in greater depth, so much the better. Learning to understand another culture is never easy, but neither is it impossible. The resources surveyed here are intended as a way to begin.

8.0 Works Cited

Albright, W. F., and C. S. Mann
    1971   *Matthew.* AB 26. Garden City, N.Y.: Doubleday.
Burke, Peter
    1980   *Sociology and History.* Controversies in Sociology 10. London: Allen and Unwin.
Carney, Thomas F.
    1975   *The Shape of the Past: Models and Antiquity.* Lawrence, Kans.: Coronado.
Elliott, John H.
    1988   "The Fear of the Leer: The Evil Eye from the Bible to Lil Abner." *Forum* 4:42–71.
    1993   *What Is Social-Scientific Criticism?* Guides to Biblical Scholarship, New Testament Series. Minneapolis: Augsburg Fortress.
Gilmore, David D.
    1982   "Anthropology of the Mediterranean Area." *ARA* 11:175–205.
_____ , ed.
    1987   *Honor and Shame and the Unity of the Mediterranean.* American Anthropological Association Special Publication 22. Washington, D.C.: American Anthropological Association.

Malina, Bruce J., and Richard L. Rohrbaugh
  1992   *Social Science Commentary on the Synoptic Gospels.*
          Minneapolis: Fortress.
Neyrey, Jerome H., ed.
  1991   *The Social World of Luke–Acts: Models for Interpretation.*
          Peabody, Mass.: Hendrickson.
Oakman, Douglas E.
  1985   "Jesus and Agrarian Palestine: The Factor of Debt."
          SBLSP 1985: 57–73.
  1987   "Forgive Us Our Debts: Agrarian Debt and the Original
          Meaning of the Lord's Prayer." Unpublished paper.
  1991   "The Countryside in Luke-Acts." In *The Social World of
          Luke–Acts: Models for Interpretation.* Ed. Jerome H.
          Neyrey. Pages 151–80. Peabody, Mass.: Hendrickson.
Peristiany, Jean G., ed.
  1968   *Contributions to Mediterranean Sociology.* Paris: Mouton.
Pitt-Rivers, Julian A., ed.
  1963   *Mediterranean Countrymen: Essays in the Social
          Anthropology of the Mediterranean.* Paris: Mouton.
Rohrbaugh, Richard L.
  1987   "Models and Muddles: Discussions of the Social Facets
          Seminar." *Forum* 3:23–33.
Schweizer, Eduard
  1975   *The Good News According to Matthew.* Trans. David E.
          Green. Atlanta: John Knox.

Part One:

Core Values

1

Honor and Shame

Halvor Moxnes
University of Oslo

1.0 Introduction

Notions about honor and shame exist in virtually all cultures. But in many Western societies these terms play a minor role in descriptions of prominent social values. Indeed, many people today regard "honor" as an old-fashioned word, while we normally associate the term "shame" with the most private aspects of our lives. In both past and present Mediterranean societies, however, honor and shame have played a dominant role in public life.

The goal of this essay on honor and shame is threefold. First, we need to get a deeper understanding of the content and function of honor-shame in the social life of Mediterranean societies. Second, in order to clarify the value of this kind of study we look briefly at examples of honor and shame in the NT. Finally, we highlight recent works in social anthropology that have focused attention on the concepts of honor and shame as a key to the social and cultural systems of the Mediterranean region.

Before beginning, however, we must put the matter in perspective. Since honor and shame have to do with people in *social* settings, they must always be studied within the larger religious, social, and economic context. One implication of this is that understanding honor and shame is crucial for almost every other topic in this volume. For example, it is possible to fathom the Mediterranean kinship system only if one understands that family honor is on the line in every public interaction. Similarly, one can understand the division between public and private space, a separation that often occurs along gender lines, only by recognizing the special roles of men and women in the honor system. Patronage, slavery, economic practices, purity rules, meal practices, and even the peculiar Mediterranean sense of identity that derives from group membership must likewise be understood in terms of honor and shame.

2.0 What Are Honor and Shame?

What then are the main characteristics of honor and shame as a system? Honor is fundamentally the *public* recognition of one's social standing. It comes in one of two ways. One's basic honor level, usually termed *ascribed* honor, is inherited from the family at birth. Each child takes on the general honor status that the family possesses in the eyes of the larger group, and therefore ascribed honor comes directly from family membership. It is not based on something the individual has done.

By contrast, honor conferred on the basis of virtuous deeds is called *acquired* honor. By its very nature acquired honor may be either gained or lost in the perpetual struggle for public recognition. Since the group is so important for the identity of a Mediterranean person (see ch. 2 below), it is critical to recognize that honor status comes primarily from *group* recognition. While honor may sometimes be an inner quality, the value of a person in his or her own eyes, it depends ultimately on recognition from significant others in society. It is a public matter. When someone's claim to honor is recognized by the group, honor is confirmed, and the result is a new social status. With this status follows the expectation of honorable behavior.

2.1 Challenge and Riposte

In Mediterranean societies interaction between people is always characterized by competition with others for recognition. Everyone must be constantly alert to defend individual or family honor. Such social interaction often takes the form of challenge and riposte, most often verbally, but also with symbolic gestures and even with the use of physical force.

Traditional societies have clear rules for this kind of exchange. A proper challenge can take place only among people who are equal or almost equal in honor. A challenge always implies recognition of the honor of the other person; hence to challenge an inferior or somebody without honor brings shame and humiliation to the challenger. Likewise, when a challenge is issued, it is accepted only if one considers the challenger worthy of respect. Accepting the challenge of an inferior is shameful. If a challenge is finally accepted, however, a response is necessary. A response in kind usually levels the playing field. One can also up the ante, of course, though not so much that the opponent cannot respond because then the exchange would end. Thus challenge and riposte are played like a game with a set of rules. Exchanges frequently lead to competition. The winner of such a competitive exchange has defended his honor, while the loser experiences shame and his standing in the community is damaged.

It is important to understand that the competitive spirit of challenge and riposte may rule many aspects of life. Not only feuds and wars might be involved, but also competitions in benefactions or in athletic games. When this competition becomes all pervasive, as it was in ancient Greece (as well as other Mediterranean societies in antiquity), we may speak of an "agonistic" culture.

2.2 Relation to Gender Separation

Honor and shame are also related to the typical Mediterranean separation between the sexes and generally reflect the power structures of ancient Mediterranean society. Since men held the dominant public position, a male perspective also dominated public discourse on honor and shame. (It is important to realize that until very recently this perspective has also influenced presentations by social anthropologists, most of whom are male. The viewpoint herein, based largely on the work of Julian Pitt-Rivers, represents this male perspective.) Since women occupied the private or domestic sphere, public discourse on honor gives little account of the way the honor and shame system functioned in the women's world.

Men competed among themselves to defend their masculinity. In order to maintain his honor a man had to be able to defend the chastity of women under his dominance and protection. If they lost their chastity it implied shame for the family as a whole. Women were therefore looked upon as potential sources of shame.

Shame also had a positive side in Mediterranean culture. In one sense it was understood as modesty, shyness, or deference. It was these virtues, often construed as feminine, that enabled a woman to preserve her chastity as well as her obedience to the male head of the family in which she was embedded. (The ancient Mediterranean world was not individualistic. The line between personal identity and family identity tended to disappear. Since family identity usually subsumed personal identity, anthropologists speak of such persons as "embedded" in the family.) In another sense, however, shame was simply social sensitivity and applied to both males and females.

To be "shameless" was to lack concern for one's honor and to be insensitive to the opinion of others.

While this description of honor and shame is rather simple and schematic, it suggests the basic way in which Mediterranean people use honor and shame to express their self-esteem or their esteem for others. As we shall see below, it is fundamental to any understanding of the world of the NT.

3.0 Honor and Shame in the New Testament

With the basic model of honor and shame in front of us, it is appropriate to ask about the importance of these values in the NT. By helping us to formulate the proper questions, the model can aid us in recognizing passages we might otherwise miss where honor and shame play an important role. It is important to ask, for example, What is considered honorable or shameful in the story world or the world of the author? Is honor based on social precedence (ascribed honor, status)? Or on merit (acquired honor), like good deeds? Is the relationship between men and women described in honor and shame categories or vocabulary? Who are the significant others in whose eyes characters seek recognition? A simple example will indicate how we can analyze biblical passages on the basis of these kind of questions.

3.1 Honor and Shame in Luke 13:10–17

Several Gospel narratives portray Jesus together with Pharisees, scribes, or other adversaries in conflicts that involve competition over honor. The immediate reason for the conflict is often an act of healing, assistance, or liberation by Jesus involving individuals or groups of people. The following story in Luke 13:10–17 (NRSV) offers a good example:

> A. Now he was teaching in one of the synagogues on the sabbath. And just then there appeared a woman with a spirit that had crippled her for eighteen years. She was bent over and was quite unable to stand up straight. When Jesus saw her, he called her over and said, "Woman, you are set free from your ailment." When he laid his hands on her, immediately she stood up straight and began praising God.

> B. But the leader of the synagogue, indignant because Jesus had cured on the sabbath, kept saying to the crowd, "There are six days on which work ought to be done; come on those days and be cured, and not on the sabbath day."

C. But the Lord answered him, "You hypocrites! Does not each of you on the sabbath untie his ox or his donkey from the manger, and lead it away to give it water? And ought not this woman, a daughter of Abraham whom Satan bound for eighteen long years, be set free from this bondage on the sabbath day?"

D. When he said this, all his opponents were put to shame; and all the entire crowd was rejoicing at all the wonderful things that he was doing.

In this narrative we see Jesus' skill at riposte. The modern reader understands Jesus' healing of the woman (A) primarily as an act of compassion. But for the culturally informed reader, Luke places the story in a different perspective. The healing took place in a synagogue on the sabbath (B). An opponent is introduced, the leader of the synagogue, who was in charge of the interpretation of the Torah and the rules surrounding the sabbath. He sees the healing not as an act of compassion but as the breaking of a law of which he was the guardian, and thus as a challenge to his authority. He therefore responds by attacking Jesus, albeit indirectly, through rebuking the people present. Jesus takes up the challenge (C) and gives a riposte that unmasks the synagogue leader's objection as hypocrisy. Furthermore, Jesus skillfully shows that he can turn Jewish law and tradition against a defender of the law. No wonder that the people present, who act as judges of the exchange (D), proclaim Jesus the winner. His adversaries are clearly "put to shame."

This is only one of many similar stories about Jesus; throughout the Synoptic Gospels challenge and riposte are a common form of interaction between Jesus and his opponents (cf. Matt 4:1–11; Mark 2:1–12; Luke 4:1–13; 10:25–37).

3.2 New Testament Terms for Honor and Shame

In looking beyond the example cited above, it is useful to know some of the terms used for honor and shame that occur in the NT. The semantic field is a broad one.

3.2.1 Words for "Honor"

Greek words for honor, esteem, recognition (τιμή, *timē;* τιμάω, *timaō*), are commonly used of humans (John 4:44; Rom 2:7, 10; 9:21; 12:10; 13:7; 1 Pet 1:7; 2:7, 17; 1 Cor 12:23–24). They can also be used in praise of God, most commonly together with other terms like δόξα, *doxa* (1 Tim 1:17; Rev 4:9).

Glory (δόξα, *doxa;* δοξάζω, *doxazō*) is mostly used of God and Jesus (John 5:44; 7:18; 8:50; Rev 4:10–11; 5:12–13; Rom 9:23; 1 Cor

2:8). It is especially common in doxologies (Rom 11:36; 16:27). But these terms are also used of human beings in the ordinary sense of honor, fame, and repute (John 5:44; 7:18; 8:50; 1 Thess 2:6).

3.2.2 Words for "Shame" and "Dishonor"

Words for shame (αἰσχρός, *aischros;* and words with the αἰσχ-, *aisch-*, stem) occur frequently (Luke 9:26; 1 Cor 1:26; 11:4–6; Rom 1:16; 5:5; 6:21; 9:33; 10:11). Words for dishonor (ἀτιμία, *atimia;* and words with the ἀτιμ-, *atim-*, stem) are also common (Mark 12:4; John 8:49; 1:Cor 4:10; 11:14; 12:23; Rom 1:24, 26; 9:21).

3.2.3 Words for Seeking Honor

Boasting was often seen as a demand for public recognition of honor. Words for "boast" and "boasting" (καύχημα, *kauchēma;* and terms with the καυχ-, *kauch-*, stem) are common in the NT (Rom 2:17, 23; 3:27; 4:2).

3.2.4 Other Relevant Terms and Situations

In addition to individual words and phrases, a much larger field of patterns and situations is relevant. Examples include honorable relationships such as "sons" or "daughters" (Matt 6:8–9; Luke 13:16), and acts of recognition (Mark 11:1–11; 14:3–9; John 6:14–15) or dishonoring (Mark 15:16–20). The model of honor and shame and the questions cited above will help those interested to identify similar patterns in other biblical passages and narratives. (For a more complete set of NT examples the reader should consult Malina and Rohrbaugh 1992; and Malina and Neyrey 1991.)

4.0 Mediterranean Studies of Honor and Shame: Development of a New Field

Among the scholars who first established Mediterranean studies in the 1960s, British social anthropologist Julian Pitt-Rivers holds a central position. Two of his theoretical essays are the most important sources for the typology of honor and shame, hence a good place to begin. The first is a concise introduction to honor and shame (1968). The second is a somewhat longer version with more examples from his field work in Andalusia (1966). Also at the introductory level, Pierre Bourdieu (1966) provides an excellent description of the typical patterns of challenge and riposte.

Pitt-Rivers (1961) gives a fascinating picture of life, social relations, and the values that governed social interaction in a Mediterranean village in Andalusia in Spain. This and the studies by Pitt-Rivers cited above represent a first attempt to identify and to describe concepts previously ignored by the social sciences. Later studies, some of them by Pitt-Rivers himself, have broadened the picture and made it more complex.

Several important essays by Pitt-Rivers and other scholars from this first period are also in the volume edited by Peristiany (1966). Here they develop the perspective on the Mediterranean, in the words of a later critic, "as united by a pervasive and relatively uniform value system based on complementary codes of honor and shame" (Gilmore 1987b:2).

The establishing of the Mediterranean as a special area of study was based on the hypothesis that this region has a certain cultural and social unity, and that honor and shame are central components of that common culture. Granted that honor and shame are widely used concepts in anthropology, do these concepts have such a special form in the Mediterranean area that they can be used to single out this region as a special unit? These questions were given thorough discussion in a more recent collection of essays edited by David Gilmore (1987c).

In his works Pitt-Rivers had raised an important question: What is the relation between honor as status and privilege on the one hand, and honor as moral virtue on the other hand (1966, 1968)? His critics argued that this tension between honor as social precedence and honor as virtue is found in many cultures, and therefore cannot be a primary basis for establishing the Mediterranean as a distinct area. Moreover, some of them (Herzfeld 1987; Gilmore 1987a) found that in many Mediterranean societies other moral values are as important as honor, especially hospitality and honesty. These values do not necessarily compete with honor; they may rather be correlative. Nonetheless, the discussion concerning what is distinctive about the Mediterranean region concluded that one aspect of honor and shame does indeed remain peculiar to the area: its strong association with sexual roles and gender division (§4.5).

The essays in Gilmore's book (1987c) show some of the changes that have taken place in anthropology since the first collection by Peristiany (1966). One important change is to speak of "culture" rather than "society." Culture here is understood as a "moral" or "symbolic" system that unites people into communities with shared values. Thus there is an important shift away from anthropology conceived of as an empirical science and toward cultural anthropology concerned with the shared "meaning" of a culture.

The most recent, major collection of essays, edited by Peristiany and Pitt-Rivers (1992), moves in a different direction on the issue of a specific Mediterranean notion of honor and shame. Here the collaborators in the 1966 volume, together with some younger colleagues and more female scholars, take a new look at the question of honor. Just as "honor and shame" was a new concept for anthropologists in the 1960s, so "grace" is now a new term in the anthropological vocabulary. It indicates the shift toward more concern with symbolism and religion noted above. The main focus is on grace as divine legitimation, particularly grace mediated through rituals that give legitimacy to honor in terms of social precedence and status. Typical examples are the coronations and funerary rites of kings in medieval France (Lafages 1992). The main contribution of this last collection is to place honor and shame in the center of the traditional religious language of "grace" and the divine.

These latest developments in the study of honor show that the predominantly American scholarship in Gilmore (1987c) has a different emphasis from the British and French scholarship in Peristiany and Pitt-Rivers (1992). The first is more oriented toward social-science theories, sexuality, and gender distinctions, whereas the second leans more strongly toward symbolism and historical studies of political institutions and religion. Between them these various approaches show both the diversity of honor and shame and related concepts, and also their central role in ordering society. In the following sections we look at some of the important issues that have been discussed in this emerging literature; we start with a question about method.

4.1 The Role of Honor and Shame in Social Conflicts

Since honor and shame were "discovered" as an important part of culture in the 1960s, much of later scholarly discussion has been concerned with the relationship between honor and shame and various social realities, including gender relations and other power relations like those between patron and client. For the question of honor and shame in the area of gender relations it has also made considerable difference that more female scholars have been involved, focusing attention on honor and shame from the perspective of women.

Honor and shame are not static, unchangeable concepts, but rather expressions of social and cultural relations. They change with various cultures and within cultures according to sex, class, status, geographic location, and so on. Being central elements in the culture of a society, honor and shame are likewise elements in the conflicts between various groups that seek to influence and dominate a society.

In two studies J. C. Baroja (1966, 1992) has argued that honor and shame on the one hand and society on the other are linked in a dialectical relationship. Different groups and classes struggle over the definition of honor and shame, and power struggles bring with them continual redefinition of these concepts. For example, Baroja shows how various concepts of honor competed in Spain from the fifteenth to the seventeenth century. First, honor was based on virtue, in accordance with ancient Christian and classical notions. The noble families, however, had a totally different concept based on conquest, competition, and revenge. Finally, with the rise of a merchant and industrialist class, still another concept of honor developed. It centered on "virtue and efficiency in work, utility, and the general good," and implied a criticism of the honor code represented by the old feudal aristocracy. The "older" concept of a competitive honor continued to dominate among the lower classes, however, in some cases surviving in a criminal lifestyle.

Baroja's work shows convincingly how concepts of honor are linked to social situations and conflicts between various groups competing over the right to be honorable. His work provides a wider perspective for the study of honor and shame among the early Christians. For example, we may see Paul's praise of the "shame of the cross" (1 Cor 1:18–31) as an attempt to give a new definition of what was honorable, in defiance of the dominant social elites of the Greco-Roman world and their values. Furthermore, when he criticized Christians for seeking honor (Rom 12), something that was commonly accepted by the Greco-Roman elite, we can assume he thereby wanted to create a separate identity for Christians as a group.

4.2 Honor and Shame in Family and Lineage

Most of us in the Western world live in societies built around individuals. Our social structures are based on voluntary participation rather than family ties. The result is a morality based on general, nondiscriminatory principles that are meant to apply equally to everyone. By contrast, studies of honor and shame in the Mediterranean region introduce us to societies that are based not on individuals but on *families, clans,* and *lineages.* The primary values are invested in these groups, not in abstract or "universal" principles. This creates a different system of values and morals from what we know in Western modern and postmodern societies.

Many of the contributors in Peristiany 1966 (Abou-Zeid, Baroja, Campbell, Bourdieu) focus on this central relation between honor-shame and *family.* They find that a collective honor, based on a system of patrilineal clans, is a common element in traditional communities all over the Mediterranean area, including Spain, Greece, Cyprus, Kayla in North Africa, and among bedouin in

Egypt. Later studies have shown the same to be true even in the modern Mediterranean state of Libya (Davis 1987). In fact, collective honor based on family and lineage is present well beyond the Mediterranean region, as shown in a recent comparison between Catalan and Japan (Asano-Tamanoi 1987).

A series of common elements can thus be described in societies in which honor and shame play an important role:

> A. The central unit of social organization is the family, and beyond that the lineage or clan. The consequences of this central position of the family are important. A person is never regarded as an isolated individual, but always as part of a group, responsible for the honor of the group and also protected by it. Because honor always derives from the group, an individual's conduct also reflects back on the group and its honor.

> B. Since honor is linked to the family and depends heavily on the way it defends its honor status, the result is an exclusive loyalty toward the family. Thus honor values are *exclusive* and *particularist* and stand in sharp contrast to the *universal* and *inclusive* values of the West. Moreover, the history of the family becomes all-important.

> C. The family plays a central role in the agonistic character of honor societies. Family honor is on the line in the continual game of challenge and riposte, be it expressed in words, gestures, acts, or ultimately in feuds between families.

> D. Even if a family or a clan presents a common front toward outsiders, there may be conflicts and tensions within the group. There can be large differences between individual lineages in terms of wealth and status, hence some members of a family can become clients of other more honorable and wealthy ones. There can be fierce competitions between them for the kind of public honors and positions that can become hereditary within the lineage.

Many of these elements are immediately relevant to the study of the NT. Notice, for instance, how important the genealogy of Jesus is to the claim to status made for him (Matt 1:1–17; Luke 3:23–38). Or again, observe how dominant the pattern of the family was in the social world of the first Christians. Even if many of the first followers experienced conflicts with their Christian communities, nonetheless these groups described themselves in terms of "surrogate family" or "fictive kinship" (Mark 3:31–35). The fundamental importance of kinship for identity and status also becomes visible in Paul's arguments. He denounces Jewish claims to a special status on the basis of their heritage (Rom 2:17, 24; 3:5), but he keeps to a Jewish kinship system when he describes the identity of believers: they are all descendants of Abraham (Rom 4; Gal 3).

4.3 Honor and Grace

"Grace" is a term that has largely gone unnoticed in anthropological studies until it was taken up in the collection of essays edited by Peristiany and Pitt-Rivers (1992). There Pitt-Rivers suggests that "grace" and "honor" both "deal with problems in the same field: the destiny of a man and his relations with other people and with God" (1992:240). The relationship of these concepts varies: sometimes they are similar, sometimes complementary, and sometimes even opposite. But even when they are contrary concepts, each contributes to the composition of the other. Grace points toward the divine, especially divine legitimation. Several recent studies therefore focus on rituals that give divine legitimacy to honor in terms of precedence and status, such as the coronation and funerary rites of kings in medieval France (Lafages 1992).

But another aspect of grace points more toward what we might speak of as the sacred side of honor, associated with honor not in an agonistic and competitive sense, but with honor as virtue. "Grace" is first of all a religious concept of great importance within Christianity, Judaism, and Islam. But outside the religious realm, derived notions like "gratuity" also play an important role. Grace "is inspired by the notion of something over and above what is due, economically, legally, or morally. It stands outside the system of reciprocal services" (Pitt-Rivers 1992:231).

When an agonistic competition for honor has been successful, the victor must "show qualities that are the contrary: generosity, moderation, forbearance." Thus one can see in Western civilization "two opposed—and ultimately complementary—registers: the first associated with honor, competition, triumph, the male sex, possession and the profane world, and the other with peace, amity, grace, purity, renunciation, the female sex, dispossession in favor of others, and the sacred" (Pitt-Rivers 1992:242). In other words, Pitt-Rivers sees "grace" as an inversion of competitive honor: one must renounce one's claim to honor as precedence to gain a privileged relationship to God.

We can see such an inversion at work in Paul's retelling of the Abraham story in Rom 4. In Jewish tradition, Abraham, the ancestor of the Jews, was an example of an honorable man who could rightly claim honor ("boast," 4:2). But not so, according to Paul: Abraham remained the honorable man and an example for all believers, but he could not claim any honor of his own making; his status rested solely on *grace* and on the promise of God (4:16).

This introduction of the notion of "grace" into social anthropology is potentially of great importance for the student of the NT. For one thing, together with studies of concepts like hospitality and honesty, it deepens our understanding of the broader context of honor and shame. We begin to see the noncompetitive aspects of honor and can show that not even in honorific societies is the agonistic side of honor all-pervasive. Moreover, it brings a religious dimension into the purview of social anthropology. In modern societies religion has become a separate sector of society, often reduced to a peripheral role, out of view for students of social structures. Thus they are often unable to recognize the religious dimensions of other cultures in which religion is deeply embedded. By focusing on a term like "grace" we become aware of how much religious beliefs have formed mentalities and social structures.

4.4 Masculinity and Honor

What is an honorable man? Our earlier definition emphasized competition among men in bravery, in their relations to women, and in defending their masculinity. Now Gilmore (1987b, c) has suggested that a contributing factor to this aggressive defense of male honor is an uncertainty among Mediterranean men about their masculine role. Gilmore also finds that there is a development as men age. The young man needs to prove himself to gain honor, often implying antagonistic behavior, whereas what is expected of the mature or older man is honesty and responsibility. The element of competition in sexual performance, so strong among young men, can among older men be transformed into fulfilling his obligations— sexual and economic—toward his wife and family.

Gilmore has further complemented the picture of an aggressive competition for honor with a description of more quiet and less agonistic values based on cooperation. For example, challenge and riposte can take the form of friendly exchange, from the informal and casual exchange of drinks at a bar, to more contractual exchanges of services, to a general solidarity between best friends. But of course even a presentation of gifts represents a challenge and requires a proper response in the form of reciprocity.

Examples like this show that a variety of ideals can be associated with the honorable man. It is important, therefore, not to assume that a single definition of honor can apply to every biblical text. It is necessary to ask how a given text or document describes or thinks of an honorable man and to identify various answers. Notice, for example, how some early Christian authors give different advice about honorable behavior to young men and those who are older (1 Tim 4:12–5:2; 3:1–7; Titus 2:2, 6; 1 Pet 5:1–5).

The importance of the honorific male role, and at the same time the uncertainties and ambiguities surrounding it, is also a theme in studies of classical antiquity. In a patriarchal society the defense of male honor is of paramount importance. In their studies of sexuality and gender roles in ancient Greece, therefore, D. M. Halperin (1990: 88–112) and J. J. Winkler (1990:45–70) show how the moral code for sexual relations between males is based on a concept of male honor. These studies are particularly useful to students of the Bible since they offer examples of applying anthropological perspectives to ancient texts.

Homosexual relations in the form of pederasty, that is, a relation between an adult man and a prepubescent male, were socially acceptable in ancient Greece; here too honor and shame play an important role. Such relations were carefully prescribed with moral rules that had to be followed. It was an absolute prerequisite that the young man should not accept money or gifts that put him in a class with paid prostitutes. If he did that he was judged according to the law of ἀτιμία (*atimia*, "shame") and lost important civic rights. The reason for this public shame was that by accepting payment a young man had acted in a way unacceptable for a free male and thus could not be trusted with the responsibility of public office. He had given up self-control and become like a slave.

Jewish and early Christian traditions were also very concerned to preserve the specific male role. In contrast to Greek culture, Jewish society strongly opposed sexual relations between men. It is commonly believed that there were specific religious reasons for this opposition; and the desire of the Jews, especially in the Diaspora, to distance themselves from the Greeks has often been emphasized. But we can notice how Paul in Rom 1 uses honor and shame language associated with concepts of masculine and feminine roles when he argues against same-sex relations.

4.5 Women's Perspective on Honor and Shame

To speak of women's perspective on honor and shame has at least two different aspects. First, it implies that in social anthropology, as in all other academic fields, female scholars have brought in new priorities as well as new methodological approaches. Some of these have questioned the models of honor and shame provided by male scholars (Wikan 1984). Second, it suggests the importance of attempts to bring into the description women's particular experiences and understandings of honor and shame. These attempts are not without considerable difficulties, however, since ancient literary material is almost exclusively written from a male perspective. Even today it is often difficult for anthropologists to gain access to the women's world.

Thus this area is in considerable flux, with old theories being questioned and new ones being tried out. While we are in no position to give definite answers, it is nonetheless important to point to some of the questions that are being discussed.

4.5.1 Gender Analysis of Honor

In line with what is happening in other fields, we find a gender analysis of honor and shame, distinguishing between male and female experiences. J. Schneider (1971) and C. Delaney (1987) try to explain the origin of the idea of female chastity or shame. Schneider suggests that the origin of the ideal of female chastity and the accompanying submission to men lies in competition for scarce resources among kinship groups. Delaney finds the basis for the strong link between men and honor on the one hand and between shame and women on the other in cosmological presuppositions. The three main religions that originated in the Middle East, Judaism, Christianity, and Islam, share the idea of a male creator god and corresponding ideas of a primary male role in procreation. Women have only a subsidiary role, which makes them inferior and creates a feeling of shame. Maureen J. Giovannini (1987) focuses on female chastity codes and finds that they belong to a common Mediterranean moral system. That chastity represents women's honor or "shame," in a positive sense, is generally accepted. Giovannini wants to bring this knowledge further by analyzing women's chastity in the context of community and class relations.

Such historical reconstructions remain conjectural, but they suggest how concepts of honor and shame are linked with power relations between men and women as well as with ideological traditions and cosmology. Paul's discussion in 1 Cor 11:1–16 is an excellent illustration of the often confusing interrelations between such varying traditions and ideologies.

4.5.2 Women's Experiences: Women's World of Modesty

The division between men's and women's space in the Mediterranean world often makes it difficult for male anthropologists to gain access to the women's world. Here works by women anthropologists play a special role. The best introduction is by Lila Abu-Lughod (1986), a study of a bedouin tribe in Egypt based on her own participation in the women's world. For the positive notion of female shame she uses the term "modesty," which sums up the female moral code of shyness, self-restraint, and a deferential attitude. The central Arabic term is *hashama*, which is translated by "a cluster of words including modesty, shame, and shyness. In its broadest sense, it means propriety" (1986:105).

Especially important is Abu-Lughod's unraveling of the links between female sexuality, modesty, and the hierarchical social structure. Threats to established bonds of sexuality are threats to the loyalties of this hierarchical society. Modesty codes (e.g., veiling) are a way of denying sexuality and showing acceptance of the existing social structure. For women the primary focus of this deferential attitude is their sexuality, but modesty is also important in other kinds of dependent relationships. For example, members of client tribes are expected to show modesty and deference toward their patrons.

4.6 Is There a Mediterranean Honor and Shame Culture?

The establishing of a special area of Mediterranean studies was strongly linked to the "discovery" of honor and shame as central cultural concepts in this region. It is therefore significant that Peristiany and Pitt-Rivers, in their last collection of essays (1992), dissociate themselves from the "Mediterranean" as a fixed cultural area, and include also western and northern Europe as belonging to "the same part of the world." The focus of several essays is on the relationship between honor as precedence and honor as virtue. That relationship is precisely the aspect of honor that is most universal and least specific for the Mediterranean. Likewise their emphasis on ritual and legitimation of honor on a state level presents a very generalized picture of honor.

So is there no distinct Mediterranean honor and shame culture after all? The growing interest in honor and shame has led to studies that have found that these or similar concepts play an important role also in many other societies. Systems of prestige and precedence are common to many social groups. So far Peristiany and Pitt-Rivers have a point when they find similarities between the Mediterranean and other parts of Europe.

But it is the specific relationship between an honor-and-shame code and male and female roles that has been put forward as distinctive for the Mediterranean region. It is this theory that is at the center of the current discussion. Both linguistically and conceptually, languages in the Mediterranean divide the world into masculine and feminine domains, and "male" and "female" thus become metaphors for other types of divisions. The outcome of this discussion appears to be that the one aspect that qualifies for a separate treatment of the Mediterranean region remains the relationship of honor and shame to masculinity, sexuality, and gender distinctions (Delaney 1987; Gilmore 1987b).

5.0 Honor and Shame in the Classical World

To use anthropological studies of present-day Mediterranean communities in the interpretation of texts from the first century CE presupposes a certain degree of cultural consistency within this region over the centuries. This working hypothesis has been supported by historical and classical studies in which the honor and shame paradigm has proved fruitful.

Most anthropological studies from the Mediterranean are of small communities, both sedentary village communities and migrating tribal groups. The insights derived from these studies are therefore mostly applicable to similar small-scale communities in earlier periods, for example, Homeric society in Greece and tribal and local communities in Palestine in first and second temple periods. These studies are especially helpful to examine honor and shame within the OT and within the village setting in Galilee in the Gospels. The focus here is on honor and shame in groups based on kinship.

5.1 Honor and Competition in the Greek World

There are many points of contact between anthropological studies of small communities with a simple organization and classical studies of Homeric society. In his seminal study, Moses Finley (1979) shows how Homeric society was characterized by a warrior's quest for honor. Moreover, this ideal was of fundamental importance to all later periods of Greek society and ethics.

The aristocratic value system of honor and shame, however, was also supplemented and balanced by "softer" values. A. W. H. Adkins (1960) traces the development of this tradition and its significant changes in later periods. He sees a conflict between society's ideal of the hero warrior who could not be restrained by ordinary men, and society's need for "quieter" values like justice and moderation (σωφροσύνη, sōphrosynē). As society became more complex in the Hellenistic period there was a need for less competitive and aggressive values and attitudes in order to keep the city-state (πόλις, polis) united.

But the urban Greek culture of the Hellenistic period preserved much of the emphasis that ancient Greece placed on honor. Central to the Hellenistic conception of the city was the notion that the community was a unit and that the individual was first and foremost a part of the community. Honor was closely linked to the upkeep of public life and the financing of common goods through benefactions toward the city.

Such benefactions were ideally made out of goodwill, but in reality there was pressure on citizens to contribute to the city expenses in exchange for honors of various kinds (e.g., public offices). This system became a source of competition for power and influence among the city elites. The system of city honors in exchange for benefactions is well known from ancient sources; the best collection of material on this topic is found in Frederick Danker (1982).

Close to the NT milieu, the Jewish historian Josephus is likewise an excellent source for understanding honor and shame. For example, at one point he gives a description of the wide range of honors that could be conferred. His example, an Athenian decree to honor the Jewish high priest Hyrcanus, also shows that foreigners could receive such honors:

> it has therefore now been decreed . . . to honour this man with a golden crown as the reward of merit fixed by law, and to set up his statue in bronze in the precincts of the temple of Demos and the Graces, and to announce the award of the crown in the theatre at the Dionysian festival when the new tragedies are performed, and at the Panathenean and Eleusinian festivals and at the gymnastic games; and that the magistrates shall take care that so long as he continues to maintain his goodwill toward us, everything which we can devise shall be done to show *honour and gratitude* to this man for his zeal and generosity (*Ant.* 14.152–54; LCL trans., emphasis added).

5.2 *Honor, Power, and Precedence in the Roman World*

With the expansion of the Roman Empire the period of the free Greek cities in the East came to an end. Although they kept many of the formalities of their former status, and though the elites in them continued with their competition for honor and power, power and honor came ultimately from outside these cities. It originated from Rome and the emperor. For their rule of the eastern provinces the emperors could draw on this Hellenistic system of competition. In a fascinating study of the emperor cult, S. R. F. Price (1984) has pointed out how this cult was an expression not just of political manipulation but also of deeply rooted religiosity and culture in the East. It continued an old eastern tradition of giving divine honors to the ruler and at the same time it was part of the Hellenistic system of competition. Leading citizens used benefactions to compete for priestly positions, and the major cities competed for the privilege to establish temples for the emperor cult.

Whereas Price placed the Roman imperial cult within the Hellenistic system of honor, in two studies of Roman history P. A. Brunt (1988, 1990) has brought forth the distinctive character of honor within Roman society. There was honor for *the nation*, the Roman people and the empire. It was related not only to individual psychology or to small-group relations, but to the relations between the Roman state and the surrounding states. It became part of official ideology, primarily for the aristocracy and the emperor. "Glory," "honor," and "prestige" (*gloria, laus, fama*; Cicero, *Pro Arch.* 12–32) were first and foremost obtained by war and by making other states subject to Rome's will. One may speak of "the glory of imperial expansion" as an official ideology (Brunt 1990:288–323).

Several NT writers view Roman power from the viewpoint of the eastern provinces and their Hellenistic honor societies. In Rom 13 Paul focuses on Roman rule as a system of honor and prestige as well as of military and political power to impose taxation. He addresses his readers as those who are subject to the authorities and urges them to show honor to and obey their superiors, above all the emperor.

The letter to the Romans reflects a period in which the Christians did not experience oppression from the authorities. The situation behind the book of Revelation, however, must have been very different. There we find none of Paul's positive view of the emperor. The conflict with Rome is couched in honor and shame terminology, but Rome is decried as a fallen Babylon covered with shame (Rev 18). All honor and glory are ascribed to God alone (Rev 19).

6.0 Conclusion

Studies of honor and shame introduce us to a world that is very different from that which most of us know from our daily lives. Those who live in Asia, Africa, or Latin America might recognize many aspects of the Mediterranean honor system, as might those with older relatives who have heard stories about traditional communities in Europe or even in North America. But for most of us in the modern West, this is new territory.

The starting point is to sufficiently immerse oneself in a culture by reading narrative descriptions of honor and shame societies. One might begin with the first collection edited by Peristiany (1966), and with Abu-Lughod (1986). A next step, engaging the reader in more theoretical discussion, is provided by Gilmore (1987c). The volume edited by Peristiany and Pitt-Rivers (1992) widens the perspectives from local communities to the realm of the state and its various institutions.

Historical studies by Finley, Adkins, Price, and Brunt show that the first Christian communities were part of a larger honor and shame culture in the Greco-Roman world of the first century. They shared many elements of this larger culture, for example, participation in the system of challenge and riposte and the division between women's and men's worlds. But like some other groups, such as the Stoic philosophical schools, they also protested against important aspects of the system. They especially opposed the emphasis on ambition that led to strife and conflict in the community. By using the literature we have reviewed the reader should be able to identify both the shared elements and also the possible conflicts between early Christianity and the social milieu in which it began.

The most exciting and useful part of a learning process is to learn by doing. The ultimate aim is to use some of this literature in studying biblical passages for oneself. But one can also get some help by looking at existing studies that introduce honor and shame perspectives into the interpretation of the NT. For beginners, three such studies are useful: Malina (1993:28–62); Malina and Rohrbaugh (1992); and Malina and Neyrey (1991:25–65).

7.0 Works Cited

Abu-Lughod, L.
  1986   *Veiled Sentiments: Honor and Poetry in a Bedouin Society.* Berkeley: University of California Press.
Abu-Zeid, A.
  1966   "Honour and Shame among the Bedouins of Egypt." In *Honour and Shame.* Ed. J. G. Peristiany. Pages 243–59. London: Weidenfeld and Nicholson.
Adkins, A. W. H.
  1960   *Merit and Responsibility.* Oxford: Clarendon.
Asano-Tamanoi, M.
  1987   "Shame, Family and State in Catalonia and Japan." In *Honor and Shame and the Unity of the Mediterranean.* Ed. D. D. Gilmore. Pages 104–20. American Anthropological Association Special Publication 22. Washington, D.C.: American Anthropological Association.
Baroja, J. C.
  1966   "Honour and Shame: A Historical Account of Several Conflicts." In *Honour and Shame.* Ed. J. G. Peristiany. Pages 79–137. London: Weidenfeld and Nicholson.
  1992   "Religion, World Views, Social Classes and Honor During the Sixteenth and Seventeenth Centuries in Spain." In *Honour and Grace in Anthropology.* Ed. J. G.

Peristiany and J. Pitt-Rivers. Pages 91–102. Cambridge: Cambridge University Press.

Bourdieu, Pierre
1966   "The Sentiment of Honour in Kabyle Society." In *Honour and Shame*. Ed. J. G. Peristiany. Pages 191–241. London: Weidenfeld and Nicholson.

Brunt, P. A.
1988   *The Fall of the Roman Republic*. Oxford: Clarendon.
1990   *Roman Imperial Themes*. Oxford: Clarendon.

Campbell, J. K.
1966   "Honour and the Devil." In *Honour and Shame*. Ed. J. G. Peristiany. Pages 139–70. London: Weidenfeld and Nicholson.

Danker, Frederick W.
1982   *Benefactor: Epigraphic Study of a Graeco-Roman and New Testament Semantic Field*. St. Louis: Clayton.

Davis, J.
1987   "Family and State in the Mediterranean." In *Honor and Shame and the Unity of the Mediterranean*. Ed. D. D. Gilmore. Pages 22–34. American Anthropological Association Special Publication 22. Washington, D.C.: American Anthropological Association.

Delaney, C.
1987   "Seeds of Honor, Fields of Shame." In *Honor and Shame and the Unity of the Mediterranean*. Ed. D. D. Gilmore. Pages 35–48. American Anthropological Association Special Publication 22. Washington, D.C.: American Anthropological Association.

Finley, Moses I.
1979   *The World of Odysseus*. 2d ed. New York: Penguin.

Gilmore, D. D.
1987a   "Honor, Honesty, Shame: Male Status in Contemporary Andalusia." In *Honor and Shame and the Unity of the Mediterranean*. Ed. D. D. Gilmore. Pages 90–103. American Anthropological Association Special Publication 22. Washington, D.C.: American Anthropological Association.
1987b   "Introduction: The Shame of Dishonor." In *Honor and Shame and the Unity of the Mediterranean*. Ed. D. D. Gilmore. Pages 2–21. American Anthropological Association Special Publication 22. Washington, D.C.: American Anthropological Association.
————— , ed.
1987c   *Honor and Shame and the Unity of the Mediterranean*. American Anthropological Association Special

Publication 22. Washington, D.C.: American Anthropological Association.

Giovannini, M. J.
1987   "Female Chastity Codes in the Circum-Mediterranean: Comparative Perspectives." In *Honor and Shame and the Unity of the Mediterranean.* Ed. D. D. Gilmore. Pages 61–74. American Anthropological Association Special Publication 22. Washington, D.C.: American Anthropological Association.

Halperin, D. M.
1990   *One Hundred Years of Homosexuality and Other Essays on Greek Love.* New York: Routledge.

Herzfeld, M.
1987   "As in Your Own House: Hospitality, Ethnography, and the Stereotype of Mediterranean Society." In *Honor and Shame and the Unity of the Mediterranean.* Ed. D. D. Gilmore. Pages 75–89. American Anthropological Association Special Publication 22. Washington, D.C.: American Anthropological Association.

Lafages, C.
1992   "Royalty and Ritual in the Middle Ages: Coronation and Funerary Rites in France." In *Honour and Grace in Anthropology.* Ed. J. G. Peristiany and J. Pitt-Rivers. Pages 19–49. Cambridge: Cambridge University Press.

Malina, B. J.
1993   *The New Testament World: Insights from Cultural Anthropology.* Atlanta: John Knox.

Malina, Bruce J., and Jerome H. Neyrey
1991   "Honor and Shame in Luke Acts: Pivotal Values of the Mediterranean World." In *The Social World of Luke–Acts.* Ed. J. H. Neyrey. Pages 25–65. Peabody, Mass.: Hendrickson.

Malina, Bruce J., and Richard L. Rohrbaugh
1992   *Social Science Commentary on the Synoptic Gospels.* Minneapolis: Fortress.

Peristiany, J. G., ed.
1966   *Honour and Shame: The Values of Mediterranean Society.* London: Weidenfeld and Nicholson.

Peristiany, J. G., and J. Pitt-Rivers, eds.
1992   *Honour and Grace in Anthropology.* Cambridge: Cambridge University Press.

Pitt-Rivers, J.
1961   *The People of the Sierra.* Chicago: University of Chicago Press.

1966   "Honour and Social Status." in *Honour and Shame.* Ed.
          J. G. Peristiany. Pages 19–77. London: Weidenfeld and
          Nicholson. Reprinted in J. Pitt-Rivers, *The Fate of
          Shechem or the Politics of Sex: Essays in the Anthropology
          of the Mediterranean.* Pages 1–47. Cambridge:
          Cambridge University Press, 1977.
1968   "Honor." *International Encyclopedia of the Social Sciences.*
          2d ed. 6:503–11. New York: Macmillan.
1971   *The People of the Sierra.* Chicago: University of Chicago
          Press.
1992   "Postscript: The Place of Grace in Anthropology." In
          Honour and Grace in Anthropology. Ed. J. G. Peristiany
          and J. Pitt-Rivers. Pages 215–46. Cambridge:
          Cambridge University Press.

Price, S. R. F.
1984   *Rituals and Power: The Roman Imperial Cult in Asia Minor.*
          Cambridge: Cambridge University Press.

Schneider, J.
1971   "Of Vigilance and Virgins: Honor and Shame and
          Access to Resources in Mediterranean Society."
          Ethnology 19:1–24.

Wikan, U.
1984   "Shame and Honor: A Contestable Pair." *Man*
          19:635–52.

Winkler, J. J.
1990   *The Constraints of Desire: The Anthropology of Sex and
          Gender in Ancient Greece.* New York: Routledge.

2

Understanding New Testament Persons

Bruce J. Malina
Creighton University

1.0 Introduction

Matthew (21:28–30, RSV) reports that Jesus once told the following story:

> What do you think? A man had two sons; and he went to the first and said, "Son, go and work in the vineyard today." And he answered, "I will not"; but afterward he repented and went. And he went to the second and said the same; and he answered, "I go, sir," but did not go.

How would an American reader respond to this story? Which of the two sons would an American think behaved like a "good" son? Which of the two behaved admirably? Which of the two ought the reader to imitate?

In answering these questions, notice how readers of the Bible react in much the same way as do TV viewers when they consider the scenes presented to them. TV viewers invariably bring to their viewing a knowledge of who people are and how people interact. Every U.S. TV watcher is well acquainted with the range of roles that people play, the rankings and statuses that people occupy, as well as the varied values that people pursue in U.S. society. They know how Americans think of themselves—as unique persons, as individualistic selves, as personalities with opinions and conscience and feelings of guilt and anxiety. Even purportedly alien people in sci-fi shows like *Star Trek* behave in line with these behavior patterns expected of all Americans.

Now just as persons bring scenarios of the self from U.S. experience to their TV viewing, they do the same with their Bible reading. The men and women who people the pages of the Bible are imagined to act like "religious" Americans—individuals in pursuit of "salvation" as they attempt to control other people and things so that they might find success. Modern Bible readers generally believe that the people around Jesus saw him as their personal Lord and Savior, their personal Redeemer. So long as Jesus' followers found that their consciences did not bother them, what they did was good. Good intentions were what counted. While only God gave success, God did help those who helped themselves, those who took the initiative, and those who persevered in their resolve.

But in fact none of these traits that Americans normally associate with persons and personhood is to be found among the people described in the Bible. We know this largely because people in the world today who live within social systems very similar to those of the first-century Mediterranean region do not for the most part have any of the traits characteristic of Americans. Yet if the ancient Mediterranean persons presented in the NT were so different, why should we bother to get to know them now?

Perhaps the first and primary reason is to be fair to the authors of the NT documents. At a minimum, fairness means to understand other persons on their own terms. And the only way to do that is to learn about how they perceived themselves in their own world. Fair reading requires a set of common scenarios shared by reader and writer. (See Malina 1991b for a full explanation of what reading entails, based on data derived from actual readers; also Malina 1991a offers a full explanation of what interpretation entails; finally, Elliott 1993 gives an excellent overview of the whole enterprise.) All too many biblical scholars, however, professional and nonprofessional alike, are selectively inattentive to the fact that reading is the first step to making contact with those who act in biblical scenarios. What is required is that one be a considerate reader. And considerate reading requires the reader to imagine what sort of persons are being presented in biblical documents. A considerate assessment of what people are up to when we see them act demands that we understand a people's social system that endows their activity with meaning.

How can one get to know and understand the social system(s) of those Mediterranean persons one reads about in the NT? Perhaps the most important step to knowing and understanding another person is to keep oneself out of the picture. To keep Americans out of our imaginary picture of ancient Mediterraneans, a most useful tool is comparison. Fully conscious of what Americans are like, we can be sure of one thing: Mediterraneans were not like that. As in the study of any alien society, the first basic requirement is a reflexive awareness of one's own society (for what Americans are like, see Stewart and Bennett 1991; and the fundamental work of Williams 1970; Augsburger 1986 offers many excellent models for such a comparative exercise). With knowledge of the structures and values of American society in tow, one can move on to ancient Mediterranean society.

It is important to note, however, that a variety of insuperable constraints are involved in dealing with individual, unique personalities in cross-temporal and cross-cultural perspective. The psychological descriptions of persons readily available in modern biographies do not seem possible for people of the past, if only because there are no adequate models available to produce such descriptions in a responsible way. While the main American approach to explaining persons and their behavior is psychological, this approach is simply not feasible relative to persons of the past (on the impossibility of psychohistory, see Stannard 1980, to whom we will return a bit later). Thus it seems that at present the best we can attempt is a type of regional character study, patterned after the national character studies of the 1940s and 1950s. Such study has picked up once again, now under the label of social psychology (see Seelye 1985, who describes contemporary comparative "character" studies; Gamson 1992 on the nature of social psychology, the study of how social systems and individual selves interpenetrate; Kagitçibasi 1989 describes the present foci of such study). For example, we can learn to compare contemporary U.S. values with those held by Middle Easterners, noticing especially how both use the same words, often with quite different meanings (as described by Abu-Hilal 1982).

A number of studies offer excellent comparative models describing modern eastern Mediterraneans and their traditional cultures. Gilmore's bibliographic overview of Mediterranean studies (1982) offers a full overview of the literature, and he later edited a collection of most useful essays by his Mediterraneanist colleagues (1987). Saunders (1981) offers some valuable characterizations, while Karmi (1993) presents a very contemporary portrait.

Available social-scientific studies, then, suggest that if our goal is to understand ancient Mediterranean persons in some comparative way, our main tool will be a social psychology. It should be built on a circum-Mediterranean "modal" or typical personality, while at the same time taking into account the idiosyncrasies of the culture and distinctiveness of social structure in any given time and place. Obviously there are distinctive cultural groups within the Mediterranean region, along with the types of personalities such groups would sanction. But such distinctions must be allowed to emerge only after we gain some understanding of the circum-Mediterranean personality in general.

Before moving to a description of Mediterranean persons, however, a caution is in order. It is important to recognize that in this discussion of circum-Mediterranean societies and their culture(s), modern Israel must be omitted, since it is in fact a central European intrusion into this culture area. Evidence for this can be found in Schwartz and Bilsky (1987), both Israelis, who have demonstrated the similarity in values held by Israelis and Germans (this is also noted by Triandis 1990:68).

2.0 Getting to Know Mediterranean Persons

In order to get to know and understand Mediterranean persons, it seems best to proceed by stages. First, we need a general orientation concerning what Mediterranean societies (unlike the U.S.) have in common with much of the rest of the world, that is, with collectivistic cultures rather than individualistic cultures. The next stage offers a perspective on Mediterranean persons as collectivistic persons. Finally, we consider some typical social-psychological scripts shared by Mediterraneans in antiquity. The first general orientation deals with the 70 percent of the world's population that believes in the group rather than the individual as the primary focus of human living. Here the value of family (or kin group) integrity far outweighs that of self-reliance. The second perspective deals with Mediterraneans as anti-introspective, as not psychologically minded, as dyadic personages bent on honor and shame. The final topic deals with ancient Mediterranean descriptions of persons and their orientation toward the world in terms of physiognomic stereotypes, encomia, in-group concerns, public selves, and three-tiered personhood.

2.1 The Collectivistic Self

Even though all people on the planet, as far as we can verify, use the word "I" and its equivalents, the meanings invested in that word in the various social systems of the world are often radically different. By the term "I," and equivalents, we refer to the "self." "The self here is defined as all the statements a person makes that include the word 'I,' 'me,' 'mine,' and 'myself.' This definition means that all aspects of social motivation are included in the self. Attitudes (e.g., I like . . .), beliefs (e.g., X has attribute X in my view), intentions (e.g., I plan to do . . .), norms (my in-group expects me to do . . .), roles (my in-group expects people who hold this position to do . . .), and values (e.g., I feel that . . . is very important), are aspects of the self" (Triandis 1990:77).

The way people deal with the self can be plotted on a line whose extreme axes are individualism (awareness of a unique and totally independent "I") on the one hand, and collectivism (awareness of an "I" that has nearly everything in common with the kinship group and its spin-offs) on the other. Cultures in which people believe in individualism are a rather recent phenomenon in recorded history (sixteenth century CE at the earliest). As Daniel Bell points out, "The fundamental assumption of modernity, the thread that has run through Western civilization since the sixteenth century, is that the social unit of society is not the group, the guild, the tribe, or the city, but the person" (1976:16; for antiquity, the essays in Veyne 1987 describe ancient persons in a number of contexts). Indeed, a common belief among historians is that individualism of the sort available in the U.S. today emerged with St. Augustine and his *Confessions,* if not earlier (so, e.g., Perkins 1992).

Like many common beliefs held by historians, however, this one too is an anachronistic, ethnocentric projection, asserted frequently but not validated. In fact, the Mediterranean selves we read about in the Bible could not have been individualistic selves in the way we are. Rather they were all group-oriented selves, very concerned to adopt the viewpoints of the groups (their in-groups) whose fate they shared. They would never have considered Jesus as a personal Lord and Savior or as a personal Redeemer. If anything, Jesus was the church's (the group's) Lord and Savior, and it was by belonging to the church (the group) that one experienced the presence of the Lord.

These were people who required other people to know who they were. "Who do people [others] say that I am?" is a typical (though most often unexpressed) Mediterranean question. And it was the answer to this question that directed a person how to feel and think about him- or herself. Such persons were not individualists but "dyadics" or "doublists," in the sense that they always thought of themselves in terms of the opinion of at least one other person (usually the central person of the group). This was not due to any radical incapacity to think individualistically. Rather, just as all normal persons are born with the capacity to speak their parent's language, so too all normal persons are born with the capacity to think of themselves and to behave as *either* individualists or collectivists. However, this capacity is realized only through a social process of enculturation (or "education" in the sense of "formation in humanity") or socialization. Due to their socialization, ancient Mediterraneans simply learned that they needed at least one other person to feel that they knew who they really were.

Such persons are said to be collectivistic rather than individualistic. "The self is coterminous with the body in individualist cultures and in some of the collectivist cultures. However, it can be related to a group the way a hand is related to the person whose hand it is. The latter conception is found in collectivist cultures, where the self overlaps with a group, such as family or tribe" (Triandis 1990:77–78).

Americans live in an individualistic culture that centers on the value of self-reliance. Individualism may be described as the belief that persons are each and singly an end in themselves, and as such ought to realize their "self" and cultivate their own judgment, notwithstanding the push of pervasive social pressures in the direction of conformity. In individualist cultures most people's social behavior is largely determined by personal goals that often overlap only slightly with the goals of collectives such as the family, the work group, the tribe, political allies, coreligionists, compatriots, and the state. When a conflict arises between personal and group goals, it is considered acceptable for the individual to place personal goals ahead of collective goals. Thus individualism gives priority to the goals of single persons rather than to group goals. What enables this sort of priority is focus on self-reliance, in the sense of independence, separation from others, and personal competence.

This focus on self-reliance is not to be equated with the ancient Mediterranean philosophic insistence on αὐτάρκεια, autarkeia, "sufficiency." The term is often translated "self-sufficiency." Whatever the term "self-sufficiency" conjures up for an individualistic reader, in the Mediterranean world αὐτάρκεια, autarkeia, is about having access to "enough"—that is, to neither too little nor too much. "Having enough" was the goal of every family and every city, since it guaranteed group integrity, which was the main value of the kinship/political institution. In philosophic usage, the word did not refer to self-reliance in the modern U.S. sense, with its psychological overtones. Rather, "having enough" allowed for nondependence on those others upon whom one was normally dependent, hence a form of nonattachment to persons to whom one was connected by social convention: parents, children, spouse, neighbors, village mates, and the like. In true Mediterranean fashion, this nonattachment was implemented in a group of like-minded persons to whom one was often quite attached: the philosophic "school," or "community." (See Malina 1993a, 1993b. By contrast, Meeks's understanding of αὐτάρκεια, autarkeia, "makes the Stoic sound like a radical individualist" [1986:50]; for a Cynic the word underscores "freedom" [54, 56]. Clearly the model of contemporary individualistic culture stands behind such an appreciation of αὐτάρκεια, autarkeia.)

Ancient Mediterraneans, and nearly all peoples before the sixteenth century CE, following Bell's (1976) suggestion, lived in collectivistic cultures. Collectivism may be described as the belief that the groups in which a person is embedded are each and singly an end in themselves, and as such ought to realize distinctive group values, notwithstanding the weight of one's personal drive in the direction of self-satisfaction. In collectivist cultures most people's social behavior is largely determined by group goals that require the pursuit of achievements that improve the position of the group. The defining attributes of collectivistic cultures are family integrity, solidarity, and keeping the primary in-group in "good health."

For a philosophic orientation on the study of the self, both individualistic and collectivistic, see Rom Harré (1980, 1984, 1989). Grace Harris has sought conceptual clarity in the study of people by noting the following distinctions: "persons in society" are studied sociologically, "individuals in environments" are studied biologically, and "selves in relations" are studied psychologically (Harris 1989). The best overview based on the actual study of "selves in relations," comparing collectivistic cultures and individualistic cultures, is that of Triandis (1990). This sort of study might be called comparative social psychology. Triandis and his colleagues continue to sharpen their data-gathering instruments, as one can read in Triandis, et. al. (1993). Their work has been subject to critique by Schwartz (1990), who is more concerned with what collectivistic and individualistic cultures have in common. For how this sort of study applies to reading the NT, see Malina (1994, 1995), who also provides further pertinent bibliography.

In order to be able to follow the directives controlling their collectivistic culture (rather than our U.S. individualism), ancient persons were enculturated to be anti-introspective, much as modern collectivistic persons are. Simply put, that meant that if persons felt badly or well, they should look outside themselves to persons around them rather than inside, into the psyche, the soul, the mind, for the cause of their feeling. For it was outside that one could find an answer to why one felt depressed or elated, anxious or at ease, worried or excited, fearful or confident, and the like.

Anti-introspective persons are not psychologically minded at all. Since positive and negative feelings were always believed to be triggered by causes outside a person, and since feelings were perceived to deal with something personal, Mediterranean persons sought the causes of feelings among persons, visible and invisible. For example, if I feel depressed it must be because of what somebody said or did to me. But if I have free-floating feelings of depression that I cannot trace back to any person I know, then it must be due to some nonhuman person, such as a spirit, a demon, or a "genius." The world is full of persons, human and nonhuman, and it is essentially persons who are responsible for all significant events in anyone's life. "Personal causality" is the rule.

One of the distinctive features of Mediterraneans, ancient and modern, is the almost total absence of interest in the individual psyche as distinctive and idiosyncratic (that is, unique). Nowadays, practicing psychiatrists are rare in Mediterranean societies; they are generally employed by the government, representing the government in government-run institutions. This nonconcern with the individual psyche is indicative of an anti-introspective bias. The individual, unique psyche and its singular development are as uninteresting as concern with a child's individuation. Codependency is the desired outcome of child rearing. In practical terms this means that personal causation and motivation are generally ascribed to external forces.

It is quite obvious that individuals are not in control of their lives; rather, the in-group group or dominating out-groups control a person's life. Such groups control individuals through their central personages: the father or surrogate father, the oldest son (or the mother) in the father's absence, the father's male relatives, and the like. Whether atop a hierarchy (in lineal, pyramidal systems) or at the center of the group (in collateral, group systems), there is always the dominant male or his surrogate.

Even though individuals are not in control, they may be either responsible for their actions or not responsible at all. Responsibility depends on the quality of the collectivistic culture. Where commonly held values are normally realized by group members, responsibility is the norm. Where commonly held values are often not realizable, however, individuals are not responsible for their actions (as in the writings of Paul, e.g., Rom 5 and 7, and the traditional Mediterranean understanding of "original sin"; see Malina 1986).

Given the anti-introspective bent of Mediterranean persons, what counts above all is what other people say, how other people assess the situation. Individuals are always playing to an audience from which they expect approval. Approval results in a feeling of honor; disapproval results in a profound sense of shame. People generally do not have to face the social sanction of internalized guilt, which is not a feature of the anti-introspective, collectivistic personality. Since persons are expected to be codependent on a range of others who dominate their ever-changing in-groups, Mediterraneans may be described as dyadic persons. They need other people to continue to know who they really are.

Perhaps the easiest way to understand these features of the Mediterranean person is to read Malina (1993a) and then do the exercises in Malina (1993b) and Pilch (1991). The next stage would involve reading reading Malina and Neyrey (1991) as well as the other essays in Neyrey (1991) for a general overview of a range of NT themes. Finally, Malina (1992) deals specifically with stereotyping and responsibility. For the values that these persons held, and who held them, see the brief and pertinent entries in Pilch and Malina (1993).

2.2. Mediterranean Collectivistic Persons

If all significant events in my life are due to persons, visible and invisible, the most important thing I can learn in life is how to evaluate other people. The previous readings demonstrate that the way to this end is to learn what is typical of persons, given their family and place of origin. Just as animals looked and behaved the way they did because of their genetic source and place of origin, so too with people. And just as animals retain those genetic and local traits no matter where they might roam, so too with people. Thus an Arabian horse is still an Arabian even when born and bred in Kentucky. So too with Poland-China hogs in Iowa. So too with Romans or Judeans or Cretans or Babylonians, wherever they may be.

The originating place and parentage of living beings is of fundamental significance. What is characteristic of places, Mediterraneans believed, was the sky with star and sun impact, the air with its health-giving or health-hindering qualities, and the water with its health and potency-affording properties. And what was characteristic of parentage is that parents hand down outstanding qualities to their offspring, such as honor, strength, reliability, and beauty. The kin group, therefore, is the most significant in-group. Kin share common qualities and make enemies because of these qualities. After all, a wolf has common qualities with other wolves in regard to sheep; hence wolves will always prey on sheep.

In-group boundaries often follow the fences of originating parentage (kinship) and originating place (village mates, city quarter mates). But in-group boundaries may be expanded to include fictive kin: clients, friends, contractual partners, and the like. In-group dimensions are very important since interpersonal obligations bind in-group members only. Out-group members are fair game for challenges, deception and lies, or general nonconcern. The question of "who is my neighbor" was generally settled to include only in-group members.

2.3 Gender Division in Mediterranean Society

For American readers of ancient Mediterranean writings, the most distinctive social feature to understand is the gender division of Mediterranean society. While family reliance is the core value supported by the prevailing social institution of kinship, yet all valued persons or objects are primarily gender defined. This means that an individual is primarily male or female (secondarily a group-embedded person, and thirdly a person with a name). Not only are selves defined by gender, but so are other things, including nature, times, and places. Other persons come in out-groups and in-groups, and these are gender assessed as well. For example, some groups describe the father's side or are father initiated (the father's patrons, friends); other groups are on the mother's side or are run by persons without legal rights (e.g., early Christian churches). Then, some animals are distinctively under male control (cattle, sheep, dogs), while others are under female control (goats). The rest are wild, out-group beings. Similarly, as regards times, women must come after men and leave before them or must be duly chaperoned. Some places are distinctively female: for example, the inside of a house, though that can have shifting boundaries (e.g., the courtyard when men are out working). Male places are those on the outside: the fields, other towns, the outside of the house, and the like.

Mediterraneans held kinship as their focal social institution. Societies with kinship as the focal point invariably have a moral division of labor based on gender. What this means is that selves were first and foremost defined by gender: persons were essentially male or female selves. There really were no parents—only fathers and mothers. And mothers never gave birth to a child but only to a male child or female child. Similarly, parents never had children but only sons and daughters.

The fact of a person being a gender-defined self in a gender-divided society embraced all aspects of life. It was the father's side of the family that was owed allegiance and that had clear rights (Bettini 1991 has spelled this out most clearly for Roman society, although there were like divisions throughout the ancient Mediterranean). The father's brothers and sisters had different "uncle" and "aunt" names from those of the mother's brothers and sisters. The father's side was the patriarchal side for the children. The mother's side was the "emarchal" side ("em" is the old English name for the mother's brother). Obviously all that people write about patriarchy today has to do with the patrilineal side of the family. The men in the emarchal or matrilineal side had quite different roles that were not rooted in rights and obligations when it came to their sister and her children. (Early Christian groups [churches], having no rights in law, were essentially "emarchal" organizations. See Malina 1978 for an explanation of the impact of this for the behavior of the Christian bishop Ignatius, who died ca. 106.) In sum, Mediterraneans have a gender-defined society in which gender determines role, rights, obligations, and behavior. It is a society in which persons of each gender for the most part live their lives apart from the other.

2.4 Assessing Mediterranean Selves

Though gender defines everything in Mediterranean society, human beings, both males and females, relate to the world in terms of three zones of activity: eyes-heart, mouth-ears, and hands-feet. In nonphilosophical writings, people are always defined in terms of these zones, as is apparent in the Bible from beginning to end (how God creates in Genesis; how the Word is described in 1 John 1:1–2). Eyes-heart refers to emotion-fused thinking; mouth-ears to self-revelation and self-communication; hands-feet to activity, doing.

To learn about these additional features of Mediterranean persons one ought to begin with the general orientations provided by Malina (1993a), the exercises in Malina (1993b), and the fuller workbook of Pilch (1991). For further specifics, especially about the dimensions of gender-based personality, see Malina (1989, 1990). How gender-based behavior figures in Jesus' new teaching ought be noted by reading Jacobs-Malina (1993). She points out how Jesus' male followers were urged to adopt lines of behavior in which females alone were socialized, such as service, being last, not striving for honor, and yielding precedence.

Since ancient Mediterraneans assessed behavior in terms of what was outwardly perceptible, their references to what we would call "internal" states always had an accompanying external activity. For us, for example, knowing, hating, loving, judging, and the like are "internal" states that take place in some psychological arena such as the mind or feelings. For the first-century Mediterranean person, locked on to the outwardly perceptible, one cannot look at a person holding a glass of clear liquid taken from a drinking fountain and say it is a glass of water. One would have to taste it and pour it out and then conclude: it is a glass of water. In other words, to know something means to experience it. "To know one's wife" is to have sexual relations. "To know right from wrong" means to be able to do what is right and what is wrong. Similarly, to hate means to do negative things to another (with or without negative feelings). And to love another means to demonstrate one's attachment by means of positive actions. To judge means to display the effects of one's assessment, usually negatively, hence to condemn another in word and behavior.

Just as we U.S. individualists became the way we are thanks to the socialization efforts of our parents, so too with ancient Mediterraneans. They had to be socialized into their group-think, communalistic, dyadic personalities. The first step has to do with ego formation and differentiation. Group-oriented individuals are kept embedded within the mother. They are neither allowed nor expected to differentiate. This keeps them within the psychological womb, first of the mother, then of the kin group, a sort of surrogate mother.

Little girls are taught household responsibilities and help their mothers in real-world tasks (not play) early on. Little boys live with their mothers but are usually not expected to help as their sisters are. The boy remains with the mother and in the female world until near puberty, when he is abruptly situated in the world of males, with little if any knowledge of how men actually do things, since the domestic world of women where boys are raised rarely touches the public, political world of men.

Consequently the boy's early range of experiences involves other males telling him that he does things just like a girl, just like a woman (which is true enough). When exactly will the boy do things like a man? What exactly does it mean to do things like a man? Such uncertainty about what is specifically masculine in given instances will stay with the boy throughout life. Mediterranean males are not expected to resolve this uncertainty. The result is fitness for the cultural value called "machismo." Machismo is exaggerated male display undertaken to prove one's masculinity.

2.5 How Ancient Mediterraneans Knew Each Other

Ancient Mediterraneans did speak about how to know persons other than themselves. That a given person may have had specific facial or bodily features was regarded as credible evidence of a constitutional or genetic predisposition to act in a particular fashion. Some learned ancients recorded such features in those categories of writing called "physiognomies" as well as those called "progymnasmata." These odd words point to the odd things the ancients thought it was important to know as well as the odd ways in which they got to know them.

Physiognomies deal with descriptions and evaluations of how people looked. What did they look like? First of all, what was their gender? Did they reveal physical characteristics of specific ethnic groups? Then as individual specimens, did they resemble particular animals, both in general and in details? The accepted truth was that what an animate being could do depended on its physique. Mice could not behave like lions, if only because they were built differently. Behavior follows physique, a term that means both physical structure and nature. All animals follow their nature, which is revealed in a given physical structure. As with animals, so too with people. Just as one knows what an animal does because of its physique, so also one can tell what people will do by paying attention to their physiques. And from where do animals get their physical traits? Obviously from genetics and environment; they have been born of given parentage and live adapted to a given environment with its characteristics of air and water. Again, so too with human beings. All depends on geniture (genealogy and gender) and geography.

However, the ancients were after more than this, if they could discover it. We learn of their specific concerns from handbooks for rhetoricians called progymnasmata (see Malina and Neyrey 1996). In a type of progymnasmaton called an encomium (praise for an individual), the scholion on Aphthonius (translated from Christian Walz, ed., *Rhetores graeci* [9 vols.; Stuttgart and Tübingen: Cotta, 1832–36. II.617.18–27]) states:

> The five divisions of an encomium are: birth, education, actions, comparison, and epilogue. Into how many parts is "birth" divided? into four: race/tribe, country, ancestors, and elders/fathers. Into how many parts is "education" divided? into three: pursuit in life, manner-craft, customs. Into how many parts is "action" divided? in what pertains to the soul, the body, and fortune. The virtues of the soul are: prudence, courage, temperance, and justice. Of the body: stature, strength, beauty and health. In addition to these (of fortune): wealth, good fortune, friendship.

What is important here is to see that "birth" forms the framework and sets the possibilities of each of the other dimensions that an encomium explores. In the Mediterranean world, genetics determined character.

2.6 Conclusion

From the foregoing readings, scenarios of typical Mediterranean persons should emerge. Given what they seek to know about others, we can safely say that such persons saw themselves as group-embedded males and females, concerned about judging others and being judged on the basis of outward behavior. They were anti-introspective, not psychologically minded, and thought in terms of stereotypes. What counted most in life was family integrity, sufficiency, in-group support, and honor.

The goal of reading the literature described above is to develop scenarios adequate to knowing and understanding the Mediterranean persons described in the NT. Success in this task should lead to a greater appreciation of our ancestors in faith. Jesus was socialized to live as a Mediterranean person. Hence it was as a Mediterranean person that the Word of God was incarnate. Without an appreciation of this way of being a person, the modern reader will simply lose many of the interpersonal dimensions of the biblical witness.

3.0 Outdated and Inadequate Approaches

Before leaving the topic of the Mediterranean person it is important to give the reader a sense of perspective. Many of the standard approaches to the topic in contemporary scholarship perpetuate ethnocentric and anachronistic understandings that can lead to misunderstanding of biblical texts.

3.1 Outdated Approaches

Perhaps the most influential statement contrasting ancient "biblical" persons and modern (British) persons was the essay by H. Wheeler Robinson concerning "corporate personality" in ancient Israel (1980; first published in 1936). Robinson's description of ancient Israelite corporate personality derived from L. Lévy-Bruhl's popularization of how contemporary primitives think. From his understanding of the primitive mentality Lévy-Bruhl (1923, 1926) deduced a distinctive primitive personality, a corporate personality. The distinctive feature of this epistemological model was that primitives never perceived themselves as single beings, but believed themselves to be irreducibly part of a larger group. To use modern jargon, such primitives were not simply codependent but totally dependent in their self-awareness.

Early anthropologists obviously intuited a number of the features of collectivism. Yet the articulation of this intuition proved to be inadequate, as did the data set on which it was based. Following Lévy-Bruhl, Robinson gets credit for using anthropology to try to understand ancient Israel, yet he never defined "corporate personality" adequately, undoubtedly because of the inadequacy of Lévy-Bruhl's articulation. Be that as it may, a number of biblical scholars took up the idea of "corporate personality" to explain various phenomena in the OT as well as in the NT (e.g., the sin of Adam in Paul, as in de Fraine 1965). Significant works similar to Robinson and based on presuppositions of different mentalities include those of of Tresmontant (1960) and Boman (1960). In this regard, the 1980 reprint of Robinson's essay includes a valuable introduction by Tucker describing the history of the influence of Robinson's work and the position taken by its critics. It also has a historically relevant bibliography. The reader should note that "corporate personality" has the same standing as "primitive mentality," which essentially serves today as a historical curiosity.

3.2 Inadequate Approaches

Before concluding, we think it is also important to warn the reader against the overwhelming temptation to project our individualistic psychology back upon NT persons. Books about the psychological temptations or personality traits of Jesus and Paul are common today. But I suggest that such statements are pure projections, without the slightest basis outside the imagination of the modern writer. The best cure for this temptation is a careful reading of Stannard's (1980) critique of the application of psychology to history. He argues in effect that since psychoanalysis is essentially and directly a therapy, to use psychological models derived from and rooted in psychoanalysis to explain behaviors rooted in cultures of the past is like using models derived from and rooted in procedures of operating rooms, emergency rooms, and first-aid clinics to explain human biological behavior. To this I would add that there simply were no individualistic cultures before the sixteenth century (see Bell 1976). Mediterraneans are still known for their anti-introspective and antipsychological approaches to life. Hence I would label models rooted in psychology as dead-end models.

Under this category I include those descriptions of ancient Mediterraneans based either on pop psychology or on modern psychology (usually in the Freudian tradition). Each approach evidences defects. The descriptions of Jesus, Paul, and early Christians based on pop psychology are essentially ethnocentric anachronisms. The descriptions based on modern psychology are methodologically unsound.

Pop psychology is quite pervasive in nearly all descriptions of ancient Mediterraneans that are still innocent of social-scientific concerns. This is true not only of the countless books offering immediate relevance to modern Americans but also of works presented as biblical scholarship. For example, Jerome Murphy-O'Connor tells of "a feeling of frustration" that was inevitable in first-century Corinth. For "what was the point of a life in which the full exploitation of one's talents was blocked by circumstances outside one's control" (1984:153). Wayne Meeks, in turn, explains that first-century Mediterraneans might join and adhere to a Pauline type church because of loneliness, anxiety, and need for social mobility. Persons afflicted with loneliness and anxiety would find a welcome refuge in the intimacy of Christian groups, while the daring, self-confident social climber would be allowed to break out of a constraining social structure

(1983:164–92). Similarly, largely ethnocentric psychological models shape the way Meeks presents ancient Mediterranean moral behavior, even though the work (1986) is largely in the words of the ancients.

In the same way, others see the world of Jesus and Paul as similar to our own. It has been characterized as one in which "a strong individualism prevails in most segments of Greek society alongside of a search for community" (Doohan 1989:49). Such retrojections of contemporary experience into the world of early Christianity do make that world relevant, but they do not accurately describe the ancient Mediterranean. Moreover, while hypothetical intuitions about early Christians personages deriving from the history-of-ideas approach are interesting (for example, Stendahl's intuition about Paul, 1963), such intuitive approaches offer little by way of testable explanation and remain in the pop-psychology category.

Equally problematic are Gerd Theissen's (1987) psychobiology and Terrence Callan's (1987, 1990) rather straightforward psychology that overlook the difficulties involved in psychological analysis (Callan 1987 gives an excellent overview of previous psychological studies; Callan 1990 is a full study). Even the insistence, for example of Doohan (1984), that it is necessary and legitimate to study Paul's unique personality in terms of modern psychology does not face up to the fundamental obstacles of applying modern psychology to the past. The question is not the obstinacy of the critic but the lack of a workable method to carry off the task in some intellectually responsible manner.

Historians as a rule give little attention to the problem of the *implicit* models they inevitably use. And this holds all the more for their selection from among the many analytic frameworks that do exist (Prochaska 1979). Moreover, these historians often ignore the formidable impediments to an adequate psychological assessment of absent, idiosyncratic subjects. We cannot interview persons from the past. These impediments have been well articulated by Stannard (1980). Stannard's arguments do not seem to faze psychohistorians, even when he quietly concludes: "The time has come to face the fact that, behind all its rhetorical posturing, the psychoanalytic approach to history is—irremediably—one of logical perversity, scientific unsoundness, and cultural naïveté. The time has come, in short, to move on" (156).

4.0 Works Cited

Note: The items marked with an asterisk (*) are judged to be inadequate for a valid understanding of ancient Mediterranean persons.

They are cited in this chapter as examples of outdated or dead-end approaches to the subject. Furthermore, all the recommended readings contain further valuable bibliographical references.

Abu-Hilal, Ahmad
    1982   "Arab and North-American Social Attitudes: Some
            Cross-Cultural Comparisons." *Mankind* 22:193–207.
Augsburger, David
    1986   *Pastoral Counseling Across Cultures.* Philadelphia:
            Westminster.
Bell, Daniel
    1976   *The Cultural Contradictions of Capitalism.* New York:
            Basic Books.
Bettini, Maurizio
    1991   *Anthropology and Roman Culture: Kinship, Time, Images of*
            the Soul. Trans. John Van Sickle. Baltimore: Johns
            Hopkins University Press.
Boman, Thorleif.
    *1960   *Hebrew Thought Compared with Greek.* Trans. Jules L.
            Moreau. Philadelphia: Westminster.
Callan, Terrence
    *1987   *"Competition and Boasting: Toward a Psychological
            Portrait of Paul." *JRelS* 13:27–51.
    *1990   *Psychological Perspectives on the Life of Paul: An*
            Application of the Methodology of Gerd Theissen. Lewiston,
            N.Y.: Mellen.
Doohan, Helen
    *1984   *Leadership in Paul.* Wilmington, Del.: Michael Glazier.
    *1989   *Paul's Vision of Church.* Wilmington, Del.: Michael
            Glazier.
Elliott, John H.
    1993   *What Is Social-Scientific Criticism?* Guides to Biblical
            Scholarship, New Testament Series. Minneapolis:
            Fortress.
Fraine, Jean de
    *1965   *Adam and the Family of Man.* Trans. Daniel Raible. Staten
            Island: Alba House.
Gamson, William A.
    1992   "The Social Psychology of Collective Action." In
            Frontiers in Social Movement Theory. Ed. Aldon D. Morris
            and Carol McClurg Mueller. Pages 53–76. New Haven
            and London: Yale University Press.
Gilmore, David D.
    1982   "Anthropology of the Mediterranean Area." *ARA*
            11:175–205.

_____ , ed.

1987   *Honor and Shame and the Unity of the Mediterranean.*
         American Anthropological Association Special
         Publication 22. Washington, D.C.: American
         Anthropological Association.

Harré, Rom

1980   *Social Being: A Theory for Social Psychology.* Totowa, N.J.:
         Rowman and Littlefield.

1984   *Personal Being: A Theory for Individual Psychology.*
         Cambridge: Harvard University Press.

1989   "The 'Self' as a Theoretical Concept." In *Relativism:*
         Interpretation and Confrontation. Ed. Michael Krausz.
         Pages 387–417. Notre Dame: University of Notre Dame
         Press.

Harris, Grace Gredys

1989   "Concepts of Individual, Self, and Person in
         Description and Analysis." *American Anthropologist*
         91:599–612.

Jacobs-Malina, Diane

1993   *Beyond Patriarchy: Images of Family in Jesus.* Mahwah,
         N.J.: Paulist.

Kagitçibasi, Çigdem

1989   "Cross-Cultural Psychology: Current Research and
         Trends." *Annual Review of Psychology* 40:493–531.

Karmi, Ghada

1993   "The Saddam Hussein Phenomenon and Male-Female
         Relations in the Arab World." In *Women in the Middle*
         East: Perceptions and Struggles for Liberation. Ed. Halef
         Afshar. Pages 146–57. New York: St. Martin's.

Lévy-Bruhl, Lucien

*1923   *The Notebooks on Primitive Mentality.* Trans. Peter
         Riviere. Reprint, New York: Harper & Row, 1975.

*1926   *How Natives Think.* Trans. Lilian A. Clare. Reprint, New
         York: Arno, 1979.

Malina, Bruce J.

1978   "The Social World Implied in the Letters of the
         Christian Bishop-Martyr (Named Ignatius of Antioch)."
         SBLSP 1978:2.71–119.

1986   *Christian Origins and Cultural Anthropology.* Atlanta:
         John Knox.

1989   "Dealing with Biblical (Mediterranean) Characters: A
         Guide for U.S. Consumers." *BTB* 19:127–41.

1990   "Mother and Son." *BTB* 20:54–64.

1991a   "Interpretation: Reading, Abduction, Metaphor." In *The*
         Bible and the Politics of Exegesis: Essays in Honor of

Norman K. Gottwald on His Sixty-Fifth Birthday. Ed.
David Jobling, Peggy L. Day, and Gerald T. Sheppard.
Pages 253–66. Cleveland: Pilgrim Press.

1991b   "Reading Theory Perspective: Reading Luke-Acts." In
The Social World of Luke–Acts: Models for Interpretation.
Ed. Jerome H. Neyrey. Pages 3–24. Peabody, Mass.:
Hendrickson.

1992   "Is There a Circum-Mediterranean Person? Looking for
Stereotypes." *BTB* 22:66–87.

1993a   *The New Testament World: Insights from Cultural
Anthropology.* 2d rev. ed. Louisville: Westminster/John
Knox.

1993b   *Windows on the World of Jesus: Time Travel to Ancient
Judea.* Louisville: Westminster/John Knox.

1994   " 'Let Him Deny Himself' (Mark 8:34//): A Social
Psychological Model of Self-Denial." *BTB* 24:106–19.

1995   "Power, Pain and Personhood: Asceticism in the
Ancient Mediterranean World." In *Asceticism.* Ed.
Vincent Wimbush and Richard Valantasis. Pages
162–77. New York: Oxford University Press.

Malina, Bruce J., and Jerome H. Neyrey

1991   "First-Century Personality: Dyadic, Not Individual." In
The Social World of Luke–Acts: Models for Interpretation.
Ed. Jerome H. Neyrey. Pages 67–96. Peabody, Mass.:
Hendrickson.

1996   *Portraits of Paul: An Archaeology of Ancient Personality.*
Louisville: Westminster/John Knox.

Meeks, Wayne A.

*1983   *The First Urban Christians: The Social World of the Apostle
Paul.* New Haven: Yale University Press.

*1986   *The Moral World of the First Christians.* Philadelphia:
Westminster.

Murphy-O'Connor, Jerome

*1984   "The Corinth That Saint Paul Saw." *BA* 47:147–59.

Neyrey, Jerome, ed.

1991   *The Social World of Luke–Acts: Models for Interpretation.*
Peabody, Mass.: Hendrickson.

Perkins, Judith

*1992   "The 'Self' as Sufferer." *HTR* 85:245–72.

Pilch, John J.

1991   *Hear the Word.* Vol. 2, *Introducing the Cultural Context of
the New Testament.* Mahwah, N.J.: Paulist.

Pilch, John J., and Bruce J. Malina, eds.

1993   *Biblical Social Values and Their Meaning: A Handbook.*
Peabody, Mass.: Hendrickson.

Prochaska, James
    1979   *Systems of Psychotherapy: A Transtheoretical Analysis.*
            Homewood, Ill.: Dorsey.
Robinson, H. Wheeler
    *1980   *Corporate Personality in Ancient Israel.* 1936. Rev. ed.
            with introduction by Gene M. Tucker. Philadelphia:
            Fortress.
Saunders, George R.
    1981   "Men and Women in Southern Europe: A Review of
            Some Aspects of Cultural Complexity." *Journal of
            Psychoanalytic Anthropology* 4:435–66.
Schwartz, Shalom H.
    1990   "Individualism-Collectivism: Critique and Proposed
            Refinements." *Journal of Cross-Cultural Psychology*
            21:139–57.
Schwartz, Shalom, and W. Bilsky
    1987   "Toward a Universal Psychological Structure of Human
            Values." *Journal of Personality and Social Psychology*
            53:550–62.
Seelye, H. Ned
    1985   *Teaching Culture: Strategies for Intercultural
            Communication.* Lincolnwood, Ill.: National Textbook Co.
Stannard, David E.
    1980   *Shrinking History: On Freud and the Failure of
            Psychohistory.* New York: Oxford University Press.
Stendahl, Krister
    *1963   "The Apostle Paul and the Introspective Conscience of
            the West." *HTR* 56:199–215. Reprinted in Stendahl, *Paul
            Among Jews and Gentiles and Other Essays.* Pages 78–96.
            Philadelphia: Fortress Press, 1976.
Stewart, Edward C., and Milton J. Bennett
    1991   *American Cultural Patterns: A Cross-Cultural Perspective.*
            Rev. ed. Yarmouth, Me.: Intercultural.
Theissen, Gerd
    *1987   *Psychological Aspects of Pauline Theology.* Trans. John P.
            Galvin. Philadelphia: Fortress.
Tresmontant, Claude
    *1960   *A Study of Hebrew Thought.* Trans. M. F. Gibson. New
            York: Desclée.
Triandis, Harry C.
    1990   "Cross-Cultural Studies of Individualism and
            Collectivism." In *Nebraska Symposium on Motivation
            1989.* Ed. John J. Berman. Pages 41–133. Lincoln:
            University of Nebraska Press.

Triandis, Harry C., et al.
    1993   "An Etic-Emic Analysis of Individualism and
              Collectivism." *Journal of Cross-Cultural Psychology*
              24:366–83.
Veyne, Paul, ed.
    1987   *A History of Private Life: From Pagan Rome to Byzantium.*
              Trans. Arthur Goldhammer. Cambridge: Belknap.
Williams, Robin, Jr.
    1970   *American Society: A Sociological View.* 3d ed. New York:
              Knopf.

3

Kinship

K. C. Hanson
Creighton University

1.0 Introduction

In a challenge to Jesus' honor and as a test of his Torah acumen, the Sadducees (referring to Deut 25:5–10) pose a hypothetical situation:

> Teacher, Moses wrote for us that if a man's brother dies and leaves a wife, but leaves no child, his brother must take the wife, and raise up seed for his brother. There were seven brothers; the first took a wife, and when he died left no seed; and the second took her, and died, leaving no seed; and the third likewise; and the seven left no seed. Last of all the woman also died. In the resurrection whose wife will she be? For the seven had her as wife (Mark 12:19–23 par. Matt 22:24–28; Luke 20:28–33).

While the Gospels relate this anecdote as a means of establishing Jesus' honor (putting aside the topic of resurrection), it raises for the modern reader the issue of cultural assumptions. What sort of family configuration does this case presuppose? Why would brothers even consider providing their sister-in-law with children? What were ancient Judean marriage strategies and regulations? What rules of inheritance does this story assume? In what ways is childbearing related to family honor? This is clearly not a middle-class U.S. family; so what would one need to know in order to understand this text on its own terms and in an ancient Palestinian context? A fundamental aspect of understanding ancient texts, such as those in the Bible, is knowing something about the kinship forms operant in the societies that produced them.

"Kinship" is an abstraction relating to the network of relationships based on birth (either real or fictive) and marriage, and it forms one of the four foundational social domains (politics, economics, religion, kinship) that social scientists analyze. While families are a universal phenomenon, they are configured in a multitude of ways, are controlled by different mechanisms, and serve different functions. Even though humans universally construct relationships with those to whom they are related by birth or marriage, "family" is a notion constructed differently in different cultures. Therefore it is perhaps the easiest set of relationships to misconstrue when observing another culture. If we look at the family ethnocentrically it is easy to confuse a cultural pattern with a biological one.

The four social spheres or domains addressed by social scientists are never discrete entities that operate in isolation from one another—they are interactive in every society. But beyond interaction, one sphere may be *embedded* in another. By this I mean that its definition, structures, and authority are dictated by another sphere. As Bruce Malina (1986) has demonstrated, religion in the ancient Mediterranean (and specifically with regard to Judean Yahwism) was always embedded in either politics or kinship.

Kinship in ancient Israel and Judah, as well as in first-century CE Palestine, was affected by the political sphere, especially in terms of law (often in regard to deviance), for example: incest (Lev 18:6–19), rape (Deut 22:23–29), adultery (Lev 20:10), marriage (Lev 21:7; Deut 25:5–10), divorce (Deut 24:1–4), and inheritance (Num 27:1–11; Luke 12:13). But kinship also affected politics, most notably in patron-client relationships (2 Sam 3:3; Josephus, *Ant.* 18.109), faction building (1 Sam 18:17–19), and royal genealogies (2 Sam 3:2–5; Matt 1:1–17). In similar fashion kinship was affected by religion in terms of purity, for example: intercourse regulations (John 7:53–8:11) and the status of spouses (Deut 7:1–4; Luke 1:5). And kinship affected religion (embedded in politics) in terms of descent, especially in the importance laid on the lineages of priests and their wives, but also by regulating cultic membership for the laity (Phil 3:5). Finally, kinship was interactive with the economic sphere in terms of occupations (Mark 1:16–20) and the distributions of dowry, indirect dowry, bridewealth, and inheritance (Luke 12:13). These configurations of kinship practices and norms are startlingly different from our modern Western experiences, and this is why they call for such detailed analysis.

It is essential for those studying other cultures to have a solid grasp of their own cultures. If one wishes to understand ancient Judean marriage strategies, for example, one must understand that under U.S. law marriage to close kin (e.g., uncles and nieces, or first cousins) is illegal, but it has been preferable in much of the Middle East throughout history. Good overviews of U.S. kinship issues are offered by Williams (1970) and Schneider (1980). For an analysis of African-American kinship, see Stack (1974). Figure 3.1 highlights a few of the more significant variables in kinship analysis, and how twentieth-century U.S. society contrasts to that of first-century Judea.

Variable	1st-century Judean society	20th-century U.S. society
Family form	Endogamous community (multigenerational)	Absolute nuclear (dual generational)
Spousal choice	Controlled by custom and parents	Free choice by couple
Marriage strategy	Endogamous (ideal)	Exogamous (required by law)
Wedding endowment	Formal: dowry, indirect dowry, and bridewealth	Informal: family gifts
Married couple lives with groom's parents	Yes	No
Inheritance distribution	Oldest son: double Other sons: single Daughters: dowries	No inheritance rules

Figure 3.1: Contrasting Kinship Variables in Judean and U.S. Society

In thinking about kinship patterns in the United States one must not underestimate how much American kinship is in the midst of change. As Jacoby's popular article points out (1990), the U.S. legal system, and U.S. society as a whole, has been confronted since the 1970s with a host of issues that challenge the very definition of family: in terms of marriage—one-parent families, same-sex marriages, high divorce rates; in terms of paternity and reproduction—in vitro fertilization, surrogate motherhood, abortion, sperm banks, and DNA and blood comparison.

For those wanting an overview of the subdiscipline of kinship analysis in the social sciences, several entry points are possible. To become acquainted with the larger field, readers should consult introductions to anthropology, which usually include sections on kinship. For example, Howard has two relevant sections entitled "Kinship" (1989:185–205) and "Sex, Marriage, and the Family" (206–38). Overview essays are also available in Sills (1968) and Kuper and Kuper (1990) on descent, family, household, kinship, and marriage.

For more thorough discussions of the theoretical issues, introductions to kinship will be helpful. Fox (1967) provides a readable overview, focusing especially on different types of descent principles.

But he also includes a detailed analysis of incest as a persistent issue in anthropological studies (54–76). Keesing's volume (1975) is also a widely used introduction. He includes excellent charts and diagrams, as well as a good introductory bibliography. Another useful feature is the inclusion of twenty-two case studies: summaries of other anthropologists' ethnographies that illustrate various kinship principles. Goode (1982) employs a sociological rather than anthropological methodology, but the overlap of the methods is evident here. He covers such issues as the biological bases of the family, legitimacy/illegitimacy, mate selection and marriage, household forms, role relations, divorce and death, and changes in family patterns. This is an excellent complement to the anthropological treatments.

For an analysis of kinship issues in contemporary Middle Eastern cultures (which have many parallels to ancient Israelite and Judean practices), one should consult Eickelmann (1989:151–78) and Hildred Geertz (1979). Eickelmann stresses how "family" is construed in a variety of ways and shows that "blood ties" are often metaphorical constructs for other types of association. His overview of marriage strategies and weddings in the Middle East is also informative. After addressing how earlier kinship studies have treated the Middle East, Geertz analyzes three sets of issues that are especially significant: living arrangements (the use of space and social networks), cultural constructs of "family"—including its relationship to patronage and friendship—and marriage strategies. This provides a more dynamic view of kinship transactions and their social significances than one finds in most studies.

For a narrative account of families in a Middle Eastern peasant village, it is difficult to overestimate the usefulness of Fernea (1965). Among the many issues relevant to kinship that Fernea describes are: marriage and weddings, dowry arrangements, polygamy, and male and female space.

One aspect of kinship studies the reader should be aware of is that they employ a highly specialized vocabulary. Terms such as "affine" (relative by marriage), "consanguineal" (relative by birth), or "endogamy" (marriage to close kin) may easily confuse the novice. The glossaries in Schusky (1964:71–79) and Keesing (1975:147–51) are concise guides through this linguistic maze. Furthermore, since each culture's kinship terms express different interests, relationships, and sometimes overlapping meanings, it is also helpful to analyze the semantics and sociolinguistics of the "native" terminology; for a helpful guide to asking these questions see Fox (1967:240–62). As an example of this type of problem, note that ʾāb (Hebrew), ʾabbāʾ (Aramaic), πατήρ, patēr (Greek), and pater (Latin) are all translated "father" in English; but each of them has a different semantic range (see Barr 1988).

Williams (1970:48) draws attention to three different aspects of kinship analysis. "Kinship structure" is the overall term referring to the full range of kinship norms and organization. The term "family system" addresses the configurations of the basic kinship unit (e.g., patrilocal residence). A biblical text that raises these first two types of questions is Lev 18, on incest regulations. Finally the term "family groups" refers to actual manifestations of kinship practices in particular forms and permutations; for example, the marriage strategies of Solomon (1 Kgs 3:1–2; 11:1–3).

At the most general level, kinship has two basic social functions: group formation and inheritance (Howard 1989:204). But group formation has a variety of dimensions: production (work and food), reproduction and child rearing, protection, worship, sociality/belonging, patronage, and play. Similarly, one should not construe inheritance too narrowly as receiving money from dead relatives. One of the most important aspects of ancient Mediterranean culture is that status, in the form of ascribed honor, is inherited from one's family (Matt 13:54–57; Mark 6:3; John 7:40–44; Malina 1993:33–39; §5.0 below). Another factor to consider is that for peasants the primary issue of inheritance was land, not money. For example, Naboth is offended at Ahab's offer of money for his ancestral land (1 Kgs 21:1–3). Women's dowries need also to be figured into this inheritance picture (§5.0).

At the most basic level of kinship is the household. Elliott's treatment of 1 Peter (1990) includes a major section analyzing households in the ancient Mediterranean as a unit of social organization of conjugal families, as well as of fictive kin groups of different types (165–266). He interprets the importance of the οἶκος, *oikos*, "household" as the unit of identity, solidarity, and status, and shows how these features affect the use of "household" as a metaphor of other types of relationships.

2.0 Family Systems

The work of Emmanuel Todd (1985) is significant because he proposes a typology of the basic family forms throughout the world. Building on the model of a nineteenth-century sociologist, Frédéric Le Play, Todd makes a bold proposal that identifies the basic family types with different ideologies:

A universal hypothesis is possible: the ideological system is everywhere the intellectual embodiment of family structure, a transposition into social relations of the fundamental values which govern elementary human relations. One ideological category and only one, corresponds to each family type (1985:17).

Whether or not one accepts Todd's hypothesis of a one-to-one correspondence between family form and ideology, his typology of family forms is useful to analyze large, cross-cultural patterns. He employs the variables of spousal choice (determined by custom, parents, or individual choice), spousal relationship (exogamy or endogamy), division of inheritance (equality or unequal shares), and cohabitation of married sons with their parents. His typology yields seven basic family forms: (1) Exogamous Community Family (e.g., ancient Rome); (2) Authoritarian Family (e.g., Japan); (3) Egalitarian Nuclear Family (e.g., Greece); (4) Absolute Nuclear (e.g., U.S.); (5) Endogamous Community Family (e.g., ancient Israel); (6) Asymmetrical Community Family (southern India); and (7) Anomic Family (e.g., Philippines).

One should keep three factors in mind when employing Todd's typology. First, these are dominant forms in a given society, not necessarily practiced by every single family. Second, the typology is significant for historical studies because family forms are relatively constant over time, especially in peasant societies. Third, Todd has not fully taken into account the role dowry systems play in inheritance practices.

3.0 Genealogy and Descent

"Genealogy" is a particular subgenre of the genre "list" (note also in the Bible: king list, administrative list, booty list, itinerary). It is a list of relatives arranged by generation, but it may skip any number of generations for a variety of reasons. Genealogies may be oral or literary in origin, and they organize relatives (literal or fictive) into their appropriate relationships by generation and parentage. They are pervasive in the biblical tradition, though they are usually embedded in narratives: in the Pentateuch (e.g., Gen 5:4–32), the Deuteronomistic History (e.g., 2 Sam 5:13–16), the Chronicler's History (1 Chron 3:10–24), the short story (e.g., Ruth 4:18–22), the Apocrypha (1 Macc 2:1–5), and the Gospels (Matt 1:1–17).

Robert Wilson has analyzed the biblical genealogies in terms of their social functions and uses in traditional cultures (1977). He provides a good cross-cultural comparison of the biblical genealogies to those of other traditional peoples; for a brief summary of his conclusions, see Wilson (1992). Wilson's work is significant not only for the specifics of his analysis but also for leading the way among biblical scholars in employing cross-cultural analysis.

Segmented genealogies (those which identify more than one member per generation) seldom extend beyond four or five generations, even in written form. However, they can serve a number of different social functions, separately or simultaneously. *Linear genealogies* (those tracing only one member per generation) are not as diverse in their interests. Wilson argues that they have one function: "to ground a claim to power, status, rank, office, or inheritance in an earlier ancestor. Such genealogies are often used by rulers to justify their right to rule and by office-holders of all types to support their claims" (Wilson 1992:931). Wilson also identifies several metaphorical uses of genealogies: political relationships, economic or cultic status, and geographical location (1992:931; see also Gottwald 1979:334–37).

It is fundamental, however, that genealogies are *always* social constructs, not objective reflections of reality. That is, a variety of factors affect genealogy construction: how many generations one covers; whom one includes, excludes, puts first and last; and whether they are patriarchal, matriarchal, or cognatic—all these issues are choices in composing genealogies and say something about the interests of those who compose or repeat them. How one composes a genealogy reflects one's social values, perspective, and specific goals. As Wilson says: "All of them are accurate when their differing functions are taken into consideration" (1975:182). But one must add to Wilson's caveat that all genealogies are only "accurate" given their particular construction of reality and cultural matrix. This comports with another of Wilson's conclusions: "All genealogies, whether oral or written, are characterized by fluidity" (1992:930), although writing tends to limit this fluidity (931). For an analysis of the Herodian family's genealogies and a discussion of descent principles, see Hanson (1989a).

Descent is the series of links that connects the members of a kin group to a common ancestor; it defines who constitutes a family intergenerationally. But Sahlins broadens our perspective here:

> Descent in major residential groups is a political ideology and not a mere rule of personal affiliation. It is a way of phrasing political alignments and making political differentiations. It is a charter of group rights and an expression of group solidarity. And quite beyond relating man to man within the group, the descent ideology makes connections at a higher level: it stipulates the group's relation, or lack of relation, to other groups (1968:55).

Thus societies are interested in different sets of ancestors. The different principles of descent exemplified throughout the world have attracted the attention of anthropologists; indeed, most overviews of kinship spend a great deal of space analyzing the possibilities (Fox 1967:77–174; Keesing 1975:9–100). The primary types are patrilineal, matrilineal, and cognatic. "Patrilineal descent" traces the kinship associations through the father's ancestors, "matrilineal descent" through the females, and "cognatic descent" through a combination of male and female ancestors (Keesing 1975:17; Hanson 1989a:81–83). For the standardized patterns of visually diagramming kinship relations, see Howard (1989:186–88).

Reading texts that refer to Israelite, Judean, Greek, Egyptian, Roman, and other families calls for attention to the variety of descent principles in these societies. For example, the consequence of eastern Mediterranean cosmology and anthropology, employed in both Israelite and Christian writings, is that descent can be passed only through the generating male (see, e.g., Delaney 1987). This limitation affects the Mediterranean customs of genealogies, inheritance, residence patterns, gender-role differentiation, and pollution ideologies.

Studying the biblical genealogies calls for attention to the reasons an author/redactor has included it, how it is structured, and whose honor and interests it manifests. Rather than just boring lists to be passed over quickly, genealogies are important texts that pass on key information to the reader. In the present text of Ruth, for example, it becomes clear that, given the genealogy in 4:18–22, the story stands in the interests of the Judean monarchy. The genealogies of Jesus in Matt 1:1–17 and Luke 3:23–38 are structured differently and have both different apical ancestors and different intentions.

4.0 Marriage and Divorce

In traditional societies, the marriage of a male and a female is seldom (if ever) an arrangement between individuals. It is a social contract negotiated between families, with economic, religious, and (occasionally) political implications that go far beyond the interests of sexuality, relationship, and reproduction. As a Moroccan informed Hildred Geertz, "Arranging marriages is a highly serious matter, like waging war or making big business deals" (Geertz 1979:363).

There are three primary strategies for choosing a spouse: custom (e.g., preference for close kin), the choice of the parents, and the choice of the marrying individuals. But even where custom is a heavy determinant, the parents or other relatives may play a key role in the precise choice. We cannot say that any one of these strategies fits all the biblical texts, however, since the Bible covers such a long time period and reflects such diverse cultural pressures. Malina (1993:129–42) has described some of the key shifts in marriage strategy one can find within the Bible and summarized them (144) in figure 3.2.

Marriage and kinship	Conciliatory	Aggressive	Defensive	Charismatic Defensive	Christian Defensive
Main symbol	Holy family	Holy land	Holy seed	Holy churches	Holy church
Period	Patriarchal	Israelite	Judean	Pauline	Post-Pauline
Head	Patriarch	Leader/king	Priest	Charismatic leaders	Church officers (bishop)
Norms	Custom	Law	Law	Custom	Law
Worship	Family	Temple/palace	Temple group activity	Group activity	Church group activity

Figure 3.2: Typology of Marriage Strategies in the Bible

In the "defensive" strategy practiced among Judeans of the second temple period, endogamy had become the dominant social practice (Hanson 1989b:143–44). Endogamy protected well what Malina identifies with the symbol "holy seed" and can be readily seen in the apocryphal books of Judith (8:2) and Tobit (1:9; 3:15–17; 4:12–13), as well as *Jubilees* (second-century BCE), which retells OT stories. Of the fifty-one known marriages within the Herodian family, twenty-four of them were endogamous (Hanson 1989b:144).

Divorce is the severing of the marriage bond. Just as marriage in the ancient Mediterranean was an expansive negotiation between and binding together of families, divorce also had broad social ramifications. It potentially affected the disposition of the woman's dowry, the change of residences, the ability to find another spouse, and the honor of the families.

The Gospel texts relating to divorce provide two different perspectives. In Mark 10:2–9 the Jesus-saying indicates that divorce was allowed under no circumstance. Matt 5:31–32 and 19:3–9 allow divorce in the case of the wife's adultery, paralleling the rabbinic school of Shammai (*m.Giṭ.* 9.10a).

For an analysis of Roman divorce practices, one should consult the essays by Susan Treggiari and Mireille Corbier in Rawson (1991:31–46, 47–78). Treggiari concludes that Roman elites exercised a great deal of freedom to divorce, and it usually carried no social stigma. Corbier sees divorce and adoption as social strategies in the larger framework of Roman acquisition of honor, power, and social networks. These factors are important to early Christian writings since they would have heavily influenced the cultural ethos of the first-century Mediterranean world. The Pauline and other epistles have a great deal to say on marriage and divorce (e.g., 1 Cor 7:1–16; Eph 5:21–6:9; Col 3:18–4:1; 1 Thess 4:3–8; 1 Pet 3:1–7).

5.0 Dowries, Bridewealth, and Inheritance

"Dowry" is the property that a bride's family provides the bride or couple (usually under the control of her husband) at the time of marriage. This might be movable property (such as bedding, cooking utensils, jewelry, animals), immovable property (land and buildings), cash, or a combination of these. It is mentioned in the Bible in the context of the patriarchal narratives as well as the early Israelite monarchy (Heb. *šillûḥîm,* lit. "those things which are sent" or "gifts"; Gen 30:20; 31:14–16; 1 Kgs 9:16). We also find evidence for dowries in the literatures of Babylonia, Nuzi, Ugarit, Greece, Rome, and Judah. For a cross-cultural analysis of these ancient societies' dowry systems, see Hanson (1990); for dowry systems in Eurasia, see Goody and Tambiah (1973).

Three cross-cultural studies of preindustrial societies inform our understanding of dowry. Goody (1973) was the first to demonstrate that dowry has broader implications than just as one aspect of a marriage transaction. It is, in fact, a payment of a daughter's share of the family inheritance (full or partial) given to the daughter at the time of marriage (see, e.g., Gen 31:14–16; Josh 15:18–19; and *m. Ketub.* 6.6).

At marriage, women in traditional, patriarchal societies shift from being "embedded" in (under the authority, legal responsibility, and care of) their fathers to a similar status in their husbands (e.g., *m. Ketub.* 4.4–5). Thus the groom was given the woman's property to administer (the legal term is "usufruct"); but it nonetheless belonged to her and was passed to her children, as distinct from the personal property of the husband, or his kin group, or his children from other marriages. This is nowhere made clearer than in the Code of Hammurabi (§§137–84), where the laws of inheritance, dowry, indirect dowry, and bridewealth are all interconnected. For examples, see Tobit (third/second century BCE), Mibtahiah's dowry arrangements in the Elephantine papyri (fifth century BCE), and the Babatha documents from the Transjordan (second century CE).

Harrell and Dickey build on Goody's work by further elucidating the functions and intentions of the dowry (1985). They argue that the dowry is not only an economic transaction but also an expression of the family's honor on the occasion of a daughter's wedding. The size of the dowry demonstrates to the community how wealthy the family is, and is one way of publicly displaying their honor. This is not hoarded wealth but transmitted wealth, providing the daughter with her portion of the family's goods, money, and property.

Schlegel and Eloul extend the discussion of honor beyond the public display of wealth: a dowry may also be the means of *acquiring* honor or a client. A son-in-law of higher status increases the family's honor, while one of lower status may be enlisted along with his family as a client (1988:301).

Schlegel and Eloul go on to define the economic character of marriage more precisely. They approach marriage transactions as "a function of the kind of property relations within the society" (294), and as a means of adjusting "labor needs, the transmission of property, and status concerns" (305). They also include a list of characteristics exhibited by societies that utilize dowry systems (294–99).

"Bridewealth" is a term covering a wide range of transfers of goods and services from the groom's kin to the bride's kin. As Goody makes clear, these diverse transactions can have a wide variety of implications for social structure (1973:2). Like dowry, bridewealth is also attested in texts from ancient Israel (Heb. *mōhar*; e.g., Gen 34:12), postbiblical Judea (e.g., *m. Ketub.* 1.2; 5.1), as well as in Babylonia, Nuzi, Ugarit, and Greece—but not Rome.

"Indirect dowry" is property and/or cash given by the groom's kin either directly to the bride or indirectly through her kin; it may be all or part of the bridewealth. The story of Isaac's betrothal to Rebekah demonstrates both indirect dowry (in the form of silver and gold jewelry, and clothing) as well as general bridewealth given to her mother and brother (Gen 24:53; see possibly Luke 15:8–10).

Dowries and indirect dowries, as already noted, originate in opposite families. They have the same (or similar) economic result, however, by bestowing property on the new couple. This gives each family a vested interest in the new couple. Bridewealth that is not handed over to the bride is utilized in some societies to secure wives for the bride's brothers, if she has any. "Indeed it involves a kind of rationing system. What goes out for a bride has to come in for a sister" (Goody 1973:5).

The place of indirect dowry in combination with dowry in agonistic societies (such as those in the Mediterranean) is a procedure for balancing honor concerns. By these means both contracting families avoid becoming too indebted to the other (i.e., becoming the client of the other); see Schlegel and Eloul (1988:303). For a collection of essays on dowry and bridewealth in cross-cultural perspective, see Comaroff (1980). In his introduction Comaroff critiques previous theories and approaches (1–47).

In her excellent historical and anthropological synthesis on the roots of patriarchy, Lerner (1986) outlines the importance of taking account of class and economics in any analysis of marriage arrangements. She makes clear that the stratification of society is perpetuated by dowries and bridewealth: homogamy (marriage within the group of one's own social level) circulates property and wealth within particular social classes (108). Furthermore, concubinage and slavery serve to keep a segment of the women disenfranchised and powerless. In this vein, it is important to note that the regulations for early Christian families assume that household slaves are an integral part of the family structure (see Eph 6:5–9 and Col 4:1).

Inheritance is the disposition of movable and immovable property, most commonly at the death of the male head of the family (e.g., Gen 25:29–34; Sir 33:23; Luke 12:13; 15:11–12). But, as discussed above, Goody has also demonstrated that dowry is a means of "pre-mortem inheritance" given to the daughters at the time of their marriage (1973).

Emmanuel Todd's methodology is demonstrably sexist when it comes to determining inheritance traditions (under his rubrics of "equality" and "inequality" [1985:7]). He fails to take two variables into account. First, in dowry-giving societies, such as those represented in the Bible and much of the ancient Mediterranean world, the dowry functions as premortem inheritance (viz., a daughter's share of the family wealth given before her father's death). Second, while Todd attempts to construct a kinship typology of the whole world, he fails to consider that in many societies (including ancient Rome and the U.S.) both sons and daughters may inherit equally at the parents' death; he speaks only of sons inheriting (see also Num 27:3–4; Job 42:15). Note that the wife is included neither in the Numbers prescriptive list nor in most ancient lists of successors. The reason is that her portion was her dowry and indirect dowry.

Note that Deut 21:17 designates a double portion for the eldest son. This was also practiced in late Judaism (*m. B. Baṭ.* 8.3–5), as well as in Nuzi and Old Babylonia, but not in Greece or Rome.

6.0 The Israelite/Judean Family

For overviews of the kinship issues in the Bible, see Patai (1959), Malina (1993:117–48), Hanson (1989a, 1989b, 1990), and the articles in the *Anchor Bible Dictionary* by Collins, Hamilton, Wilson, and Wright (1992). Among those treating the biblical texts, only Patai, Malina, Hanson, and Wilson consciously employ social-scientific methods. The others take a basically descriptive or historical approach; the usefulness of these others resides in their identification of historical shifts and the listing of texts.

Patai (1959) aims to provide a comprehensive overview of biblical texts related to kinship; his citation of texts is nearly exhaustive for each topic: marriage and divorce, sexuality, childbearing and child rearing, childhood, the life cycle, and inheritance.

Malina provides the reader with a brief introduction to kinship analysis along with its importance for biblical studies (1993:117–48). Besides the synchronic/diachronic chart of marriage strategies (see fig. 3.2 above), one of the most helpful features of Malina's treatment is his comparison of the main structural features of ancient Judean and modern U.S. kinship systems (119–26).

For a detailed analysis of the levels of Israelite society as it relates to kinship (tribe, clan, extended residential family) one should consult Gottwald (1979). Goody provides an analysis of the marriage strategies in Genesis and Ruth and their implications (1990:242–60). Pilch contrasts the parenting styles and strategies of the modern United States to those articulated in the Bible, especially in Proverbs and Ben Sirach (1993).

Using the Herodian family as a test case, I explore the main issues in kinship studies with regard to ancient Israel and Judah through the second temple period: genealogy and descent (Hanson 1989a), marriage and divorce (1989b), and the economics of kinship (inheritance and dowry) systems (1990). Each article includes cross-cultural comparisons to Mesopotamian, Ugaritic, Greek, Roman, and U.S. practices.

7.0 The Greek Family

A wide-ranging analysis of the family in archaic and classical Greek society is carried out by W. K. Lacey (1968). The macrostructure of the book is historical and geographical in sequence. The microstructure is synchronic, dealing with the οἶκος, *oikos*, "household," marriage strategies, children, property, the life cycle, aristocracy, law, the status of women, and so on. An important complement to Lacey's study is that of Hunter (1993), who explores the social implications of law in comparison to the actual practice of Greek kinship structures and the impact both of these had on the lives of Greek women.

J. K. Campbell provides an outstanding ethnography of kinship among modern Greek peasants kinship (1964:36–212). His analysis is especially illuminating with regard to family structure and roles. Ernestine Friedl (1962) provides a useful complement to Campbell. She covers issues of family economics, consumption, dowries, and inheritance (18–74). Though modern, these works are helpful because of the many historical continuities in Greek social structure.

The examples they employ are from real families in real situations and nicely complement historical reconstructions from law codes, literary works, and archaeological remains.

The importance of Greek kinship issues for biblical studies is twofold. First, Greek culture affected the entire eastern Mediterranean world (and as far east as India) through the hellenization policies of Alexander the Great and his successors—especially the Seleucids in Syria and the Ptolemies in Egypt, who controlled Judah for approximately two hundred years. Second, many of the earliest Christian communities we read about in the NT were formed in Greece itself: Corinth, Thessalonica, and Philippi.

8.0 The Roman Family

The details of Roman kinship have been of particular interest to anthropologists through the years for several reasons: the specificity of Latin legal terminology for kinship relations and arrangements, the comprehensiveness of Roman law, and the influence of Roman law on Western culture. For a brief overview of the Roman family and household, see Garnsey and Saller (1987:126–47).

Two volumes of collected essays edited by Beryl Rawson provide detailed studies of Roman kinship issues. In the first (Rawson 1986) nine scholars contribute essays ranging from general overviews (Rawson, "The Roman Family," 1–57) to examinations of individual cases for their broader implications (e.g., Suzanne Dixon, "Family Finances: Terentia and Tullia," 93–120). The bibliographic essay by Binkowski and Rawson (243–57) will guide the researcher through the massive literature, and the extensive bibliography will be of special interest to those wishing to pursue detailed issues (258–72).

The second volume (Rawson 1991) offers nine more essays. Again, they range from overviews (e.g., Rawson, "Adult-Child Relationships in Roman Society," 7–30) to very focused ethnographic/archaeological analyses (e.g., Andrew Wallace-Hadrill, "Houses and Households: Sampling Pompeii and Herculaneum," 191–227). One should note that all the contributors to these two volumes are classicists or social historians rather than anthropologists.

9.0 Conclusions

In examining kinship issues (or any other social phenomena), one should not treat them in isolation. Social institutions always interact with, overlap, and change in response to other institutions. They form a network or web of relationships. Thus economics at the local level in ancient Palestine was controlled largely by kinship institutions. What a person's parents did for a living usually determined what that person did: farmers' children became farmers, potters' children became potters. Kinship also interacted with politics since traditional monarchies followed patrilineal descent principles. And religion affected kinship in that membership in both the Israelite cultic community and the priesthood was based on birth.

10.0 Works Cited

Of course, the nuances of laws, group regulations, and preferences are distinctive in each society and historical period. But kinship studies provide an analytical framework within which to ask the necessary questions, organize data, and make cross-cultural comparisons. Obviously the characters we find in the Bible lived and worked in families far different from our own. If we want to understand their experiences, perspectives, and values, then we must understand the different kinds of families in which they were socialized.

Barr, James
    1988   " 'Abba' Isn't 'Daddy.' " *JTS* 39:28–47.
Campbell, J. K.
    1964   *Honour, Family, and Patronage.* New York: Oxford
              University Press.
Collins, Raymond F.
    1992   "Marriage (NT)." *ABD.* 4:569–72. New York: Doubleday.
Comaroff, John, ed.
    1980   *The Meaning of Marriage Payments.* Studies in
              Anthropology 7. London: Academic Press.
Delaney, Carol
    1987   "Seeds of Honor, Fields of Shame." In *Honor and Shame
              and the Unity of the Mediterranean.* Ed. D. D. Gilmore.
              Pages 35–48. American Anthropological Association
              Special Publication 22. Washington, D.C.: American
              Anthropological Association.
Eickelmann, Dale F.
    1989   *The Middle East: An Anthropological Approach.* 2d ed.
              Englewood Cliffs: Prentice-Hall.
Elliott, John H.
    1990   *A Home for the Homeless: A Social-Scientific Criticism of
              1 Peter, Its Situation and Strategy.* 2d ed. Minneapolis:
              Augsburg Fortress.

Fernea, Elizabeth Warnock
  1965   *Guests of the Sheik: An Ethnography of an Iraqi Village.*
          Garden City, N.Y.: Doubleday.
Fox, Robin
  1967   *Kinship and Marriage: An Anthropological Perspective.*
          New York: Penguin.
Friedl, Ernestine
  1962   *Vasilika: A Village in Modern Greece.* Case Studies in
          Cultural Anthropology. New York: Holt, Rinehart and
          Winston.
Garnsey, Peter, and Richard Saller
  1987   *The Roman Empire: Economy, Society, and Culture.*
          Berkeley: Univ. of California Press.
Geertz, Hildred
  1979   "Family Ties." In *Meaning and Order in Moroccan Society.*
          Ed. C. Geertz, H. Geertz, and L. Rosen. Pages 315–91.
          Cambridge Studies in Cultural Systems. New York:
          Cambridge Univ. Press.
Goode, William J.
  1982   *The Family.* 2d ed. Foundations of Modern Sociology
          Series. Englewood Cliffs: Prentice-Hall.
Goody, Jack
  1973   "Bridewealth and Dowry in Africa and Eurasia." In
          Bridewealth and Dowry. Ed. Jack Goody and Stanley J.
          Tambiah. Pages 1–58. Cambridge Papers in Social
          Anthropology 7. Cambridge: Cambridge University
          Press.
  1990   *The Oriental, the Ancient, and the Primitive: Systems of
          Marriage and the Family in the Pre-Industrial Societies of
          Eurasia.* Studies in Literacy, Family, Culture, and the
          State. Cambridge: Cambridge University Press.
Goody, Jack, and Stanley J. Tambiah
  1973   *Bridewealth and Dowry.* Cambridge Papers in Social
          Anthropology 7. Cambridge: Cambridge University
          Press.
Gottwald, Norman K.
  1979   *The Tribes of Yahweh: A Sociology of the Religion of
          Liberated Israel, 1250–1050 B.C.E.* Maryknoll, N.Y.: Orbis.
Hamilton, Victor
  1992   "Marriage (OT and ANE)." *ABD.* 4:559–69. New York:
          Doubleday.
Hanson, K. C.
  1989a   "The Herodians and Mediterranean Kinship. Part I:
          Genealogy and Descent." *BTB* 19:75–84.

1989b   "The Herodians and Mediterranean Kinship. Part II:
         Marriage and Divorce." *BTB* 19:142–51.
1990   "The Herodians and Mediterranean Kinship. Part III:
         Economics." *BTB* 20:10–21.

Harrell, Stevan, and Sara A. Dickey
1985   "Dowry Systems in Complex Societies." *Ethnology*
         24:105–20.

Howard, Michael C.
1989   *Contemporary Cultural Anthropology.* 3d ed. Glenview,
         Ill.: Scott, Foresman & Co.

Hunter, Virginia J.
1993   "Agnatic Kinship in Athenian Law and Athenian Family
         Practice: Its Implications for Women." In *Law, Politics
         and Society in the Ancient Mediterranean World.* Ed. B.
         Halpern and D. W. Hobson. Pages 100–21. Sheffield:
         Sheffield Academic.

Jacoby, Tamar
1990   "Families." *Lear's.* April, 68–73.

Keesing, Roger M.
1975   *Kin Group and Social Structure.* New York: Holt,
         Rinehart and Winston.

Kuper, Adam, and Jessica Kuper, eds.
1996   *The Social Science Encyclopedia.* 2d ed. London:
         Routledge & Kegan Paul.

Lacey, W. K.
1968   *The Family in Classical Greece.* Aspects of Greek and
         Roman Life. Ithaca, N.Y.: Cornell Univ. Press.

Lerner, Gerda
1986   *The Creation of Patriarchy.* New York: Oxford University
         Press.

Malina, Bruce J.
1986   " 'Religion' in the World of Paul." *BTB* 16:96–101.
1993   *The New Testament World: Insights from Cultural
         Anthropology.* Rev. ed. Louisville: Westminster/John
         Knox.

Patai, Raphael
1959   *Sex and Family in the Bible and the Middle East.* New
         York: Macmillan. (Also published as: *Family, Love and
         the Bible.* London: MacGibbon & Kee, 1960.)

Pilch, John J.
1993   " 'Beat His Ribs While He Is Young' (Sir 30:12): A
         Window on the Mediterranean World." *BTB* 23:101–13.

Rawson, Beryl, ed.
1986   *The Family in Ancient Rome: New Perspectives.* Ithaca,
         N.Y.: Cornell University Press.

1991   *Marriage, Divorce, and Children in Ancient Rome.*
Canberra: Humanities Research Centre; Oxford:
Clarendon.

Sahlins, Marshall D.
1968   *Tribesmen.* Foundations of Modern Anthropology
Series. Englewood Cliffs, N.J.: Prentice-Hall.

Schlegel, Alice, and Rohn Eloul
1988   "Marriage Transactions: Labor, Property, Status."
American Anthropologist 90:291–309.

Schneider, David M.
1980   *American Kinship: A Cultural Account.* Chicago:
University of Chicago Press.

Schusky, Ernest L.
1964   *Manual for Kinship Analysis.* Studies in Anthropological
Method. New York: Holt, Rinehart and Winston.

Sills, David L., ed.
1968   *International Encyclopedia of the Social Sciences.* 18 vols.
New York: Macmillan.

Stack, Carol B.
1974   *All Our Kin: Strategies for Survival in a Black Community.*
New York: Harper & Row.

Todd, Emmanuel
1985   *The Explanation of Ideology: Family Structures and Social
Systems.* Trans. D. Garrioch. Family, Sexuality and
Social Relations in Past Times. Oxford: Basil Blackwell.

Williams, Robin M., Jr.
1970   *American Society: A Sociological Interpretation.* 3d ed.
New York: Knopf.

Wilson, Robert R.
1975   "The Old Testament Genealogies in Recent Research."
JBL 94:169–89.

1977   *Genealogy and History in the Biblical World.* New Haven:
Yale University Press.

1992   "Genealogy, Genealogies." In *ABD.* 2:929–32. New
York: Doubleday.

Wright, C. J. H.
1992   "Family." *ABD.* 2:761–69. New York: Doubleday.

4

Clean/Unclean, Pure/Polluted, and Holy/Profane: The Idea and the System of Purity

Jerome H. Neyrey
University of Notre Dame

1.0 Pervasive Importance of This Topic

In the Hebrew and Christian scriptures we often read of some thing, person, or place labeled as "unclean," "common," or "polluted." In regard to foods, Israelites prohibited the eating of some animals (Lev 11). When Peter saw the contents of the sheet lowered from heaven and was told to eat those animals, he responded, "I have never eaten anything common or unclean" (Acts 10:14). Paul twice wrote to communities in which some members considered certain foods permissible and others proscribed (1 Cor 8 and 10; Rom 14–15). Someone who ate food labeled "unclean" could be "defiled" (1 Cor 8:7). Paul himself stated, "I know . . . that nothing is unclean in itself; but it is unclean for anyone who thinks it is unclean" (Rom 14:14). Pharisees became mightily upset that Jesus or his disciples ate with "unclean" hands (Luke 11:38; Mark 7:2–4). For his part, Jesus criticized as hypocritical the Pharisaic concern for the cleanness of the "outside" of the cup (Matt 25:25–26). And Jesus himself shocked the Pharisees when he "declared all foods clean" (Mark 7:19). What is meant when people label foods "clean" or "unclean"? This is clearly not a matter of hygiene or concern for viral or bacterial contamination. Why are people who eat unclean foods themselves considered as "defiled"?

Purity concerns also arise in relation to the physical body. In Leviticus priests are expected to examine and declare whether certain persons are "clean" and so fit to stand and worship, or whether they are "unclean" and so are to be excluded (Lev 13; see Mark 1:44). Much attention is given to the skin and surface of the body, but also to its wholeness as a precondition for access to holy space and holy tasks. For example, according to Lev 21:16–21, priests with particular bodily defects may not function in the temple. This prescription also extended beyond the ranks of priests and labeled those outside the group (see 1QSa 2:3–10 and 1QM 7:4–7). It is precisely these folk whom Jesus commanded to be invited to table (Luke 14:13–14, 21). In several places, Josephus recorded a fight between two high priests, one of whom mutilated his opponent and so disqualified him from further priestly service:

> Hyrcanus threw himself at the feet of Antigonus, who with his own teeth lacerated his suppliant's ears, in order to disqualify him for ever, under any change of circumstances, from resuming the high priesthood; since freedom from physical defect (ὁλοκλήρους, *holoklērous*) is essential to the holder of that office (*War* 1.269–70; see *Ant.* 14.366; *War* 5.228).

Philo also explained the law of physical integrity, which, because of its importance for this study, we cite in full:

> With regard to the priests there are the following laws. It is ordained that the priest should be perfectly sound throughout, without any bodily deformity. No part, that is, must be lacking or have been mutilated, nor on the other hand redundant, whether the excrescence be congenital or an aftergrowth due to disease. Nor must the skin have been changed into a leprous state or into malignant tatters or warts or any other eruptive growth (*On the Special Laws* 1.80; see also 1.117).

Why were such people labeled "unclean," and why should this exclude them from priestly service in the temple? The issue is hardly one of handicapped inability to perform the tasks.

The mighty deeds of Jesus included the casting out of "unclean" spirits (Mark 1:23; 3:11; Luke 6:18; 9:42). One might ask why the evangelist labeled the demon "unclean." Does this add anything to our perception of it? Moreover, the leper asked Jesus to make him "clean," not simply to heal him (Mark 1:40–42). Although the menstruating woman in Mark 5:24–35 is not labeled "unclean," that would have been the common perception of the bystanders. Jairus's daughter, who was dead when Jesus came to her (Mark 5:35–42), was unclean and all who touched her would become unclean as well, since death is one of the "Fathers of Uncleanness." Jesus' critics cannot credit him with the holy role of a prophet when he has bodily contact with a woman known to be a sinner (Luke 7:39). A wide variety of issues and problems, then, are connected with the language of "unclean," "common," and "polluted" in the Hebrew and Christian scriptures.

While attending to what is "unclean," "polluted," and "common," we should also ask what is meant by the label "holy," especially when applied to God ("Be ye holy as I am holy," Lev 11:44–45; 1 Pet 1:16). Paul stated that the will of God is our "sanctification" (1 Thess 4:3), which he clarified by adding, "God has not called us for uncleanness but in holiness" (4:7). To be holy as God is holy, ancient Jews performed extensive washing rites. The water that Jesus turned into wine was in jars kept there "for purification" (John 2:6). We read of controversy between disciples of John the Baptizer and other Jews "over purification" (John 4:25). But why are some persons and objects declared "pure"? It is more than their being separated and consecrated for temple use.

Although we mentioned three contrasting pairs of labels, "pure and profane," "clean and unclean," and "pure and polluted," the semantic word field for this topic is broad, including the following terms (Neyrey 1990:54–55, 1991:275–76).

1.1 Terms for "Purity"

1. clean, to cleanse, cleanness (καθαρός, *katharos;* καθαρίζω, *katharizō;* καθαρισμός, *katharismos*): Luke 2:22; 5:12; 11:41; Acts 10:15; 15:9; Rom 14:20; 2 Cor 7:1

2. sweep (σαρόω, *saroō*): Luke 11:25 par. Matt 12:44

3. pure, to purify, purity (ἁγνός, *hagnos;* ἁγνίζω, *hagnizō;* ἁγνότης, *hagnotēs*): Acts 21:24, 26; 24:18; 2 Cor 6:6; 7:11; 11:2, 3; Phil 4:8

4. holy, to make holy, holiness (ἅγιος, *hagios;* ἁγιάζω, *hagiazō;* ἁγιότης, *hagiotēs;* ἁγιασμός, *hagiasmos*):

   ἁγιάζω, *hagiazō:* Rom 15:16; 1 Cor 1:2; 6:11; 7:14; 1 Thess 5:23

   ἁγιασμός, *hagiasmos:* Rom 6:19, 22; 1 Cor 1:30; 1 Thess 4:3, 4, 7

   ἅγιος, *hagios:* Rom 1:7; 7:12; 8:27; 11:26; 12:1, 13; 15:25; 16:2; 1 Cor 1:2; 3:17; 16:1, 15, 20; 2 Cor 1:1; 8:4; 9:1; 13:12; Phil 1:1; 4:21–22; 1 Thess 3:13; 5:26–27; Phlm 5, 7 (references to "Holy" Spirit not included)

   ἁγιότης, *hagiotēs:* Heb 12:10

5. pure (πιστικός, *pistikos*): Mark 14:3; John 12:3

6. innocent (ἀκέραιος, *akeraios*): Matt 10:16; Rom 16:19; Phil 2:5

7. spotless (ἀμίαντος, *amiantos*): Heb 7:26; 13:4; Jas 1:27; 1 Pet 1:4

8. unstained (ἄσπιλος, *aspilos*): Jas 1:27; 1 Pet 1:19; 2 Pet 3:14

9. blameless (ἄμωμος, *amōmos*): Eph 1:4; 5:27; Phil 2:15; Col 1:22; 1 Pet 1:19

10. blameless (ἀνέγκλητος, *anenklētos*): 1 Cor 1:8; Col 1:22; 1 Tim
    3:10; Titus 1:6–7
11. faultless (ἀνεπίλημπτος, *anepilēmptos*): 1 Tim 3:2; 5:7; 6:14
12. innocent (ἄμεμπτος, *amemptos;* ἀμέμπτως, *amemptōs*): Phil 2:15;
    3:6; 1 Thess 2:10; 3:13; 5:23
13. innocent (ἀθῷος, *athōos*): Matt 27:4, 24
14. innocent (ἄκακος, *akakos*): Rom 16:18; Heb 7:26.

1.2 Terms for "Pollution"

1. defilement, to defile (μιασμός, *miasmos;* μιαίνω, *miainō;* μίασμα,
   miasma): John 18:28; Titus 1:15; 2 Pet 2:10, 20
2. defilement, to defile (μολυσμός, *molusmos;* μολύνω, *molunō*): 1 Cor
   8:7; 2 Cor 7:1; Rev 3:4
3. unclean (ἀκάθαρτος, *akathartos;* ἀκαθαρσία, *akatharsia*):
   ἀκαθαρσία, *akatharsia:* Rom 1:24; 6:19; 2 Cor 12:21; Gal 5:19;
      1 Thess 2:3; 4:7
   ἀκάθαρτος, *akathartos:* 1 Cor 7:14; 2 Cor 6:17; Eph 5:5
4. spot (σπίλος, *spilos;* σπιλόω, *spiloō*): Eph 5:27; 2 Pet 2:13; Jas 3:6;
   Jude 23
5. stain (μῶμος, *mōmos*): 2 Pet 2:13
6. common, to make common (κοινός, *koinos;* κοινόω, *koinoō*): Acts
   10:14–15, 28; 11:8–9; 21:28; Rom 14:14
7. defilement (ἀλίσγημα, *halisgēma*): Acts 15:20.

Even this list should be expanded to include labels such as "whole"
or "divided" and "complete" or "incomplete" (Elliott 1993:71–72).

The positive labels ("holy," "clean," and "pure") and the negative ones ("profane," "unclean," and "polluted") are pervasive throughout the Christian scriptures and the literature of second temple
Judaism. Moreover, they serve as potent weapons that can include or
exclude. They pertain to the fundamental ways in which Jesus, Paul,
James, and other Jews perceived and classified persons and things in
their world.

Yet what do they really mean? Why are they so potent? So
pervasive? This chapter offers a survey of pertinent literature that
aims at equipping a reader of the Hebrew and Christian scriptures to
appreciate these labels in terms of the culture of the ancient writers.
Thus when we examine these labels we are not simply conducting a
word study, but looking at the broad cultural system that finds
expression in these terms. That broad cultural context, or symbolic
universe, is called a "purity system."

Those unfamiliar with the topic may indeed be confused by the terminology just noted and by the very idea of examining "clean" and "unclean" together. In the literature, all the above words and terms tend to be understood and discussed under the general rubric of "the language of purity." This is so partly because the discussion has been shaped by concentration on the term "purity" in the Hebrew scriptures (*thr*) and partly because "purity" is an abstract code word for what is culturally acceptable. Although Jews and Christians regularly used the language of "clean" and "unclean," the umbrella concept for this discussion is the abstract notion of "purity."

Students of late Judaism and early Christianity have been busy investigating these matters. The approaches to issues of "unclean," "common," and "polluted" seem to have taken two different but compatible directions, one descriptive and historical and the other anthropological and social.

2.0 Historical and Descriptive Approaches

Although the material may at first seem strange and difficult to understand, the Mishnah contains valuable data on "clean" and "unclean." We recommend the Danby translation because it contains (a) an excellent index to trace key terms such as "Father of Uncleanness," and (b) an appendix on "The Rules of Uncleanness" from *Eliyahu Rabbah* (pp. 800–804), which is a most useful summary of the topic. In particular, one should read *Kelim* 1.1–9, which contains elaborate lists of things clean and unclean, all of which are ranked in hierarchical order, which is another aspect of "purity systems."

We start our survey with several general dictionary articles. L. E. Toombs (1962) began his survey with an attempt to deal with the words "clean" and "unclean," first in terms of general religious language and then in terms of what they have in common with Canaanite and Babylonian religion. His main interest lay in an extensive exposition of their occurrence and use, especially in the ritual or cultic parts of the Hebrew scriptures. Toombs's article typifies a descriptive approach to the concepts of "clean and unclean," namely, what objects or persons come under the label "clean" and "unclean" in regard to the temple and cultic ritual.

A much more enlightened article by D. P. Wright (1992) identifies the relevant terminology for "clean" and "unclean" in the Hebrew scriptures, then distinguishes between permitted and proscribed impurities. Permitted impurities are those which occur naturally and

necessarily (i.e., those related to death, sex, disease, and cult); proscribed impurities are controllable and unnecessary (i.e., idolatry,
murder). Wright then examines each class in detail, noting how each
is a "father of impurities," and what is the appropriate remedy for
each (on this key term, see *m.Pesaḥ.* 1.6; *Šeqal.* 8.4; *ʿEd.* 2.1; *Meʿil.* 4.4;
Kelim 1.1; *Ṭohar.* 1.5; *Makš.* 4.2, 8 and *Ṭ. Yom* 1.4, 5; 2.1, 8; 3.1). He then
examines bodily excretions, blemishes, foods, and mixtures as these
are labeled "unclean." What sets Wright's article apart from other
surveys is his attention to the meaning of these labels, which takes
him into the realm of cultural anthropology. In discussing the "rationale" for impurities, he notes seven traditional reasons that are
not entirely satisfactory for explaining the function of impurities in
religious communities. Then he succinctly presents a model of purity
from the works of anthropologist Mary Douglas, which both he and
other OT scholars have profitably adapted for interpreting of Leviticus and Deuteronomy. He digests Douglas's work into three key
insights: (a) purity is related to wholeness and normality; (b) the
definition of purity derives not from observed reality but from the
cultural understanding of particular societies; purity is a language
expressing social concerns; and (c) the physical body manifests the
purity concerns of the social body. He applies this material to the P
tradition and its concerns with space and sacrificial foods. This
article supplies excellent data about the occurrence, classification,
and treatment of impurities in the OT. Moreover, it is sensitive and
informed about the meaning of the data in terms of a "system" of
cultural perceptions. It is an enlightened and necessary introduction
to the topic.

Jacob Neusner turned his attention to this topic first in a book
(1973b), then in an article (1975). Ever the careful historian, in his
book he distinguishes three blocks of texts in terms of their historical provenance: the biblical legacy, texts from the second temple
period, and talmudic materials. As had been frequently noted, the
materials from the Hebrew scriptures dealing with "clean and
unclean" treat mainly of priestly texts and temple matters. In
describing the literature of the second temple period, Neusner
basically catalogues the various associations of "unclean," with
either idolatry or moral defilement, especially sexual sins. "Clean"
is linked to temple, especially ritual imagery and praxis at Qumran. In regard to the talmudic materials, Neusner notes that concern over "clean and unclean" is still linked with temple, but that
the rabbis were increasingly interested in the moral or allegori-
cal meaning of these concepts for home life. Throughout, Neusner
deals with the material descriptively and from a historical perspective. Yet he does raise a critical social issue: according to his historical and descriptive analysis, the language of "clean" and "unclean"

tended to differentiate one sect from another. Although Neusner was adapting Douglas's seminal work on purity, he ignored the model of the body that was central to her presentation of purity. His book, then, supplies a reader with a careful historical classification of material pertaining to purity.

In examining what is "clean" and "unclean," scholars since the mid-1970s have concentrated either on specific topics or on specific texts and communities. For example, Roger P. Booth (1986) focuses on the washing of hands incident in Mark 7. His interest is in historical questions, such as the tradition history behind Mark's account, as well as the general legal issues involved. Neusner (1976) likewise investigates the history of the accusation in Matt 25:25–26 that Pharisees are concerned with the washing of the outside of cups; he shows that there was a lively debate on the issue between the followers of Hillel and Shammai. Michael Newton (1985) took up the investigation of cultic or ritual cleanness. The first part of his book surveys the terminology of "purity" at Qumran, the basic understanding of that group as "holy" or separated, and the ritual actions that embodied this holiness, either washing rites or concerns over food and meals. In regard to Paul, Newton deals first with cultic terminology in Paul and its relationship to his notion of "purity." He then takes up the issue of washing and entrance rites, which are described in terms of "clean" and "pure." Finally, he discusses moral issues, including table fellowship and the purity of food, sexual uncleanness, corpse uncleanness, and separation from evil people. Although Newton knows of anthropological studies of these concepts, his own work is basically descriptive and comparative.

For obvious reasons, Qumran texts, which contain numerous references to the language of purity and pollution, have become the object of many studies (e.g., Isenberg 1975; Newton 1985). Comparably, studies of the Hebrew scriptures regularly give attention to food laws (Milgrom 1963; Soler 1979) and to the priestly issues related to cult and temple (Neusner 1973b; Newton 1985). These studies, however, remain basically (a) *historical* (How ancient were such customs as the washing of hands or vessels? How widespread was the Jewish refusal to eat with Gentiles?) or (b) *descriptive* (What issues came under the rubric of "clean" and "unclean"?). Such approaches dominate critical biblical scholarship and are indeed valuable. Yet they are not the only approach to this topic. Nor do they answer the basic question of what "clean" and "unclean" *mean* in Judaism and early Christianity or why such labeling takes place at all. These questions require different methods of analysis.

3.0 Anthropological and Social Approaches

Alongside historical and descriptive approaches to "clean and unclean," other scholars have come to the biblical texts asking different sorts of questions. What basically is meant by "purity" or by "clean" and "unclean"? What is the social significance of labeling something "pure" or "polluted"? On one level, we can observe that all peoples declare some persons or things "unclean" or taboo (for examples of Greek labeling, see Parker 1983:357–65). Rather than merely compile descriptive lists of these objects, however, we can inquire about the very process of labeling itself. Labeling is a symbolic action that encodes considerable information about the way the labelers view the world. What is the rationale for these categories vis-à-vis specific persons or objects? The inquiry into "unclean," "common," "polluted," and "taboo" takes us into the realm of cultural anthropology.

The effort to understand the social and cultural meanings of "clean" and "unclean" leads the reader to consider the overarching "system" of a culture or to reconstruct its "symbolic universe." For example, Neusner, although he is primarily interested in the history of the material, urges us to consider historical data such as mishnaic material on sacrifice and sanctuary in terms of a "complete system" (1979:105). His presentation of this material is done systematically in terms of a "mapping," that is, the social "construction of worlds of meaning." Although the temple lay in ruins, mishnaic authors still constructed an orderly world, classifying all things in terms of "clean" and "unclean" in relation to the sanctuary remembered and expected. Physical geography gave way to ideological geography. Neusner's article is an important orientation for readers on this topic because it reminds us that "purity" has two meanings: (a) the general sense of an orderly cosmos and an elaborate system of classification, and (b) the specific Jewish system of labeling in ancient times. This is not strictly anthropology but more a matter of social description; yet it orients a reader to begin asking sociological questions about the broader meaning of "purity" in terms of cultural systems.

British anthropologist Mary Douglas offers an alternate way of investigating the general language of "clean" and "unclean" and its specific forms in Jewish and Christian literature. Her writings, especially *Purity and Danger* (1966), have greatly influenced biblical scholars, and are of such seminal importance for analyzing this topic that no scholar dares treat Lev 11 without engaging her discussion. Because her approach offers a productive line of investigation of the language of purity, we pause here to familiarize readers with its basic concepts and models. This material figures prominently in studies by biblical scholars whose works we will shortly survey.

In *Purity and Danger,* Douglas begins by surveying the standard anthropological explanations of defilement, but then suggests that we view defilement in primarily symbolic terms. Her key insight lies in an analysis of what people generally perceive as "dirt," which is her code word for what we are discussing under the terms "polluted," "unclean," or "taboo." "Dirt" is itself a relative term which basically means that something is "out of place" in the perception of the labelers. Objects and persons may be "clean" in one situation but "dirty" in another. The issue lies in the social situation, namely, in the sense of order or the system of classifications that people use to organize their world. "Reflection on dirt," she argues, "involves reflection on the relations of order to disorder, being to non-being, form to formlessness, life to death" (1966:5). Elsewhere she states:

> Lord Chesterfield defined dirt as matter out of place. This implies only two conditions, a set of ordered relations and a contravention of that order. Thus the idea of dirt implies a structure of idea. For us dirt is a kind of compendium category for all events which blur, smudge, contradict, or otherwise confuse accepted classifications. The underlying feeling is that a system of values which is habitually expressed in a given arrangement of things has been violated (Douglas 1975:50–51).

In the context of the military, then, dirt would mean insubordination to a commanding officer. In a hospital it would mean unsterile material in the operating room. Something is out of place in each particular cosmos. The analysis of "dirt," then, is a matter of social perception and interpretation.

In *Purity and Danger,* Douglas takes up some specific considerations of dirt: (a) the classification of animals in Leviticus as clean and unclean, and (b) the physical body vis-à-vis clean and unclean. The classification of animals in Judaism reveals fundamental values encoded in Gen 1, the Priestly account of creation. God made "perfect" creatures in paradise that were distributed, some to the air, some to the land, and some to the sea. By "perfect" Douglas means that, for example, an "air" creature is expected to *stay* where it belongs (in the air, not the sea), *move* as an air creature should move (fly), and *eat* what air creatures should eat (seeds, not carrion). A bird that does not meet these criteria is "unclean." At stake therefore is a cultural perception of order—proper space, proper behavior, proper diet, and so on—in which the sense of what is "proper" derives from the culture.

What the Creator God did in Gen 1, then, defines the meaning of "holy" or "in place." Therefore what does not perfectly fill those categories is "unholy" or "unclean." The issue lies in knowing the symbolic categories of the culture so as to identify what does not fit them perfectly. Since perfect fit in a single category is essential, hybrids which cross boundaries and fit in two categories are obviously "unclean." Similarly, what is not "whole" is "unclean"—which clarifies why animals must be whole and unblemished for sacrificial offering (Lev 22:20–25), or why persons with bodily defects must stand apart from holy space and rites (Lev 21:16–20). Persons with mutilated bodies are unwhole and so in some sense "unclean," a concept important for understanding Jesus' miracle stories.

The taxonomy that Douglas developed for defining clean and unclean animals subsequently enjoyed a healthy scholarly conversation. She absorbed the insights of other anthropologists and eventually published a richer version of her analysis of the diet of the Israelites (1975a:261–73). She now adds to her examination of the classification of birds, fish, and animals the importance of looking at the multiple dimensions of Hebrew culture. Douglas then states three rules for classifying meat: (a) rejection of some animal kinds as unfit for table (Lev 11; Deut 14); (b) of those admitted as edible, the separation of the meat from blood before cooking (Lev 17:10; Deut 12:23–27); and (c) the total separation of milk from meat, which involves the minute specialization of utensils (Exod 23:19; 34:26; Deut 14:21). Analyzing dietary restrictions, Douglas could then identify what makes an animal an abomination, a classification that now includes notions of suitability for temple sacrifice and consumption as food.

A second major thrust of *Purity and Danger* reminds us that since so many taboos are connected with the physical body (e.g., leprosy, menstruation), further consideration of the body is especially necessary. Douglas urges us to see the grand sense of social order (macrocosm) mirrored in the physical body (microcosm).

The body is a model that can stand for any bounded system. Its boundaries can represent any boundaries that are threatened or precarious (1966:115). Just as the social body is perceived in some way as an ordered, structured system that is concerned to affirm and protect its order and its classifications, so the physical body of individuals in that same society mirrors the social sense of order and structure. Just as the social body is concerned about its boundaries (frontiers, city walls, gates), so too the physical body is the object of concern regarding its surface (skin, hair, clothing) and orifices (eyes, mouth, genitals, anus). What crosses the frontier, the city walls, and the door of the house is of great concern: strangers are always suspect. What flakes off the body surface and what pours from its orifices are of equally great concern. All these substances are matter that is "out of place," hence "unclean," even dangerous. This might suggest why the washing of hands was so important in Jesus' world. Hands feed the mouth, and since the mouth is the object of great concern, either in regard to what speech may exit or what foods may enter, then "clean" hands contribute to "cleanness" of mouth and person.

Douglas's overriding concern is with the *meaning* of purity and pollution classification. What is communicated by this type of language? Hence she asks about the social function of such labels and their relationship to the social construction of reality by a group. Labeling things or persons "pure" or "polluted" serves to establish identity and to maintain the group, which now has power to include or exclude. It can also reinforce the moral code of a group (1966:133). "In so far as they [labels] impose order on experience, they support clarification of forms and thus reduce dissonance" (1968:339). She sums up the significance of controlling bodily orifices this way:

> When rituals express anxiety about the body's orifices the sociological counterpart of this anxiety is a care to protect the political and cultural unity of a minority group. The Israelites were always in their history a hard-pressed minority. In their beliefs all the bodily issues were polluting, blood, pus, excreta, semen, etc. The threatened boundaries of their body politic would be well mirrored in their care for the integrity, unity and purity of the physical body (1966:124).

Douglas's work had an immediate and profound impact on biblical scholarship. Interpreters were quick to see her observations on purity and pollution as a clue to investigating the symbolic universe of the ancients. For example, Jean Soler employed many of Douglas's insights in a penetrating study of Gen 1 (1979). He demonstrated the replication of the Jewish cultural values of "wholeness" and "perfection" in the creation story, in the temple system, and in daily life. He clarified how a value such as "clean" = "whole/perfect" pervaded the Bible. And in a sense he made explicit what Douglas had occasionally stated but not really explained: how the basic labeling of something as whole and perfect is replicated throughout a culture. This is true not only in regard to the temple as the major religious symbol, but also in terms of food and dietary rules observed in homes, and in terms of the kashrut laws that keep separate the yoking of ox and ass, ban the interweaving of wool and flax, and so on. The same sense of wholeness or perfection of category occurs redundantly in all areas of life.

Additional studies have explicitly taken up Douglas's insights in greater detail and thereby offer a way to examine how pervasive the concepts of "clean" and "unclean" are and how extensively they are replicated in the culture of second temple Judaism and early Christianity. Among these Bruce Malina (1993) develops a comprehensive anthropological model of clean and unclean, which is illustrated from first-century Judaism, especially in terms of an analysis both of marriage and physical anomalies. He then applies the material to the issue of sacrifice, introducing into the discussion ideas about rites of passage that permit boundary crossings into areas normally "out of place" to "clean" people. Elsewhere Malina has also developed the concept of a "limit breaker" who crosses forbidden and dangerous boundaries in rites of passage pertaining to clean and unclean boundaries (1986:143–54). This helps to explain the apology in the Gospels for Jesus' commerce with the "tax collectors and sinners" of his world (see Mark 2:17). Finally, Malina considers specifically Christian purity arrangements, which would necessarily conflict with Jewish considerations.

Malina's work advances Douglas's discussion of "clean" and "unclean" by indicating how purity concerns are replicated in a variety of areas and how one needs a model of ritual to explain why and how people lapse into unclean states and come out of them. Like Douglas, Malina does not focus on a specific document, but illustrates the pervasiveness of this labeling throughout the Bible. The modeling is rich and productive, and the illustrations indicate the replication of such concerns throughout a symbolic system. Douglas's own works, while profound and stimulating, needed to be shaped into a workable model—which is the paramount value of Malina's discussion. It is an excellent introduction to the concept and function of purity systems.

Concerning the issue of holy people dealing with the unclean, Jerome Neyrey applies Douglas's material to the perception of Jesus in Mark's Gospel (1986b). Jesus is proclaimed by some as holy and sinless, yet others perceive him as constantly "out of place" because: (a) he has commerce with unclean people (lepers, menstruants, sinners, etc.); (b) he does not observe sacred times such as the sabbath or sacred places such as the temple; or (c) he disregards food rules and washing customs. Douglas's abstract ideas about "pollution" as matter "out of place" can be fleshed out in terms of the general cultural expectations about what it means to be "whole," "perfect," or "in place." The temple constituted the chief symbol for the order of the universe for first-century Jews, a symbol articulated by priests and described in Priestly writings in the scriptures. Using the Priestly documents, one can gain a sense of the basic cultural lines whereby second temple Jews classified and located persons, times, places, and things. These classifications can be expressed in a set of "maps" such as a "map of persons" (*t. Meg.* 2.7), "map of places" (*m. Kelim* 1.6–9), "map of times" (*m. Moʿed*) and "map of things" (*m. Kelim* 1.3). "Maps" come from the endless lists of things found throughout Jewish, Greek, and Christian literature. The four "maps" or lists in figure 4.1 are characteristic examples of pervasive classification systems. Such maps indicate what is meant by "clean" and "unclean" both in the temple context and also in various other areas of life: food and table fellowship, body emissions, kashrut laws, and agricultural customs.

Maps of Places, Persons, Things, and Times

A. *Map of Places*

"There are ten degrees of holiness. The *Land of Israel* is holier than any other land. . . . The *walled cities* [of the Land of Israel] are still more holy. . . . *Within the walls* (of Jerusalem) is still more holy. . . . The *Temple Mount* is still more holy. . . . The *Rampart* is still more holy. . . . The *Court of the Women* is still more holy. . . . The *Court of the Israelites* is still more holy. . . . The *Court of the Priests* is still more holy. . . . *Between the Porch and the Altar* is still more holy. . . . The *Sanctuary* is still more holy. . . . The *Holy of Holies* is still more holy" (*m. Kelim* 1.6–9).

B. *Map of Persons*

A list of the persons who may hear the scroll of Esther: priests, Levites, Israelites, converts, freed slaves, disqualified priests, netzins (temple slaves), mamzers (bastards), those with damaged testicles, Those without a penis (*t. Meg.* 2.7).

C. *Map of Things*

"There are things which convey uncleanness by contact (e.g., a dead creeping thing, male semen). They are exceeded by carrion. . . . They are exceeded by him that has connexion with a menstruant. . . . They are exceeded by the issue of him that has a flux, by his spittle, his semen, and his urine. . . . They are exceeded by [the uncleanness of] what is ridden upon [by him that has a flux]. . . . [The uncleanness of] what is ridden upon [by him that has a flux] is exceeded by what he lies upon. . . . [The uncleanness of] what he lies upon is exceeded by the uncleanness of him that has a flux" (*m. Kelim* 1.3).

D. *Map of Times*

The tractates on "time" are collected in the section of the Mishnah called *Moʿed: Šabbat* and *ʿErubin* (Sabbath), *Pesaḥim* (Feast of Passover), *Yoma* (Day of Atonement), *Sukka* (Feast of Tabernacles), *Yom Ṭob* (Festival Days), *Roš Haššana* (Feast of New Year), *Taʿanit* (Days of Fasting), *Megillah* (Feast of Purim), *Moʿed Qaṭan* (Mid-Festival Days)

Figure 4.1: Maps of Places, Persons, Things, and Times

With the aid of such maps Neyrey demonstrates how frequently Jesus was "out of place" according to the perceptions of his culture. So much of the conflict in the Gospels has to do with peer censure of Jesus as "unclean" for his breach of cultic and bodily purity rules. Yet, of course, his followers perceived him as authorized to cross these lines; they acclaimed him "the Holy One of God," innocent, sinless, and fully within God's camp. Throughout this study of Mark Neyrey clearly depends on the theory of Douglas and the modeling of Malina.

In a subsequent analysis of Mark 7, Neyrey further develops the model of purity for a "symbolic interpretation" of the conflict between Jesus and the Pharisees (1988a). This article examines why the Pharisees are said to be concerned with washing rites and with things external, and conversely, Jesus is credited with both abolition of food concerns and espousal of things internal. As Neusner observes:

> The Houses' rulings pertaining either immediately or ultimately to table-fellowship involve preparation of food, ritual purity relating directly to food or indirectly to the need to keep food ritually clean, and agricultural rules concerning the proper growing, tithing, and preparation of agricultural produce for table use. The agricultural laws relate to producing or preparing food for consumption, assuring either that tithes and offerings have been set aside as the law requires, or that conditions for the nurture of crops have conformed to biblical taboos. Of the 341 individual Houses' legal pericopae, no fewer than 229, approximately 67 per cent of the whole, directly or indirectly concern table-fellowship. . . . The Houses' laws of ritual cleanness apply in the main to the ritual cleanness of foods, and of people, dishes, and implements involved in its preparation (1973a: 86).

In order to understand the conflict between Jesus and the Pharisees over these matters, it was also necessary to develop a model of the physical body, especially the notion that control of the individual physical body replicates issues of social control of the group. With the help of this model it is possible to recognize that the Pharisees' guarding of the mouth in regard to food and the relative unconcern for it by Jesus symbolizes the relatively closed or open boundaries of each group. This social strategy embodies and replicates a more complete ideology of each group (see fig. 4.2). Thus using models both of Jewish purity concerns and of the physical body, Neyrey argues for a thorough correlation between socio-political strategy and bodily concerns (see fig. 4.3):

	Pharisees	Jesus and Followers
Core value	God's holiness (Lev 11:44)	God's mercy (Exod 33:19)
Symbolized in	Creation-as-ordering	Election and grace
Structural implications	Exclusivistic strategy	Inclusivistic strategy
Legitimation in Scripture	Exodus, Leviticus, Numbers, Deuteronomy	Genesis and prophets

Figure 4.2: Group Ideology of the Pharisees and of Jesus

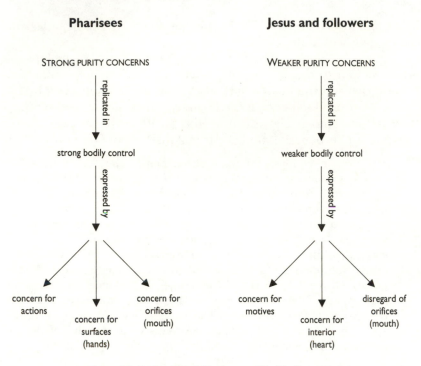

Figure 4.3: Sociopolitical Strategy and Bodily Concerns

Later Neyrey applies his model of purity to the interpretation of Luke–Acts (1991). Most of his attention focuses on boundaries, either social or physical, which Jesus is portrayed as ignoring or transgressing. Again employing "maps" to indicate the classification system of Luke's world, he summarizes the typical social perceptions concerning purity and pollution as applicable to persons, places, times, and things in Luke–Acts (282).

Even as he describes Jesus transgressing Jewish purity rules, Neyrey shows how Luke's Jesus established new maps and so new boundaries and new rules. These new rules are grounded on a new view of the "holy" God of Israel, one that includes God's loosening of boundaries for a more inclusive membership in the covenant community.

Yet "clean" and "unclean" are not labels exclusively pertaining to cult and temple, however central they were to the the values and structures of Israel. The human body can also be classified in these terms. John Pilch's study (1981) first pursues historical issues: What "leprosy" did Jesus heal? Scientific (rather than biblical) investigation indicates that biblical leprosy is not the modern disease *(mycobacterium leprae)*. Further pursuing the issue of disease from a cross-cultural perspective, Pilch comes to an anthropological understanding of body and hence of bodily surfaces. Using Douglas's materials, as well as other perspectives on purity and body symbolism, Pilch explains how in particular conflictual social situations there tends to be great concern over both social and bodily boundaries. Douglas herself suggests that when "rituals express anxiety about the body's orifices the sociological counterpart . . . is a care to protect the political and cultural unity" of a group (1966:124). Pilch's examination gives full scope to this kind of intuition; the issue of "leprosy" (bodily surface or boundary) functions in a larger social world where social boundaries are threatened and need to be guarded. The importance of Pilch's article lies in showing how purity concerns are not exclusive to cult and temple, but are replicated in the symbolic world of a culture and especially in the way the physical body is perceived.

Apropos of the physical body, Neyrey applies Douglas's suggestions about "clean" and "unclean" to body symbolism in Paul's first letter to Corinth (1986a:129–70, reprinted in 1990:102–46). The same concern for order, wholeness, and boundary defense found in the macrolevel of society is replicated on the microlevel in the way the physical body is perceived and controlled. Since what crosses boundaries is dangerous and potentially polluting, it is not surprising that Paul focuses intently on bodily surfaces, in particular hairdos (1 Cor 11). Men wearing feminine hairstyles and women wearing masculine hairdos blur the categories of male and female, and so are considered "unclean" and are proscribed. The orifices of the body (eyes, ears, mouth, genitals) are likewise the object of Paul's concern and control because they are the gates and portals whence cross foods, speech, semen, and menses. Especially in regard to bodily orifices, Paul strongly regulates (a) the sexual orifice (1 Cor 5–7), (b) the oral orifice for eating (1 Cor 8–11), and (c) the oral orifice for speech (1 Cor 12–14). His concern is with what goes in or comes out, that is, with what is "in place" or "out of place." Some sexual unions are a pollution. Some foods corrupt the innocent conscience. Some speech offends the "wholeness" of the body. Thus these are perceived as "unclean" and proscribed. Comparably, other foods (i.e., the Eucharist), other sexual unions (i.e., marry in the Lord), and other speech (i.e., confession of Jesus as Lord or prophecy) are "clean" and so prescribed. Paul's strong control of the physical body mirrors his urgent need to control the chaotic social relations of the Corinthians.

Moreover, "holiness" is related to "wholeness," which helps to explain Paul's dedication to the unity or wholeness of the social body. Any mutilation or defection would endanger its wholeness and so its holiness before God. Hence Paul is greatly concerned over events or behavior that cause division in the body or that might lead to a divorce, that is, a divided body, or that tend to exclude others.

"Clean" and "unclean," then, define what is bodily "out of place" or what threatens bodily wholeness.

4.0 Miscellaneous Studies Worth Noting

Other studies deserve attention. Their brief mention here is not intended to slight their value and importance. In regard to discussions of creation, we recommend first the brief article of Michael Barré (1981). He is unconcerned here with issues of purity but focuses on the sense of "order" pervasive in Jewish Wisdom literature. Most importantly, he demonstrates the pervasive desire for and articulation of "order" over "chaos" in the Bible. Without using the jargon of anthropology, he urges that we attend to the cultural value of order and its systematic replication in various aspects of Hebrew ideology and praxis: "But from the view of antiquity the 'order' of the created world is not merely physical. The physical aspect is only one manifestation of an all-pervasive orderliness that lies at the heart of creation. Religious, social, moral order—these too are simply facets of the fundamental world-order" (41). The task of "wise" persons, then, is to find their proper place in the orderly scheme of things. Recognizing that the study of "purity" is an investigation of both the macrosystem of order in a given culture and its microclassification of specific things as "clean" and "unclean," Barré here orients a reader to think abstractly in terms of large cultural patterns that are the social construction of the biblical writers.

Howard Eilberg-Schwartz digests and revises Douglas's analysis of the abominations of Leviticus in a study of the ideological relationship of Priestly materials and accounts of creation (1987). He attempts to show the intrabiblical relationship of texts from Gen 1 and Lev 11 and Deut 14, allowing his analysis to be guided constantly by concerns for "classification systems" and correspondences between ideology and practical issues. He argues that the biblical and mishnaic taxonomies move progressively away from mere physical criteria for uncleanness and toward "human activity" in the creation of elaborate classification systems. Anthropological categories, while present and determinative of the argument, are lightly used, which makes this a recommended article for readers more inclined to historical and textual discussion. Nevertheless, Eilberg-Schwartz insists that readers begin understanding taxonomy and classification systems as the creation of the community, and so he urges that we be open to the various links between social structures and symbolic thought.

Dietary issues in both testaments remain a constant focus of discussion. Apropos of this interest, the article of Gordon Wenham

(1981) provides an excellent survey of the food laws, with special attention to their explanation in terms of Douglas's study of their symbolic meaning. Additional historical studies are also worth noting that deal with questions such as eating with "unclean" hands in Mark 7 (Dunn 1985; House 1983), the cleanness of vessels used in eating in Matt 23 (Neusner 1976; Maccoby 1982), or the cleanness of those who could share a Jewish or Christian table (Dunn 1983).

In regard to issues of marriage and sex, several publications commend themselves. Bossman's (1979) brief analysis of Ezra's marriage reforms, although it does not use the anthropological concept of purity, calls attention to issues of endogamy, the stages of the history of prohibited marriages, and the relationship of marriage issues to the values and the larger cultural system of Israel. He shows that marriage rules replicate concern for group identity and coherence. Wenham's (1983) brief note on the defilement of sexual intercourse in Lev 15:18 is important, for it specifically adapts Douglas's analysis of purity/pollution to the Israelite values of life/death. Loss of blood, menses, or semen involves a loss of "life fluids." Because God is whole, alive, and perfect, only those who are themselves clean and who enjoy full life (i.e., no loss of "life fluids") may approach this living God. No investigation of the Hebrew Bible would be complete without some reference to the pollution attached to menses and semen. Eilberg-Schwartz's article (1990) offers a sophisticated interpretation of these materials using the works of Douglas.

In discussing sexual ethics, L. W. Countryman spends the first third of his book on "dirt" and its counterpart, "purity" (1988:11–143). The study begins with acknowledgment of Douglas's influence in shaping our understanding of clean and unclean. Countryman then surveys the shifting notions of purity in ancient Israel, first-century Judaism, the Gospels, and finally Paul. He argues that although Christianity retained the dynamic of labeling things clean and unclean, it paid less attention to physical purity (i.e., bodily integrity or fluid emission) than its parent, Judaism. Moreover, he attends to the interpretation of sexual issues in the NT in a way that both relativizes their stringency and explains their plausibility in terms of a specific culture. "Purity of heart" is identified as the determining factor in consideration of behavior. One need not accept Countryman's conclusions to appreciate his careful focusing on issues of purity, especially in relation to the physical body.

The monograph of John Gammie examines the concept of "holiness" in the Hebrew scriptures (1989). He attempts to show that "holiness" meant one thing in the context of the temple and its priests, another to the prophets, and still another to the individuals in villages and cities. Thus Gammie is sensitive to the different meanings that "clean" and "unclean" have for groups in differing social locations. Moreover, the whole study is cognizant of the anthropological contributions of Douglas and others, and so offers a satisfying historical and cultural examination of the topic.

In regard to NT documents, several studies should be noted. In terms of the idea of purity Neyrey turns from investigating the Gospels to the letters of Paul. In two articles he employs the hybrid model of "witchcraft accusations" derived from Douglas to interpret social conflict, first in 2 Cor 10–13 (1986c) and then in Galatians (1988a). At the heart of a society that makes accusations of sorcery or witchcraft lies a pervasive sense of purity and pollution. A witch is someone who appears externally to be pure, but who is internally polluted. The witch seeks to corrupt what is clean or to suck the life from what is living. By identifying someone as a witch, the accuser alerts the listening social group to a threat to its very life, namely, the unwarranted presence of a corruption that will destroy it. Neyrey shows how Paul labels his rivals at Corinth as either Satan or disguised as angels of light and his opponents in Galatia as those who "bewitch" the orthodox group. By labeling them as sorcerers who threaten the group's "purity," Paul can then invoke intolerance toward them and demand their expulsion from the group. These two studies articulate the power of labels of "uncleanness," especially their ability to motivate people to respond intolerantly in ways they may not wish to in other circumstances. Likewise they indicate how groups view their cosmos and all reality in dualistic terms, that is, in terms of purity and pollution or what is permitted and what is proscribed.

In yet another study of the symbolic universe or "purity system" of Paul's letters, Neyrey (1990:21–74) applies Douglas's model of purity to the patterns of order and disorder in 1 Corinthians. He shows that Paul tends to perceive the world like any first-century Pharisee in terms of a highly ordered cosmos, with an appropriate place for every person, thing, or time. Thus we are not surprised at Paul's (a) persistent inclination to list things and persons in hierarchical order, which is a characteristic sign of purity; (b) maps of persons, places, times, and things; and (c) endless comparisons and rankings. Neyrey argues that the rationale for such labeling and classifying lies in Paul's attempt to exercise control over his congregations.

In addition, he describes Paul's perception of "sin" and "cosmology." Sin is understood both as a pollution threatening the pure group (1 Cor 5:6–8) and a violation of specific rules (6:9–10). As a life-threatening corruption, it warrants intolerance and so excommunication of the offender (5:3–5, 13). Paul's world is described as a cosmos of competing cosmic powers of good and evil, which are pure and polluted, respectively. Thus Paul's symbolic universe is

structured around a radically dualistic perception. It is replicated in
the order (or disorder) of the cosmos and the community, the control
or noncontrol of the body, the understanding of sinful pollution
corrupting a pure body, and a cosmic war between the forces of God
and those of Satan. Purity and pollution, then, are replicated at
every level of Paul's perception. He holds the first-century perceptions of purity common to Jews and Christians alike.

Most recently John Elliott (1993) has examined the letter of
James in terms of purity and pollution. Quoting Jas 1:2–4, he notes
that James casts his argument in the formal terminology of wholeness and incompleteness, which is but a specification of the more
general labels of clean and unclean. He explains what is meant by
these symbolic terms and indicates their social function:

> Cultures variously use purity and pollution schemes in order to or-
> ganize everything in its proper place, to define and demarcate what is
> complete or incomplete, who is damaged or whole, sick or sound,
> what is allowable or forbidden, who belongs to the society and who
> does not, what preserves the society and what endangers it. Accord-
> ingly, to call a person or a social unit impure, unclean, or unholy is to
> identify and evaluate the object as out-of-order, damaged, incomplete
> (1993:73).

This statement indicates clearly that Elliott is attentive to the
social control exercised by the use of these labels. He shows how
James invokes these labels when he addresses issues of personal,
social, and cosmic disorder and order. Noting how the letter presents
an extended series of contrasts, Elliott shows that these contain both
the author's diagnosis of an unclean or unwhole situation and his
prescription for cleanness or wholeness.

Elliott pays acute attention to the way that value classifications of wholeness and incompleteness are replicated throughout
the document in regard to crises occurring on the personal, social,
and cosmic levels. He indicates how moral exhortation such as the
letter of James is fundamentally structured around the notions of
purity/wholeness and pollution/incompleteness. In doing so, he
gives salience to the notion of "perfection" of holiness both in
regard to God and to the church.

Finally, Neyrey applies his highly developed model of purity
and pollution to the unfamiliar documents of Jude and 2 Peter (1993).
Indeed, he interprets both documents specifically in terms of social-
science models, including purity/pollution concepts and a model of
the physical body. Here Neyrey weaves together anthropological
models of purity and pollution and their incarnation and illustration
in Greco-Roman literature. Then he carefully uses this lens to interpret the numerous passages in Jude and 2 Peter concerning "corrup-

tion," sexual perversions, self-control, and the like. He uses the same method for presenting the way Jude and 2 Peter urge control of the physical body as an indication of orthodox theology.

Although this survey has focused thus far exclusively on the use of purity and pollution in regard to Israelite, Jewish, and early Christian literature, readers should be cognizant of a thorough study of pollution concerns in Greek religion. Robert Parker's (1983) magisterial investigation of taboo, pollution, and purification takes up birth and death, the shedding of blood, sacrilege, curses, and disease. Besides a fine analysis of each of these topics, the book is distinguished for its appendices and indices, which will serve as guidance for identifying new vocabulary in regard to "clean" and "unclean," as well as a keen sense of the wider Mediterranean nature of the idea of purity.

5.0 Where Does This Leave a Reader?

This chapter has identified studies of some passages and documents from the Bible the interpretation of which has been the focus of authors concerned with issues of "clean" and "unclean." In the Hebrew scriptures, scholars regularly give attention to the creation story in Gen 1, the "abominations" in Lev 11, pollution materials in Deut 14, and bodily impurity in Lev 21:17–20. In the Christian scriptures, Mark 7 has attracted attention for its concern over washing rites, dietary rules, and concern for externals. Both Mark and Luke have been interpreted in terms of a model of purity, and 1 Corinthians in terms of a model of bodily control.

What does one know if one knows this? Historical and descriptive studies richly inform a reader about a specific issue in a specific document. Anthropological studies contribute by suggesting the common cultural perceptions of the way the world was perceived to be ordered, classified, and structured. They also indicate how pervasive purity concerns were, not only in cult and temple but in various other areas of social life: illness, hygiene, sexuality, food, eating, agriculture, and so forth.

The specific use of the two anthropological models of (1) "clean" and "unclean" and (2) body symbolism can equip a reader to understand a wide but interconnected series of issues such as dietary concerns (Acts 10–11), the mission to "unclean" people (Mark 5; Acts 8), sexual morals (1 Thess 4:1–9), and hand washings (Mark 7). A reader knowing this material has a firm basis for sympathetically understanding the conflicts between Jesus and Pharisees that run through the Gospel stories. Moreover, in learning this code the reader not only learns particular details of specific conflicts, but also begins to sense the coherence of different theological and social points of view in the first century. It is possible to see how the ancient classification system worked because one understands its general principles and how they are replicated again and again in specific areas.

How readers begin and what they might choose to read will probably depend on the intellectual aesthetic of the individual reader. If history and description are paramount concerns, then the works of Neusner are excellent places to begin. If cultural concerns loom large, then Douglas's writings are important; we commend in particular *Purity and Danger*, chs. 3, 6–8. Her writings, while perennially fruitful, are not easy to mold into a workable model for interpretation of biblical texts. Hence the materials of Malina and Neyrey should be consulted precisely for their digestion and application of anthropological approaches to the biblical material. Neyrey's studies of Mark, Luke, Paul, and Jude and 2 Peter consciously present the issue of "purity" both in its abstract sense of order and system and in its specific and detailed realization in the world of early Christianity. Precisely because he focuses on interpretation of texts, Neyrey's writings indicate the underlying importance of purity language for correct understanding of ancient documents and offer readers a refined series of models for their own further reading.

6.0 Works Cited

Barré, Michael
> 1981   " 'Fear of God' and the World of Wisdom." *BTB*
> 11:41–43.

Booth, Roger P.
> 1986   *Jesus and the Laws of Purity.* Sheffield: JSOT Press.

Bossman, David
> 1979   "Ezra's Marriage Reform: Israel Redefined." *BTB*
> 9:32–38.

Countryman, L. William
> 1988   *Dirt, Greed, and Sex: Sexual Ethics in the New Testament
> and Their Implications for Today.* Philadelphia: Fortress.

Danby, Herbert, trans.
> 1933   *The Mishnah.* Oxford: Oxford University Press.

Douglas, Mary T.
> 1966   *Purity and Danger: An Analysis of the Concepts of
> Pollution and Taboo.* London: Routledge & Kegan Paul.

1968   "Pollution." *International Encyclopedia of the Social Sciences.* 2d ed. 12:336–42. New York: Macmillan.

1975a   "Deciphering a Meal." In *Implicit Meanings.* Pages 249–75. London: Routledge & Kegan Paul.

1975b   "Pollution." In *Implicit Meanings.* Pages 47–59. London: Routledge & Kegan Paul.

Dunn, James D. G.

1983   "The Incident at Antioch (Gal 2:11–18)." *JSNT* 18:3–57.

1985   "Jesus and Ritual Purity: A Study of the Tradition History of Mk 7,15." In *A Cause de l'Evangile: Etudes sur les Synoptiques et les Actes offertes au P. Jacques Dupont.* Pages 251–76. Lectio divina 123. Paris: Cerf.

Eilberg-Schwartz, Howard

1987   "Creation and Classification in Judaism: From Priestly to Rabbinic Concepts." *HR* 26:357–81.

1990   "Menstrual Blood, Semen, and Discharge: The Fluid Symbolism of the Human Body." In *The Savage in Judaism: An Anthropology of Israelite Religion and Ancient Judaism.* Pages 177–94. Bloomington: Indiana University Press.

Elliott, John H.

1993   "The Epistle of James in Rhetorical and Social Scientific Perspective: Holiness-Wholeness and Patterns of Replication." *BTB* 23:71–81.

Gammie, John G.

1989   *Holiness in Israel.* OBT. Minneapolis: Fortress.

House, Colin

1983   "Defilement by Association: Some Insights from the Usage of ΚΟΙΝΟΣ/ΚΟΙΝΟΩ in Acts 10 and 11." *AUSS* 21:143–53.

Isenberg, Sheldon R.

1975   "Mary Douglas and Hellenistic Religions: The Case of Qumran," SBLSP 1975:179–85.

Maccoby, Hyam

1982   "The Washing of Cups." *JSNT* 14:3–15.

Malina, Bruce J.

1986   *Christian Origins and Cultural Anthropology.* Atlanta: John Knox.

1993   "Clean and Unclean: Understanding Rules of Purity." In *The New Testament World: Insights from Cultural Anthropology.* Rev. ed. Pages 149–83. Atlanta: John Knox.

Milgrom, Jacob

1963   "The Biblical Diet Laws as an Ethical System: Food and Faith." *Int* 17:288–301.

Neusner, Jacob
 1973a *From Politics to Piety.* Englewood Cliffs, N.J.:
    Prentice-Hall.
 1973b *The Idea of Purity in Ancient Judaism.* Leiden: Brill.
 1975 "The Idea of Purity in Ancient Judaism." *JAAR* 43:15–26.
 1976 " 'First Cleanse the Inside': The Halakhic Background
    of a Controversy Saying." *NTS* 22:486–95.
 1978 "History and Purity in First-Century Judaism." *HR*
    18:1–17.
 1979 "Map Without Territory: Mishnah's System of Sacrifice
    and Sanctuary." *HR* 19:103–27.
Newton, Michael
 1985 *The Concept of Purity at Qumran and in the Letters of Paul.*
    Cambridge: Cambridge University Press.
Neyrey, Jerome H.
 1986a "Body Language in 1 Corinthians: The Use of
    Anthropological Models for Understanding Paul and
    His Opponents." In *Social-Scientific Criticism of the New
    Testament and Its Social World.* Ed. John H. Elliott. Pages
    129–70. *Semeia* 35. Decatur, Ga.: Scholars Press.
 1986b "The Idea of Purity in Mark's Gospel." In
    *Social-Scientific Criticism of the New Testament and Its
    Social World.* Ed. John H. Elliott. Pages 91–128. *Semeia*
    35. Decatur, Ga.: Scholars Press.
 1986c "Witchcraft Accusations in 2 Cor 10–13: Paul in Social
    Science Perspective." *Listening* 21:160–70.
 1988a "Bewitched in Galatia: Paul and Cultural
    Anthropology." *CBQ* 50:72–100.
 1988b "A Symbolic Approach to Mark 7." *Forum* 4(3): 63–91.
 1990 *Paul, in Other Words: A Cultural Reading of His Letters.*
    Louisville: Westminster/John Knox.
 1991 "The Symbolic Universe of Luke–Acts: 'They Turn the
    World Upside Down.' " In *The Social World of Luke–Acts:
    Models for Interpretation.* Ed. Jerome H. Neyrey. Pages
    271–304. Peabody, Mass.: Hendrickson.
 1993 *2 Peter, Jude.* AB 37C. Garden City, N.Y.: Doubleday.
Parker, Robert
 1983 *Miasma: Pollution and Purification in Early Greek Religion.*
    Oxford: Clarendon.
Pilch, John
 1981 "Biblical Leprosy and Body Symbolism." *BTB* 11:108–13.
Soler, Jean
 1979 "The Dietary Prohibitions of the Hebrews." *New York
    Review of Books* June 14:24–30. Reprinted in *Food and Drink*

in History. Ed. Robert Forster and Orest Ranum. Pages 126–38. Baltimore: Johns Hopkins University Press, 1979.

Toombs, L. E.
1962 "Clean and Unclean." *IDB.* 1.641–48. Nashville: Abingdon.

Wenham, Gordon
1981 "The Theology of Unclean Food." *EvQ* 53:6–15.
1983 "Why Does Sexual Intercourse Defile (Lev 15.18)?" *ZAW* 95:432–34.

Wright, David P.
1992 "Unclean and Clean (OT)." *ABD.* 6.729–41. New York: Doubleday.

Part Two:

Social Institutions

5

The Preindustrial City

Richard L. Rohrbaugh
Lewis and Clark College

Whatever the provenance of Jesus and his earliest followers, the principal writers (and presumably readers as well) of the NT were urban persons. Exactly what happened to the Christian movement and its incipient literary corpus as it shifted (almost exclusively) to this urban environment has been a subject of sporadic interest among NT scholars over the years. Relatively little of that work, however, has been informed by a social-scientific understanding that allows us to distinguish the preindustrial cities of antiquity from the industrial ones of the modern world. Since most modern readers who encounter the term "city" in the NT undoubtedly envision the large and diverse industrial cities in which they themselves live, it is worth thinking about the differences between cities then and cities now if we are to read with understanding.

1.0 Using the Term "City"

Before we jump into a discussion of the social-science literature on cities, however, it might be helpful to think about the way the term "city" has been used in the Bible. Of the 164 references to the city (πόλις, *polis*) in the NT, fully half are in the Lukan writings, about equally divided between the Gospel and the book of Acts. Throughout the NT some ninety different places are named that may have been cities, though not all of them can be identified today. Among those that can, several on the list are worthy of comment. Note that Luke (2:4) calls Bethlehem a "city" (πόλις, *polis*), while John (7:42)

calls it a "village" (κώμη, kōmē). Similarly, Bethsaida is called a city by
Luke (9:10) but a village by Mark (8:23). Josephus reflects this same
inconsistency, calling Jotapata a city at one place and a village at
another. He also labels Hebron and Gischala both "city" and "hamlet" (πολίχνη, polichnē) at different times.

Places that almost certainly were not cities are sometimes
designated as such in the NT. For example, a location Luke exclusively designates a city was Nazareth. In Jesus' day it was off the
main roads of lower Galilee and was probably no more than a
hamlet of a few hundred people. At the same time Capernaum,
which Luke also consistently calls a city, is a name that literally
means "village of Nahum." Scholars usually assume that misdesig-
nations such as these betray Luke's lack of familiarity with the
actual situation in Roman Palestine. That is possible, but it may
also be that like many ancient authors he is simply using the term
"city" in a nontechnical sense. For readers of the NT in English the
problem is compounded because translators frequently render the
same Greek word (πόλις, polis) as both "city" and "town" (cf. Luke
8:1 and 8:4 in the RSV), words that can have significantly different
connotations for the modern reader.

In antiquity a city was nearly always linked to a group of
surrounding villages, which the Hebrew Bible sometimes calls its
"daughters" (bnwt; cf. Judg 1:17; see also 1 Macc 5:65, "He struck
Hebron and its villages"; Mark 8:27, "the villages of Caesarea
Philippi"). The exceptions were the cities of the Levites, which were
given pastureland rather than villages (Num 35:1–8). Josephus likewise mentions this phenomenon, indicating that Julia was the capital
of a toparchy that had fourteen villages associated with it (Ant.
20.159). These villages often provided the city with a major portion
of its income; Nazareth may have been just such a village belonging
to the nearby city of Sepphoris.

In the Hebrew Bible the city is distinguished from the village
by having surrounding walls (Lev 25:31). Legal distinctions in the
disposition of property were actually drawn on the basis of this
definition. While a village house could never be sold in perpetuity
and could always be redeemed, after the sale of a house in the city
a buyer had only one year to change his mind (Lev 25:13–17,
25–31). In the NT this distinction between cities and villages is
maintained (Matt 9:35; 10:11; Mark 6:56; Luke 8:1; 13:22), though
no criteria for the distinction are provided. In the period after the
NT, the Jewish rabbis came to designate a village as any place
lacking a synagogue.

While we have no classical definitions of a city as such, Pausanias (late second century CE) reveals something of the Greco-
Roman understanding. In a kind of travel guide to the Greek cities of

Phocis, a region opposite the Peloponnesus near Delphi, Pausanias first calls Panopeus a "city," but then raises doubts by wondering "if indeed one can give the name of city to those who possess no public buildings, no gymnasium, no theater, no market-place, no water descending to a fountain, but live in bare shelters just like mountain huts on the edges of ravines" (10.4.1). Obviously he expects cities to be more than simply containers for large numbers of people. If Latin texts from the imperial period are taken as the measure, the glory and extent of public buildings count as much in describing what a city is as does extent of population, commerce, or any other item. By contrast, in his instructions for preparing an encomium to praise a city, Menander Rhetor (*Epideictic Discourses*, Treatise I, 346–51) places far more emphasis on a city's "origins, actions, and accomplishments" than he does on its location, size, or physical appearance. As with individuals, the honor of a city is what really matters.

Exactly how the term "city" should be used is something even contemporary social theorists have been unable to decide. Over the years there have been elaborate attempts in the social-science literature to provide clear and precise criteria for distinguishing cities from towns and villages. Physical, social, and demographic criteria have all been tried, yet clarity on the matter has been not really been achieved (Blanton 1976:250).

2.0 Anachronistic Understandings of the Concept

In the same way that our understanding of what a city is can cause confusion, so also can projection of the patterns and dynamics of modern cities back onto those of antiquity. For example, Wayne Meeks (1983) tries to imagine what led the city dwellers of the Greco-Roman world to join Christian communities like those described in the book of Acts. He thinks of a harried city life not unlike that in the fast-paced cities of today.

> Urban life in the early Roman Empire was scarcely less complicated than our own, in proportion to the scale of knowledge available to an individual and the demands made upon him. Its complexity—its untidiness to the mind—may well have been felt with special acuteness by people who were marginal or transient, either physically or socially or both, as so many of the identifiable members of Pauline churches seem to have been (1983:104).

It does not take too much thought, however, to realize that the city being described here is one from the twentieth century rather than the first. Overwhelming complexity, physical and social mobility, and information overload are things we today deal with all the time. They produce in us strong feelings of loneliness, anxiety, and alienation. "Finding" such feelings in the ancient city, Meeks uses them in an attempt to explain why these ancient city dwellers joined the Christian movement (1983:191). Yet what he is really doing is projecting modern popular psychology back onto the situation of antiquity.

In part Meeks is led into this error by uncritically applying a theoretical concept, the notion of "status inconsistency" (e.g., poor but honored, rich but despised) designed to study the social tensions of *modern* societies to the societies of the ancient Mediterranean. He thereby imagines in ancient cities the rising social aspirations and accompanying emotional stresses of socially mobile groups in modern America. Jerome Murphy-O'Connor takes a similar tack in his otherwise excellent descriptions of the ancient city of Corinth. Citing status inconsistencies in Corinth, he writes, "A feeling of frustration was inevitable; what was the point of a life in which the full exploitation of one's talents was blocked by circumstances outside one's control" (1984:153). Modern notions of self-actualization are not hard to spot here, nor are modern assumptions about the character of urban life.

But equally problematic in these comments are the assumptions made about the ancient city itself. Information overload was not much of a problem in ancient cities and social mobility was nearly nonexistent. Mobility was not a conceivable expectation for most people any more than was the idea of "full exploitation of one's talents." It is highly unlikely that these things were prime causes of alienation and social isolation for ancient city inhabitants. Since the social mobility that did occur was usually downward, and since ancient people imagined the struggle to be hanging on to what they had, not gaining more, fear of loss or depression over having lost out already was more likely a motivator than rising aspirations.

Typical would have been the artisans who inhabited preindustrial cities. As Gerhard Lenski has shown, in most preindustrial cities the artisan class "was originally recruited from the ranks of the dispossessed peasantry and their non-inheriting sons and was continually replenished from these sources" (1966:278). He adds that they were lower on the status scale than peasants and had lower incomes. Having lost their connection to the land and to their extended families when they migrated to the cities, artisans inevitably lost the status and protection of their previous family and village connections. Since connection with a group of some sort was often a matter of survival, getting reconnected would have had little to do with the psychology of harried and overly complicated city life or rising social expectations. It would have had much to do with fear for the next meal.

Indeed, ancient cities differed markedly from modern ones in almost every respect. In excess of 90 percent of the American population is urban, yet in ancient Palestine 90 percent was rural. Cities were not production or market centers in the modern sense, nor were they configured in demographic patterns similar to ours. Social dynamics were different both because cities then contained different types of population than do ours now and also because the relation between the city and the rural areas of antiquity was fundamentally unlike anything existing today.

What we need, then, to understand the world of the NT is a picture of cities and the broader urban system of which they were a part that is appropriate to the preindustrial world rather than to our own. We need to learn how to distinguish ancient cities from modern cities, not only in physical appearance but also in patterns of social interaction. Who occupied what types of urban space? Why? Who wasn't there or wasn't allowed to be there? Where did city populations come from? How big were they? What functions did the city perform? On whose behalf? What were urban social relations like? Who controlled the patterns of urban-rural interaction and what means did they use? In asking these and questions like them, our concern throughout must be how ancient cities differ from those we know today and what we risk in importing modern preconceptions into our reading of the NT.

What follows is a brief survey of the literature on preindustrial cities that will assist the reader in this endeavor. Two types of literature are surveyed. First, the more traditional literature provides historical information on the rise and spread of preindustrial cities, especially in the NT world. Second, and more important, the social-science literature on preindustrial cities enables the reader to distinguish the cities of the preindustrial world from those of modern times.

To understand why these two types of literature have been chosen it is necessary to make one more preliminary observation. Like most other historians, biblical scholars have been trained to look at the particular and unique. We are at pains to discriminate between the Roman and the Greek, the Egyptian and the Hebrew. We know all the ways the ancient Jews were atypical in the Mediterranean world. By contrast, the social sciences seek the commonplace and generic. Their focus is not on details but on generalizations. They are interested in what the Greek, Roman, Egyptian, and Hebrew might have had in common as inhabitants of what anthropologists call the "Mediterranean culture-continent." Neither the questions nor the answers of the social scientist are those of the historian, and the result is that conversation between historians and social scientists is often what Peter Burke has called a "dialogue of the deaf" (1980:14).

The problem, of course, is one of level of abstraction. At the high level of abstraction at which social-science models work, for example, there is indeed a broadly generic thing called the preindustrial city. It displays common characteristics throughout the NT period. Yet at the lower level of abstraction at which the historian works, no such thing exists. There we have to distinguish between the classical city on the one hand and the oriental city on the other, or perhaps even between Jerusalem and Tiberias. At a low level of abstraction they are not alike at all. For all the uniqueness of particular cities that historians love to uncover and that requires data from each particular site under study, there is also a common set of cultural patterns that pervaded all the cities of the ancient Mediterranean culture-continent, Jerusalem and Tiberias included.

The reader is thus forewarned that historians and social scientists working on ancient cities frequently misunderstand each other's work. Historians complain that social scientists pay no attention to the data from cities that actually existed (Finley 1977:307–10), while social scientists complain that historians gather data without discriminating models as a guide for doing so and thereby tend to lose sight of the forest among the trees. The survey that follows mentions both kinds of literature. We begin by looking at the historical literature, though we do so somewhat briefly because it is already better known to students of the NT than is the social-science material that is our primary interest.

3.0 The Rise of Cities in Antiquity

While an enormous historical literature exists on the ancient Mediterranean city, much of it predates the recent, more sociologically sophisticated studies of urban life in Mesoamerica and ancient China. Nonetheless, this historical literature serves to introduce the reader to important basic information on the cities of the NT world. While some of this literature uses the term "city" uncritically, technical definition and theoretical concerns need not trouble us for the moment. Historical information about the actual cities of the Mediterranean region is what is needed. When did cities develop? Why? How many were there and where did they emerge? How were they organized? What were their major institutions? What were the typical patterns of the classical city? How did the oriental city differ from the classical city?

These are basically historical questions. Our task is thus to locate key literature that can supply this historical information and then provide the reader with some sense of what is essential and what is secondary in light of the questions we are asking.

The foundational study underlying much modern work on the ancient (classical) city was that of Numa Denis Fustel de Coulanges (1873, first published in 1864). While the modern reader will be put off by its notions of Aryan evolution and its frequently simplistic treatment of causal factors in urban development, it is nonetheless a massive collection of information from the Greek and Roman sources. A more recent treatment of the history and development of the classical city is that of A. H. M. Jones (1940). It provides not only the historical data from Alexander to Justinian, but also good descriptions of civic institutions, economic patterns, and political and administrative arrangements. It is especially helpful in citing the Greek and Roman primary sources that the student may wish to have available for further work. Other noteworthy works of this sort include Mason Hammond (1972) and Lewis Mumford (1961). Hammond covers Mesopotamia, Syria, Egypt, and Anatolia along with the classical world of Greece and Rome. Mumford's treatment is necessarily more superficial since it covers the entire period of urban history up to the modern era. It does serve, however, to remind the reader of some of the changes in the city wrought by the industrial revolution. For the original revolution that produced cities in the first place, see V. Gordon Childe's well-known article (1950) summarizing his work on the origin of cities. A good survey of the development of urban planning in the Greco-Roman world can be found in E. J. Owens (1991).

Paul Lampl (1968) provides much of the background necessary for understanding the oriental cities of that time and place. Of special value for understanding the oriental city in the biblical world is the thorough work by Frank Frick (1977). It covers not only the spread of urbanization and the physical characteristics of Israelite cities, but also the religious evaluation of the city by the writers of the Hebrew Bible. On the distinction between the classical and oriental city the reader will also want to check Ira Lapidus (1986), who describes key variables in their different development.

In addition to the historical surveys cited above, information on particular regions or particular cities may be of interest to some readers. An important special treatment of this sort is by A. H. M Jones (1971). It serves as a detailed historical description of urbanization in the eastern provinces, including both Asia Minor and Syria-Palestine. Jones's article (1931) summarizes what can be gleaned from Josephus about the urbanization process during the Roman period. Earlier we raised a question about how classical and oriental cities might differ. At just this point the reader will find Victor Tcherikover's work (1979) of special interest. It offers a survey of the thirty cities in Palestine and environs known to have been Greek rather than oriental. Some of these emerged as Greek cities during the Hellenistic period, while others were oriental cities that were reconstituted along Hellenistic lines.

Sean Freyne (1980) covers Galilean cities in the NT period, while Joachim Jeremias's important work (1969) is a valuable description of nearly every aspect of life in Jerusalem in the first century. Equally interesting is Jerome Murphy-O'Connor (1983). Of special value because of the distinctions it draws between cities and villages, as well as its descriptions of the relations between the two, is George Harper (1928). Richard Tomlinson (1992) offers a unique historical account of the architectural development of selected Greek and Roman cities that relates those developments to patterns of political and social organization. John Stambaugh (1988) provides the most thorough description in English of the physical and social environment of Rome, as well as briefer treatments of additional classical cities. Classical texts on Rome are collected in Donald Dudley (1967). A similar description of the often grim life in ancient Antioch can be found in Rodney Stark (1991). He provides much detail on the misery of everyday life for most ancient city residents.

While the archaeological literature on particular cities of interest to NT scholars is too vast to mention in any detail, summary information is available in Richard Stillwell (1976) and in Edwin Yamauchi (1980). The collection of visual materials and site information by Helmut Koester and Holland Hendrix (1987) is helpful as well.

All the studies cited to this point are historical in orientation. They concentrate on data, on information. They are generally devoid of comment on social theory, sometimes to the point of naïveté about the way modern assumptions about cities have governed their collection and organization of historical data. Since this same naïveté places us in danger of anachronistic and ethnocentric readings of the NT, we have argued that recourse to urban studies by social scientists who focus on the differences between ancient and modern cities is a necessary next step. Before moving in that direction, however, comment is in order about prioritizing the suggestions offered above.

For those unfamiliar with the rise of cities, Childe (1950) would be a good place to start. For most readers, however, the first priority should be basic historical information on both the classical and oriental city. Jones (1940) provides this for the classical world. For the oriental city, the wider view is in Lampl (1968). Those especially interested in Israel might substitute Frick (1977). For one who has read either Jones and Lampl, or Jones and Frick, Lapidus's article (1986) comparing the classical and oriental city would provide good perspective on this basic distinction that any historian must make.

Other literature cited above can be considered a search for detail, for comment on matters of particular concern, or for information about particular sites. Prioritizing it is a matter of individual need and interest.

4.0 Social-Science Literature

Shifting to our second type of literature, that from the social sciences, we must offer brief comment to give the reader perspective. Earlier social-science works (Childe 1950, Wirth 1951, Redfield 1947, et al.) concentrated on attempts to find those distinctive characteristics of cities that allow us to provide definition for them over against towns and villages (see especially Childe 1950, Wirth 1951). Models of preindustrial cities were then developed that highlighted these purportedly distinctive elements and set off the city from the rural hinterland. Seminal in this regard were studies of the so-called folk-urban dichotomy early in the century by Pitirim Sorokin. Later its widely known counterpart, the "folk-urban continuum," was developed by Robert Redfield (1947) from the work of the so-called Chicago school of urban studies in the 1920s.

One result of this concept was the development of models of preindustrial cities as discrete phenomena, as worlds unto themselves. Much was made of a supposed urban social psychology that imagined the city and the urban way of life as a key force in ongoing social change. But more sophisticated recent research has recognized the problem with this approach: in both the modern and ancient worlds the city has never been an isolated construct. Its connection to the villages and hinterlands is widely attested in ancient texts. In fact, social scientists and historians alike now recognize a systemic relationship between city and countryside that cannot be ignored. Urban domination of ancient societies was an indisputable fact of life despite the relatively small percentage of the population that inhabited the cities. How that domination worked and the mechanisms by which it was maintained have become as important to urban studies as the shape and character of the city itself. For critical reviews of this classic debate see the articles by Horace Miner (1952), Oscar Lewis (1965), and P. M. Hauser (1965).

To say that cities stand in a systemic relation to the rural areas, however, is not to imply that there was no conflict between city and country. That conflict was often severe and was the subject of frequent comment by classical writers. G. E. M. de Ste. Croix (1981) provides a full accounting of that conflict along with an excellent description of the hierarchical patterns of city-country relations. Additional detail on city-country relations can be found in Peter Garnsey's work on famine and food supplies (1987). Especially noteworthy is his description of peasant survival strategies in the face of city demands on their agricultural surplus.

What is needed, therefore, is to set the city within the urban system of which it was a central, often parasitic, part. In doing so a variety of items on urban theory warrant careful study. Much of this work stems from theory about the city as "central place," that is, a node or center in a wider system. John Collis (1986) offers a review of that concept, together with bibliography on the seminal sources. Though central place theory began as a means of understanding market towns in late medieval Europe, the concept has been extended to recognize that cities can often be considered "central" for other than market reasons. Political and religious central places are examples. The latter can be seen in the case of oriental temple cities such as Jerusalem or Amarna and the former in classical cities such as Athens or Rome.

Several sources conveniently summarize the broader contours of modern urban "systems" theory. An appropriate starting place is with the theoretical issues involved in any attempt at conceptualization of the city. Paul Wheatley (1972) gives an excellent review of these issues along with a critical look at city definitions and city models that social scientists have used. Bruce Trigger (1965) demonstrates the sharply different dynamics that led to preindustrial cities as compared to those of the modern era. In the process he also demonstrates the necessity of seeing city and hinterland as components of a single system. M. G. Smith's brief study (1972) is helpful here as well.

Of course, not all urbanized regions have organized the relationship between city and country in exactly the same fashion. Moreover, the list of ecological, political, cultural, and economic factors contributing to these regional patterns of organization has varied. Eric Lampard (1965) reviews this rural-urban relationship in historical perspective. Two articles by Anthony Leeds are especially important in this regard. Leeds 1979 shows how the varying interests of the dominant urban elite can create different patterns of organization within the total system. He demonstrates crucial ways in which industrial and preindustrial cities differ, especially in the manner in which they require and appropriate sources of labor. Leeds 1980 presents the hierarchical character of urban-rural relations in the preindustrial world, along with a model of such urban systems in relation to complexity and size.

Before leaving the topic of cities in relation to the surrounding countryside, we should mention an ongoing theoretical debate between those who take a Weberian approach (e.g., Finley 1977), contrasting the ancient "consumer city" with the "producer city" of medieval Europe, and those who consider the contrast to be overdrawn. The volume edited by John Rich and Andrew Wallace-Hadrill (1991) contains a fine series of articles on Greek and Roman cities in which the various authors discuss the issues and the evidence. While most authors strongly reaffirm the Weber/Finley model, several argue that the contrast has been overdrawn. In a volume aimed at this same debate T. K. Cornell and K. Lomas (1995) have collected the papers from a 1991 conference on the ancient city held at the University of London. In addition to evaluating the "consumer" and "producer" urban models, a number of the articles address recent proposals about "service" cities in antiquity. Here one will also find up-to-date comment on urban theory.

Recent discussions among those doing Galilean archaeology have centered on the extent and type of urbanism in lower Galilee in the first century. A related debate has occurred over the degree and type of hellenization. The works of James Strange (1992), Eric Meyers (1992a, 1992b), and Sean Freyne (1992) can lead the reader into this debate, though the reader should be forewarned that a solid grounding in urban theory does not always inform the conclusions of all participants in these discussions. Lenski, Lenski, and Nolan (1991) and Sjoberg (1960) should therefore be read alongside these recent discussions of urbanism in Galilee.

Finally we must come to the preindustrial city itself. If we have followed modern theorists in resisting the temptation to treat the city as an isolated construct, nonetheless the shape and character of the city itself is an important concern. The classic work in this area is Gideon Sjoberg's *The Preindustrial City* (1960), and few works will repay more careful study by NT scholars. Sjoberg's study has, of course, come under heavy fire from later critics on several grounds. Most criticized are its perception of a unilinear, evolutionary development of the city, its tendency to treat the city apart from the wider urban system, and its insistence that cities and literacy are inseparable phenomena. Historians have also complained that this city of Sjoberg's, a composite construct that draws on common characteristics of preindustrial cities from a wide range of times and places, exists nowhere in actual fact. It is an "ideal" model in the sense that it summarizes generalizations about the city that may or may not be true of any actual city.

Nonetheless, the work is invaluable for understanding the cities of antiquity. After a brief historical survey of the development and spread of cities (note the critique above), Sjoberg provides a detailed and comprehensive characterization of all aspects of preindustrial city life: demography, ecology, social stratification, kinship, economics, politics, religion, and education. Because Sjoberg's work is cross-cultural and comparative, it serves as an overwhelming demonstration of the anachronistic and ethnocentric assumptions modern readers from industrialized areas bring to an understanding of the urban world in which the NT emerged.

Few readers of the NT today, for example, understand the social significance of the spatial organization of ancient cities. In the modern city the elite live at the outskirts and the poor live in the ghetto in the center. In the ancient city it was the opposite. The elite, usually no more than 2 or 3 percent of the population, lived at the center near the temple and palace, while the poor lived on the periphery. Outcasts lived outside the city along with others whose presence in the city during the day was necessary or tolerated (tanners, prostitutes, beggars, traders), but who were unneeded and unwelcome at night. Internal city walls separated ethnic or occupational groups, and doors between these population areas were usually locked at night.

Unlike the modern city in which capital attracts labor and thereby promotes urban growth, with few exceptions (e.g., Rome, Alexandria) urban populations in antiquity were limited to those serving the needs of the elite. It became a major interest to keep others *out* of the cities; indeed, in most agrarian societies legal restrictions on city residence were enacted to keep peasants away. Replenishment of nonelite populations, to the degree that was necessary, came from the dispossessed of the countryside whose lack of skills often relegated them to menial tasks as day laborers. Physically and socially, therefore, the preindustrial city was quite unlike its modern counterpart.

Sjoberg's work is thus critical in understanding how these ancient cities were physically and socially shaped. The reader should understand, however, that Sjoberg uses an "ideal type" as his model of the city. Ideal types are *hypothetical* constructs created from the common characteristics of many actual examples. Thus Sjoberg's preindustrial city should not be misconstrued as a description of an actual city. It is not. It is a set of generalizations drawn from the comparison of many actual preindustrial cities the world over. For an excellent review of the way such ideal models work, together with additional cross-cultural models of life in the preindustrial city, there is the under-utilized book by Thomas Carney (1975). Carney has the rare combination of a historian's eye for the particular and unique and a sociologist's awareness of context and commonality.

Finally, it is necessary to place all this attention on the preindustrial city in the wider context of agrarian societies. We are, after
all, trying to draw the contrast between a phenomenon we know
well in our own day, the industrial city of the modern West, and a
somewhat similar but also vastly different one, the preindustrial
city of the NT world. Preindustrial cities existed in what are called
"agrarian" (*not* a synonym for "agricultural") societies. Few students of the NT have taken seriously the watershed changes
wrought by the industrial revolution, which changed not only the
shape and character of the city but also our perception of the
world. Understanding how ancient agrarian societies differ from
what we know today will help to sharpen the contrast between the
two types of cities we are considering as well. The macrosociological studies by Lenski, Lenski, and Nolan (1991) should be considered fundamental in this regard. Valuable too is the second study
by Lenski alone (1966). Both books offer comparative studies of
agrarian and industrial societies.

5.0 Conclusion: Issues and Priorities

In using studies of either the urban system or the preindustrial city, we
are trying to re-imagine the cities of antiquity. Projecting modern city
life backward when thinking about the cities of the NT is common
among contemporary scholars, but it leads to misunderstanding.

While the use of social-science models of the preindustrial city
in studying the NT is not yet very far along, an example may be
found in Richard Rohrbaugh's (1990) work on the parable of the
Great Banquet in Luke 14. It demonstrates how different the text can
look when set in a preindustrial urban context.

In reading this social-science literature, one should focus on
several issues. Older attempts to define the term "city" on the basis
of its shape or size can be left behind. Much better is an attempt to
see how a city functions in the regional system that surrounds it.
Gaining a sense of that should be a key objective of reading the
social-science literature because the dynamics that shape the urban
system often play a key role in NT stories. Of special importance here
is the relationship between the city and the rural areas, especially the
way their respective populations interacted.

We are likewise concerned with the characteristics of the preindustrial city itself. Its spatial configuration, size, appearance,
traffic patterns, and population types are all important. So also is
the ability to sort out the urban elite from nonelite and both of those

groups from rural peasants. Anachronistic attempts to do so on the basis of imagined income (e.g., "middle-class" carpenters) are inappropriate. Above all, we need to concentrate on the patterns of social interaction among the various population groups that inhabited these cities and the means by which that interaction was shaped. Throughout more recent urban studies this concern for social dynamics is central, and this same concern promises the most new insight to those who read the NT.

Before concluding our survey it might be helpful to prioritize this social-science literature as we did with the material providing the basic historical information. In doing so it is necessary to remember that while theoretical issues can be an endless tangle that many would prefer to avoid, disinterest in theory does not allow us to escape the issues. Preconceptions simply replace considered judgment.

If the reader's time is sharply limited, no work can substitute for a thorough reading of Sjoberg (1960). It should take priority over all other works cited above because it draws most clearly the contrast between ancient cities and those that inhabit our preconceptions. Second priority might be given to four articles: the one by Wheatley (1972) on the concept of urbanism, that by Trigger (1965) on the growth dynamics of preindustrial cities, and the two by Leeds on social urbanization (1979) and village-city relations (1980). These will provide both theoretical clarity and a sense of perspective that allows readers to discriminate among theoretical claims and also to assess the disclaimers about theoretical interest that are so common among historians and NT scholars. Together with Sjoberg, they offer a solid foundation for using the social sciences to understand NT cities.

Those with more time might consider both a wider and a closer view. Gerhard Lenski, Jean Lenski, and Patrick Nolan (1991) provide the wider view. While everything in it will interest some readers, the chapters on agrarian and industrial societies are those on which to concentrate. For a closer view of the value of doing this kind of social-science work in exegetical studies, Rohrbaugh (1990) provides ample illustration.

We may conclude, then, that cross-cultural work on preindustrial cities can be a significant tool to help us imagine the environment all NT writers anticipated among their ancient readers. The literature described above is intended to equip the reader to envision the urban scene more as an ancient counterpart might have seen it. In whatever measure it helps us do that, it may also help us as modern readers to let the Bible speak to us on its own first-century terms rather those we inadvertently import into it.

6.0 Works Cited

Historical Literature

Dudley, Donald R.
    1967   *Urbs Roma*. London: Phaidon.

Finley, M. I.
    1977   "The Ancient City: From Fustel de Coulanges to Max
        Weber and Beyond." *Comparative Studies in Society and
        History* 19:305–27.

Freyne, Sean
    1980   *Galilee from Alexander the Great to Hadrian: 323 BCE to
        135 CE*. University of Notre Dame Center for the Study
        of Judaism and Christianity in Antiquity 5.
        Wilmington, Del.: Glazier; South Bend, Ind.:
        University of Notre Dame Press.
    1992   "Urban-Rural Relations in First-Century Galilee: Some
        Suggestions from the Literary Sources." In *The Galilee
        in Late Antiquity*. Ed. Lee I. Levine. Pages 75–91.
        Cambridge: Harvard University Press.

Frick, F. S.
    1977   *The City in Ancient Israel*. SBLDS 36. Missoula, Mont.:
        Scholars Press.

Fustel de Coulanges, N. D.
    1873   *The Ancient City*. Trans. W. Small. Garden City, N.Y.:
        Doubleday, Anchor Books, 1976).

Hammond, Mason
    1972   *The City in the Ancient World*. Cambridge: Harvard
        University Press.

Harper, George
    1928   "Village Administration in the Roman Province of
        Syria." *Yale Classical Studies* 1:105–68.

Jeremias, Joachim
    1969   *Jerusalem in the Time of Jesus*. Trans. F. H. Cave and C. H.
        Cave. Philadelphia: Fortress.

Jones, A. H. M.
    1931   "The Urbanization of Palestine." *JRS* 21:78–85.
    1940   *The Greek City from Alexander to Justinian*. Oxford:
        Clarendon.
    1971   *The Cities of the Eastern Roman Provinces*. 1937. 2d ed.
        Reprint, London: Oxford University Press.

Koester, Helmut, and Holland Hendrix, eds.
    1987   *Archaeological Resources for New Testament Studies.* Vol. 1,
            A Collection of Slides on Culture and Religion in Antiquity.
            Philadelphia: Fortress.
Meeks, Wayne
    1983   *The First Urban Christians.* New Haven: Yale University
            Press.
Meyers, Eric M.
    1992a   "The Challenge of Hellenism for Early Judaism and
            Christianity." *BA* 55/3:84–91.
    1992b   "Roman Sepphoris in Light of New Archeological
            Evidence and Recent Research." In *The Galilee in Late
            Antiquity.* Ed. Lee I. Levine. Pages 321–38. Cambridge:
            Harvard University Press.
Mumford, L.
    1961   *The City in History: Its Origins, Its Transformations, and
            Its Prospects.* New York: Harcourt and Brace.
Murphy-O'Connor, Jerome
    1983   *St. Paul's Corinth: Texts and Archaeology.* Wilmington,
            Del.: Glazier.
    1984   "The Corinth that Saint Paul Saw." *BA* 47(3):147–59.
Owens, E. J.
    1991   *The City in the Greek and Roman World.* New York:
            Routledge.
Russell, D. A., and N. G. Wilson
    1981   *Menander Rhetor.* Oxford: Clarendon.
Stambaugh, John E.
    1988   *The Ancient Roman City.* Baltimore: Johns Hopkins
            University Press.
Stark, Rodney
    1991   "Antioch as the Social Situation for Matthew's Gospel."
            In *Social History of the Matthean Community:
            Cross-Disciplinary Approaches.* Ed. David L. Balch. Pages
            189–210. Minneapolis: Augsburg Fortress.
Stillwell, Richard, ed.
    1976   *The Princeton Encyclopedia of Classical Sites.* Princeton:
            Princeton University Press.
Strange, James
    1992   "Six Campaigns at Sepphoris: The University of South
            Florida Excavations, 1983–1989." In *The Galilee in Late
            Antiquity.* Ed. Lee I. Levine. Pages 339–55. Cambridge:
            Harvard University Press.
Tcherikover, Victor
    1979   *Hellenistic Civilization and the Jews.* 1959. Reprint, New
            York: Atheneum.

Tomlinson, Richard
1992   *From Mycenae to Constantinople: The Evolution of the Ancient City.* New York: Routledge.

Yamauchi, Edwin
1980   *The Archaeology of the New Testament Cities in Western Asia Minor.* Grand Rapids: Baker.

Social-Science Literature

Blanton, R. E.
1976   "Anthropological Study of Cities." *ARA* 5:249–64.

Burke, Peter
1980   *Sociology and History.* London: Allen & Unwin.

Carney, T. F.
1975   *The Shape of the Past: Models and Antiquity.* Lawrence, Kans.: Coronado.

Childe, V. Gordon
1950   "The Urban Revolution." *Town Planning Review* 12:3–17.
1957   "Civilizations, Cities and Towns." *Antiquity* 31:36–38.

Collis, John
1986   "Central Place Theory Is Dead: Long Live the Central Place." In *Central Places, Archaeology and History.* Ed. Eric Grant. Pages 37–40. Sheffield: Department of Archaeology and Prehistory, University of Sheffield.

Cornell, T. J., and K. Lomas, eds.
1995   *Urban Society in Roman Italy.* London: UCL Press.

Garnsey, Peter
1987   *Famine and Food Supply in the Graeco-Roman World.* Cambridge: Cambridge University Press.

Hauser, P.M.
1965   "The Folk-Urban Ideal Types: B. Observations on the Urban-Folk and Urban-Rural Dichotomies as Forms of Western Ethnocentrism." In *The Study of Urbanization.* Ed. P. M. Hauser and L. F. Schnore. Pages 503–17. New York: John Wiley & Sons.

Lampard, Eric E.
1965   "Historical Aspects of Urbanization." In *The Study of Urbanization.* Ed. P.M. Hauser and L. F. Schnore. Pages 519–54. New York: John Wiley & Sons.

Lampl, Paul
1968   *Cities and Planning in the Ancient Near East.* New York: George Braziller.

Lapidus, I. M.
    1986   "Cities and Societies: A Comparative Study of the
            Emergence of Urban Civilization in Mesopotamia and
            Greece." *Journal of Urban History* 12(3): 257–93.
Leeds, Anthony
    1979   "Forms of Urban Integration: Social Urbanization in
            Comparative Perspective." *Urban Anthropology* 8:227–47.
    1980   "Towns and Villages in Society: Hierarchies of
            Order and Cause." In *Cities in a Larger Context*. Ed.
            Thomas W. Collins. Pages 6–33. Athens: University of
            Georgia Press.
Lenski, Gerhard
    1966   *Power and Privilege: A Theory of Social Stratification*. New
            York: McGraw-Hill.
Lenski, Gerhard, Jean Lenski, and Patrick Nolan
    1991   *Human Societies*. 6th ed. New York: McGraw-Hill.
Lewis, Oscar
    1965   "The Folk-Urban Ideal Types: A. Further Observations
            on the Folk-Urban Continuum and Urbanization with
            Special Reference to Mexico City." In *The Study of
            Urbanization*. Ed. P. M. Hauser and L. F. Schnore. Pages
            491–503. New York: John Wiley & Sons.
Miner, Horace
    1952   "The Folk-Urban Continuum." *ASR* 17:529–37.
Redfield, R.
    1947   "The Folk Society." *ASR* 52:296–97.
Redfield, R., and M. Singer
    1954   "The Cultural Role of Cities." *EDCC* 3 (1954):30–46.
Rich, John, and Andrew Wallace-Hadrill
    1991   *City and Country in the Ancient World*. New York:
            Routledge.
Rohrbaugh, Richard L.
    1990   "The Pre-industrial City in Luke-Acts: Urban Social
            Relations." In *The Social World of Luke-Acts: Models for
            Interpretation*. Ed. Jerome Neyrey. Pages 125–50.
            Peabody, Mass.: Hendrickson.
Sjoberg, Gideon
    1960   *The Preindustrial City*. New York: Macmillan.
Smith, M. G.
    1972   "Complexity, Size and Urbanization." In *Man,
            Settlement and Urbanism*. Ed. P.J. Ucko, Ruth Tringham,
            and C. W. Dimbleby. Pages 567–74. London:
            Duckworth.

Ste. Croix, G. E. M. de
    1981   *The Class Struggle in the Ancient Greek World*. Ithaca,
            N.Y.: Cornell University Press.

Trigger, Bruce
    1972   "Determinants of Urban Growth in Pre-industrial
            Societies." In *Man, Settlement and Urbanism*. Ed. P. J.
            Ucko, Ruth Tringham, and C. W. Dimbleby. Pages
            575–99. London: Duckworth.

Wheatley, Paul
    1972   "The Concept of Urbanism." In *Man, Settlement and
            Urbanism*. Ed. P.J. Ucko, Ruth Tringham, and C. W.
            Dimbleby. Pages 601–37. London: Duckworth.

Wirth, Louis
    1938   "Urbanism as a Way of Life." *Journal of Sociological
            Studies* 44:1–24.
    1951   "The Urban Society and Civilization." *American Journal
            of Oriental Studies* 45:743–55.
    1938   "Urbanism as a Way of Life." *AJS* 44 (1938):1–24.

6

The Ancient Economy

Douglas E. Oakman
Pacific Lutheran University

1.0 Introduction

Economics, commonly defined today as the allocation of scarce resources, has been a constant preoccupation of twentieth-century people in Western societies. Thus economic questions overshadow our political and domestic lives. Some modern writers (e.g., Marcuse) have highlighted *homo economicus* as a special type of human being in modern times. The modern economic system—with its networks of free markets, transportation facilities, commercial institutions, banks, monetary systems and policies, industrial and corporate organizations, gross national products, salaries and wages—is a social system all to itself, able to dominate other social institutions. This fact of modern experience and social consciousness is the first stumbling block for thinking about ancient economic life and investigating its manifestations within the biblical writings.

Consider for a moment a story that appears in two of our four Gospels (Matt 25:14–30; Luke 19:12–27), and in another form in an early Christian work outside the Bible. The so-called parable of the Talents (Matthew) or Minas (Luke) may strike the modern reader as an apology for capitalism. The reward of the servants who increase the master's wealth, the punishment of the servant who refuses to risk his master's wealth, can fit right in with the modern corporate value system.

In 1925, during the heyday of the old American liberalism, Bruce Barton wrote a book about Jesus Christ called *The Man Nobody Knows.* It can still epitomize how modern Americans might think about economics in the Bible. Barton thinks of Jesus in classic liberal terms as a man who "did not come to establish a theology but to lead a life" (136). This sentiment appears in a chapter entitled "His Advertisements." Barton reads Jesus' parables as illustrating modern principles of advertising: "Every advertising man ought to study the parables of Jesus in the same fashion, schooling himself in their language and learning these four big elements of their power" (146).

In like manner, Barton approaches Jesus as "The Founder of Modern Business" (the title of ch. 6). The book's title page contains an inscription from Luke 2:49 (in the quaint language of the KJV): "Wist ye not that I must be about my Father's business?" For Barton, this "business" has much to do with modern corporate capitalism: Thus we have the main points of his business philosophy:

1. Whoever will be great must render great service.
2. Whoever will find himself at the top must be willing to lose himself at the bottom.
3. The big rewards come to those who travel the second, undemanded mile (177).

This last point suggests how Barton might have interpreted Jesus' story about the Talents (though Barton does not explicitly say so). In the similar case of the Rich Fool (Luke 12:20), Barton concludes that the story criticizes selfish satisfaction. He thinks the problem with Judas Iscariot was that he only looked out for number one; stinginess led to his downfall. So Barton sees Jesus as an advocate of philanthropy, a picture that would have been appealing in many corporate boardrooms of the 1920s.

A very different picture of the parable of the Talents emerges through Bruce Malina and Richard Rohrbaugh's *Social Science Commentary on the Synoptic Gospels* (1992). They point out (regarding Matt 25:14–30) that "the elitist reading of the parable is congenial to Westerners conditioned to treat gain as both legitimate and proper" (150). To ancient ears, however, especially those of peasants, the story speaks of something else. It highlights the shamelessness of a "hard man" in a world of limited good, and comments on the dishonorable behavior of taking even more away from the many who have nothing. For the agrarian (agriculturally based) audiences whom Jesus addressed, the hero of the story was the third servant, who maintained honor in a world of shameless behavior. A very early version of the story preserved in the *Gospel of the Nazoreans* (according to Eusebius, *Theophania* 22) praised this third servant, the one who hid the talent. The other two slaves were respectively rebuked and thrown into prison (Malina and Rohrbaugh 1992:149–50). The economic meaning of such a story shifts within an agrarian social setting.

The work done by economic historians and comparative economists since the 1940s has demonstrated conclusively that ancient economics, indeed any economic life prior to the industrial revolution of the late eighteenth century, was a different phenomenon from what moderns have come to think of under the term "economics." Therefore it is necessary to acquire a special set of conceptual lenses when reading ancient literature, including the Bible, in order to perceive appropriately the nature and character of ancient economics. The present essay has as its primary aim to introduce the reader to a select number of books that will supply these conceptual tools. Secondarily, this exposition gives some brief indications of how these conceptual tools can help in seeing characteristic economic emphases in the biblical writings.

Three major areas of reading are in store for the intrepid student who ventures into what has been called the "dismal science" as it applies to the Bible. The first area is the province of a single preeminent scholar; the second, the sphere of economic anthropologists; the third, the world of classical historians and biblical scholars.

2.0 Karl Polanyi

Perhaps the most important thinker and writer for the present topic is Karl Polanyi (1886–1964). His importance derives from his concern both with economic history and with comparative economics—the study of economics across a broad range of societies. His most representative and accessible book is probably *The Great Transformation* (1944), which attempts to chronicle the modern rise and fall of the free market, an institution that was nearly unknown in earlier economic history. The value of the book also extends to the illumination of several important concepts that concern the student of ancient economics. Thus Polanyi shows how markets, which are central in modern capitalism, played only a limited role in the economic affairs of premodern societies. There, economic activities were always socially restrained or constrained. No society before the industrial revolution was willing to allow markets to dominate other social institutions.

The ancient economy was also embedded in (subordinate to) other social institutions, notably political and kin institutions. The Greek words behind the term "economy," in fact, mean "household (οἶκος, *oikos*) management (νομία, *nomia*)." For this reason, one needs to speak of the ancient political economy or the ancient domestic economy as somewhat distinct economic spheres, but not of economics per se—as a separate sphere of life with free markets, capital institutions like banks, impersonal exchange values, and so forth. Market exchange in antiquity was limited to some special cases, usually monopolized by specific groups (Phoenicians on the eastern Mediterranean, Nabataeans in Arabia), and benefited only the most powerful elements of society. Ancient monarchs in the biblical period, for example Solomon (1 Kgs 10), virtually monopolized the benefits of trade arrangements.

Polanyi also points to reciprocity and redistribution as crucial economic alternatives to the market. The two dominant forms of economic exchange in antiquity were reciprocity within kinship relations and redistribution in political economies, and it is critical to understand both. *Reciprocity* means exchange on a gift or barter basis. It is characterized by informal dyadic contracts—social give-and-take—within household and village. A gift accepted implies an obligation owed (e.g., Luke 11:8). In contrast to market exchanges (e.g., getting food for money at the supermarket) in which the transaction implies no personal obligation, reciprocity exchanges often involve one commodity being traded for another (e.g., wine for grain) and implicit personal obligations as well. Reciprocity ensures not only that goods on the average will be equitably distributed, but also that help will be available in hard times.

By contrast, *redistribution* was characteristically observed in the institutions of state and religious taxation. It involved the politically or religiously induced extraction of a percentage of local production, the storehousing of that product, and its eventual redistribution for some political end or another. Here for illustrative purposes one can mention Roman taxation in Jesus' day (Mark 12:13–17), the Jewish tithe (Deut 14:22–26), and the Jewish temple considered as a redistributive institution. While the modern supermarket seems analogous to the ancient storehouse, the parallel inappropriately suggests the operation of supply and demand in ancient redistributive institutions and overlooks their politically extractive nature. The essential notion of redistribution is (en)-forced collection of economic surplus to a central point and redistribution at another time or place.

Polanyi (along with other students of ancient economies) has pointed toward some other characteristic shifts of emphasis in ancient economies. The dominant means of livelihood in preindustrial societies was agriculture. Around 80 to 90 percent of the populace was engaged in some way on the land. Since land was the major factor of production, control of land was the chief political question of antiquity. Consider the political direction, for instance, of the Jubilee laws in Lev 25:23, 25–28, and contrast them with 1 Sam 8:14 or 1 Kgs 21:1–29.

There was no industry as we think of it today. The division of labor had not been "rationalized" to the same degree as in modern societies. Like other economic factors, labor was embedded in other institutions, especially kinship and household contexts. Industry was normally small-scale and conducted by families and their slaves (or "hired servants," Mark 1:20).

Money appeared in antiquity after the eighth century BCE (Lydia), but it did not have the same significance it has today. Ancient money was generally hoarded and had real value only for some things: to pay mercenaries or taxes, to acquire land if legally possible (from other landowners who had it), or to create new dependencies through loans. It possessed only a rudimentary form of abstract exchange value. Moreover, it did not eliminate the need for personal exchanges between trading parties. Money was mostly available to and in the hands of the political elites. They did not work for it; such capital was obtained through slave-based mining of raw materials and wars of conquest. Those who worked for a wage were regarded as dependent or degraded—a form of slave. These in turn were generally restricted in the uses they could find for money.

Money also facilitated long-distance commerce and trade. Because of its potentially disruptive social effects, long-distance trade was normally insulated from local commerce. For the sake of economic security, local oligarchs prevented the incorporation of local markets into long-distance trade networks (Polanyi 1944:60). Land, as has been said, was the most precious commodity for the ancient elites; for them control or ownership of land implied honorable lineage and was the material basis for household (economic) security. Thus people in antiquity who acquired wealth through commerce or other means normally attempted to achieve respectability by investing in land. Ancient societies as a rule resisted placing a money value on land precisely to protect the status of longstanding elite groups and to discourage newcomers from obtaining respectability.

Two other books edited or authored by Polanyi are helpful for thinking about ancient economics. First, the collection of essays in *Trade and Market in the Early Empires* is the classic work that brought comparative economics to the attention of ancient historians and classicists (Polanyi, et al., 1957). This is heavy reading: essays range from the economic history of Mesopotamia to Aristotle's discovery of the economy, from comparative studies of South American, African, and Indian economic worlds to the modern economic theories of Parsons and Smelser. Second, Polanyi's posthumously published volume on human economies summarizes his lifetime of scholarship on economic history (Polanyi 1977). Here one finds discussions of formal and substantive economics, of the embedded economies in archaic societies, the origin and function of markets in antiquity, trade and money in ancient Greece, and so on.

3.0 Economic Anthropology

The second major area of reading pertinent for the student of ancient and biblical economics emerges from economic anthropology. Two types of literature are commented on here. First are general surveys of economies in preindustrial societies. Next are works that concentrate especially on peasants and peasant life.

3.1 General Surveys

Polanyi himself gleaned numerous comparative insights from the early work of Richard Thurnwald (1932) and Bronislav Malinowski (1961), who demonstrated that the economic life of "primitives" was socially controlled in complex ways. The classic study in this genre, however, is undoubtedly Melville Herskovits's *Economic Anthropology* (1952).

Herskovits states his objective in this book very simply: "The purpose of this book [is] to provide information concerning the economic life of nonliterate peoples" (1952:vii). After an introductory section (part 1), which contains a helpful essay "Anthropology and Economics," Herskovits proceeds to treat "Production" (part 2), "Exchange and Distribution" (part 3), "Property" (part 4), and "The Economic Surplus" (part 5). Herskovits finds that the differences between modern and preindustrial economy types are in degree, not in kind, because "practically every economic mechanism and institution known to us is found somewhere in the nonliterate world" (1952:488). Nevertheless, special approaches need to be designed to study economic processes and institutions not clearly differentiated from other social phenomena. Herskovits pays particular attention to the questions of economic determinism (whether economic processes affect other social processes and values) and self-interest within the economic activity of nonliterate peoples.

Manning Nash (1968) supplies another useful summary of themes of economic anthropology. He identifies four important economic dimensions in primitive and peasant societies: (1) technology and division of labor, (2) structure of productive units, (3) the system and media of exchange, and (4) the control of wealth and capital. Nash's (1) and (2) correspond to Herskovits's part 2; (3) and (4) correspond to Herskovits's part 3.

During the postwar period, there has been an explosion of works on themes of economic anthropology. Some of this work has been aligned with investigation of the underdevelopment of the so-called Third World. Notable here are the books by Doreen Warriner (1965) and by Colin Clark and Maurine Haswell (1970). These show in various ways why traditional agriculture throughout the globe has resisted change ("development") and shown relatively limited productivity. Clark and Haswell also provide valuable quantitative data to reveal the conditions under which traditional agriculture operates. By contrast, Stuart Plattner's collection of essays (1989) traces how the integration of traditional societies into global markets has modernized village life in a variety of respects. Much global agriculture has been carried on by peasants, hence a huge literature has come into being on this subject.

3.2 Peasant and Agrarian Studies

Peasants have been the predominant social type in most of the agrarian societies of history, including especially those of the biblical period. Robert Redfield, the dean of peasant studies because of his early effort in this area, still deserves reading. His *Peasant Society and Culture* (1956) illuminates the general values and outlook of peasants, as well as proposes the influential concepts of "Great" and "Little Traditions." Also helpful at getting at the social world and values of peasantry is the collection of essays edited by Jack Potter, May Diaz, and George Foster (1967). Foster's influential article "Peasant Society and the Image of Limited Good" illuminates the zero-sum nature of peasant economics. Because goods are always perceived in such societies to be in limited quantities, anyone who gets ahead is thought to have done so at the expense of everyone else. These perceptions lead to a variety of village social mechanisms designed to keep everybody more or less on the same social level. From a materialist perspective, the works of Eric Wolf have contributed a great deal to the study of peasant types, subsistence and land concerns, religious orientation, and so forth. Wolf's *Peasants* (1966) is an accessible summary of what has been learned about various aspects of peasant life.

In peasant or agrarian societies social stratification, best defined as social categorization measured by differences in social wealth and power, is pronounced. Gerhard Lenski helps us to understand why. In his *Power and Privilege* (1984), Lenski examines the general social makeup of the agrarian and maritime societies (among others) and shows how a variety of social phenomena are interrelated because of the technoeconomic level of such societies. Biblical

society belongs within agrarian society; this type depends techno-
logically on the plow and harnessed animal energy. The work of the
many (90 percent) supports a small (10 percent) ruling elite. Agricultural surpluses with this technology cannot support more people not
directly working the land. Lenski's discussion thus provides an evolutionary and broad, macrosociological view, which can be useful in
keeping details in perspective.

4.0 General Economic History

For those who seek a map of what has been done historically in the
study of economics, the bibliographic essay by Hoselitz (1959) is still
useful. He gives a rather full list (but not always much annotation) of
works that deal with economic analysis through history. He also
organizes his bibliography to reflect schools of economic thought.
Robert Heilbroner (1985) provides a lucid survey of economic activities and organization through history and down to the present. His
chapter on "Premarket Economy" is brief, but underscores many of
the points emphasized throughout the present essay. V. Gordon
Childe (1964) is especially useful in tracing technical and structural
factors in the economic development of ancient societies. Childe
gives the big picture on economics, tracing for instance the general
negative impact of money on societies based on agricultural production. His book reminds us that focus on details sometimes obscures
the obvious generality.

5.0 Classical Historians, Biblical Scholars, and the Ancient Economy

Several works by classical historians offer helpful summaries of results of the study of economics in antiquity. T. F. Carney (1975)
devotes a chapter to " 'Economics' in Antiquity" and details the
hard-won results of Polanyi's and others' work. As the subtitle of the
book suggests, Carney is especially interested in developing explicit
conceptual models for the investigation of significant institutions of
antiquity (including the bureaucratic states of the ancient Near East).
This important strength allows Carney, unlike authors who adopt
purely historical-descriptive treatments, to investigate in a controlled way the extent of "marketization" and "monetization" on
ancient economies. (The former refers to how far prices are set in

price markets; the latter refers to how far prices are established in money.) With a clear sense of the controlling social structures of the ancient world, Carney paints a picture of economic stagnation and gross inequality in the sharing of any economic advantages. Carney's perspective helps us to understand the moral outrage, say, of the biblical prophets or Jesus over the plight of the many.

By contrast, Moses Finley (1973) restricts attention to Greco-Roman antiquity, and while he is not as self-conscious as Carney in the development and justification of explicit models for the study of ancient societies, he does make some use of the conceptual categories and results of modern economic anthropology. Nevertheless, in a preliminary discussion of "The Ancients and Their Economy," Finley takes pains to argue that modern economic conceptions are largely inappropriate. At a number of points he stresses the irrelevance of the modern notion of economic class. He does, however, provide valuable historical sketches of agricultural production, estates, tenancy, slavery, peasants, organization of labor, banking, loans-at-interest, debts, and so on.

Older, but still of great value for a general understanding of ancient economic history, are the writings of Max Weber, who like Polanyi combined classical training with comparativist study. Weber's magnum opus was *Economy and Society* (1978), posthumously pieced together from manuscripts in various stages of completion. This massive work offers dense and highly theoretical reading on the subject.

Three other works of Weber are probably more useful and accessible. His *General Economic History* (1950), originally part of a series of lectures on universal history, is oriented to understanding the development of Western capitalism and economic "rationalism." While he focuses primarily on medieval and modern economic developments in Europe, the ever-thorough Weber is always attentive to their foundations in antiquity. He takes up, for example, a discussion of the ancient plantation, noting that it always depended on slave-hunting. Weber then draws on comparative material, for this instance examining southern U.S. slave plantations in the nineteenth century.

An equally illuminating study by Weber, full of historical detail, is *The Agrarian Sociology of Ancient Civilizations* (1976). This work, unlike *General Economic History*, gives sustained attention to ancient Near Eastern and classical social and economic organization. Weber is primarily concerned to interpret the operation of basic social values and institutions. His rich sociological imagination often makes stunning connections that mere historical description would overlook. One example of this interpretive activity has to suffice: Weber accurately characterizes ancient "capitalism" as relatively unproductive because of its alignment with power groups and because investments were limited only to certain socially acceptable outlets. Capital, because socially restricted, did not lead in antiquity to industrial production as the modern period has known it.

Ancient Judaism (1952), while somewhat dated in critical detail, surveys the sociological development of Judaism—from an agricultural people of the biblical period to a "pariah," commercial people of the talmudic period. Weber is particularly intent upon showing the relationship between specific biblical traditions and particular social groups and institutions (see Gottwald 1979, 1985).

All three of these books repay careful study and consideration, but all three require a great deal of effort on the part of the student.

More advanced students want to know about works that make available the ancient source material for economic study. A useful treatment of classical Greek society and economics, including a substantial number of texts in translation relating to these matters, is by M. M. Austin and P. Vidal-Naquet (1977). Michael Rostovtzeff's two great works (1941, 1957) are still unsurpassed for their thoroughness and scope. The weakness of these volumes lies less in their knowledge of the ancient data than in their failure to use the results of comparative social and economic study. Both sets reflect Rostovtzeff's encyclopedic knowledge of Hellenistic-Roman realities through both text and artifact. Each set contributes to our knowledge of the general social context of early Judaism and Christianity. The 1957 work especially specifies how the provinces of Judea and Syria fit within Roman imperial society.

Richard Duncan-Jones (1982) provides a wealth of data on Roman economy. As the subtitle indicates, Jones is concerned with prices, weights, measures, equivalent values, and so forth. Another massive collection of data, though older, is available in the volumes edited by Tenney Frank (1933–40). The section by Fritz Heichelheim (1938) on "Roman Syria" is especially valuable for students of the NT. Like Duncan-Jones, Heichelheim collects specific archaeological and textual data on agricultural production, population, wages and prices, taxation, municipal finances, industry, various kinds of crafts, and so on. This data represents study only up to 1938. Heichelheim offers preliminary interpretations, but does not employ sophisticated social models.

From a thoroughgoing Marxian perspective, G. E. M. de Ste. Croix (1981) provides rich fare. He devotes the first part of this massive book to the importance of Karl Marx's work for ancient historiography. As the book's title suggests, Ste. Croix pursues the notion of "class struggle" in emphasizing how much ancient history was in fact a result of the exploitation of the many-who-labored by the few-who-enjoyed-leisure. Ste. Croix's reading of apocalyptic literature as "protest literature" and his contextualizing of the Jesus movement as a protest of countryside against exploitative city present understandings of early Christianity radically different from theological approaches. He offers extensive bibliographic survey and discussion—further grist for the enterprising student's mill.

For the societies of the ancient Near East in general, Karl Wittvogel (1957) shows how the construction and maintenance of large-scale irrigation works led to such societies' typical bureaucratic shape. Another incisive book explicating the relationship between politics and economy in antiquity is by John Kautsky (1982). This book is especially important for tracing the imbalance of power in traditional, agrarian societies like those of the biblical period. Kautsky analyzes, for instance, the overall structuring of power in "aristocratic empires," showing how elites maintain their position with relatively few members in such societies and why peasant uprisings are so rare.

Norman Gottwald (1979, 1985) has investigated economic dimensions in the formation of Israel and the OT tradition generally. *The Tribes of Yahweh* (1979) is a comprehensive, technical study that argues against seeing early Israel as nomadic invaders of Canaan. Gottwald presents a convincing case for the transformation of a variety of social groups, including Canaanite peasants, into the early tribes of Yahweh. Religion here is firmly linked with subsistence agricultural concerns. Gottwald's *The Hebrew Bible* (1985), designed for college and seminary classrooms, incorporates the insights of *Tribes of Yahweh,* then traces developments down through the period of the Hebrew Bible. The Israelite monarchy represents the return to centralized state structures familiar throughout the ancient Near East. The exilic and postexilic materials are read through the lens of colonial experience. Gottwald's works show the interrelationship of power and economy in the development of Israelite faith.

Turning to the NT, Bruce Malina (1993) provides many examples of how to apply cultural anthropology to NT texts. Of special interest to the student of ancient economy is Malina's chapter "The Perception of Limited Good: Maintaining One's Social Status," which shows among other things that economic poverty was subordinate in biblical society to the concern for public reputation. There was no disgrace in poverty, but the inability to maintain one's honor was a serious liability. Not to have the means to do so would be thought of as shameful. Malina reminds the reader that economy was not a freestanding social institution in ancient societies; he points thus to the cultural meaning of wealth *within* an honor-shame framework. This meaning is not identical to perceptions within modern capitalist societies.

The collaborative work by Malina and Rohrbaugh (1992), mentioned at the beginning of this essay, gives much attention to the ancient economy in the Bible. Especially valuable are their textual notes and reading scenarios. They devote attention to what people ate, the kinds of money they used, how taxation was organized, and how lopsided power arrangements structured most social relations. This excellent resource brings together a wealth of information about Mediterranean societies pertinent for reading the Bible.

Halvor Moxnes (1988) employs models from economic anthropology to explore Luke's "moral economy of the peasant." Through this lens Moxnes sees the Lukan Jesus as an advocate of peasant values. The Pharisees are represented by Luke as those who are in league with the forces that oppose this moral economy. Douglas Oakman (1986) carries out a similar moral economic analysis with reference to the historical Jesus. Oakman focuses on production and (re)distribution from the viewpoint of the village, arguing that Jesus spoke against the exploitative political economy of Roman Palestine while advocating economic values based on general reciprocity and redistribution under a vision of God's reign.

For Palestinian and Jewish economic history, specifically, Shimon Applebaum's "Economic Life in Palestine" gives an excellent summary of first-century Palestinian economy based on Jewish and archaeological materials (Safrai and Stern 1976:2:631–700). Older, but still useful, are Joachim Jeremias (1969) and Joseph Klausner's chapter "Economic Conditions" (1925). These two authors amass from rabbinic traditions a substantial amount of information about economic realities in Roman Palestine at the turn of the eras. Jeremias gives details about commerce in the pilgrim city Jerusalem during the time of Jesus and shows how this commerce was controlled by wealthy priestly interests. Klausner supplies a lengthy description of the varieties of artisans and craftspeople in Jesus' environment. While these volumes do not have explicit social-theoretical frameworks, they give the reader valuable insights into economic realities and structures in the biblical world.

6.0 The Conceptual Payoff

By reading some or all of the works of Polanyi especially, as well as the foregoing economic anthropologists and historians of ancient economy, the biblical student can discern significant differences between the economies of the biblical period and the present. The major institutions of industrial or corporate capitalism are missing in the historical societies that hosted the biblical tradition. Economic issues and concerns do not have the same salience in the biblical writings as they do today. Some of these necessary shifts of perception and emphasis have already been indicated. However, a brief foray into some additional biblical material may serve to suggest payoffs from this type of study.

The narrow margin between subsistence and starvation is everywhere attested in the biblical literature (Deut 15:11; Mark 14:7 and par.). Biblical laws and moral injunctions were generally phrased to preserve the status of poor Israelites or poor Christians within the covenant community (see also Exod 20:1–17; 21–23; Deut 15:11; 2 Cor 9:12; Jas 2:6). As already suggested, biblical religion could function to undergird or to oppose either reciprocal household economy or redistributive political economy: throwing religious influence on the side of redistribution (Deut 14:22–29; 18:1–8; Mal 3:8–12; John 13:29; Acts 4:35; 6:1–3), or against redistributive economy (1 Sam 8:10–20; Mark 11:17).

The traditions of the OT laws and prophets show a profound concern with the economic conditions of the Israelites, but within the covenant or household metaphor. Economic concerns are always embedded within a larger social framework. Moreover, the biblical concern with economics is characteristically couched in agrarian terms. The Jubilee laws of Leviticus, as we have already seen, acknowledge the preeminence of land and family (Lev 25:10). The degraded status of labor and the prevalence of slavery in ancient Israel are also to be observed (Deut 15:12, 16–17). Moreover, one of the typical paths to slavery in the absence of war is indicated. Increasingly asymmetrical power relations lead to loss of ability to maintain one's status in the community (Lev 25:39). Biblical laws attempt to counteract the corrosive social effects of debt in covenant relationships (Deut 15:1–2). Loans must never be made at interest (Exod 22:25–27). The general picture is: debts should never get so large that they endanger the community fabric.

The political and redistributive economic machinery of the Israelite monarchy is well illustrated by the Deuteronomic account of Solomon's reign (1 Kgs 4:7, 22–23). This account makes clear that this economy was a political economy with a domestic form. Like all ancient monarchs, Solomon considered his kingdom his own household to do with as he pleased. He monopolized the lines of trade such that the notion of a free market would not apply to Solomonic commerce (10:2, 11, 14–25). Solomon used commercial ties for his own aggrandizement. 1 Kgs 9:15–22 indicates the generally unfree quality of labor in antiquity and the differential treatment accorded Israelites and non-Israelites under Solomon. Forced labor was reserved, according to the account, for non-Israelites. Nonetheless, the cause of the division of the monarchy was precisely the displeasure of Israelites with the Solomonic order (12:1–16).

The Jesus tradition, like the pre- or antimonarchic Israelite tradition, emphasizes reciprocity in economic exchanges and opposes or discourages a redistributive economy. Thus Jesus speaks of sharing freely with others (Matt 5:42; Luke 6:35), but he speaks critically of the temple institution in its economic aspects (Mark 11:17 and par.; cf. Mark 13:1–2). The rich man who seeks to found his security upon self-sufficiency and a large estate (redistributive economy) is labeled a fool (Luke 12:20). The early Christian movement itself may have lived out an economic lifestyle of familial reciprocity (Acts 4:34–35). Again we see economic exchanges embedded within other relationships and sanctioned by religious values. Debt is also abhorred in the Jesus movement, and forgiveness of debts (sins) assumes the rank of a core value in the Gospel tradition (Matt 6:12 = Luke 11:4; Matt 18:23–35; Luke 7:41–42; Matt 5:25–26 = Luke 12:58–59).

We return, finally, to Jesus' parable of the Talents. This story illustrates as well as any NT text how little modern notions of capital and investment apply to ancient economics. The narrative recalls two of the three prevalent uses for "capital" in antiquity: money on loan (Matt 25:16) or money hoarded (Matt 25:18). The third regular employment for the money elites was purchase of land. (On these typical uses, see Finley 1973:118.) Narrative developments revolve around these two options. Peasants would likely relate to the servant entrusted with one talent (although no peasant would ever see such an amount). Not only should such entrustments be hidden to avoid village envy, but peasants would always seek the economically secure course over risky loans. Peasant and Jewish values are trampled upon, however, when the rewards go to the two servants who brought back their trust with interest. As we have seen, interest was forbidden by Jewish law; such loans implied increasingly dependent and nonreciprocal relationships. The loans are not to help folks acquire a major appliance, but lead to dominance and control over others. Luke's version of the parable brings this out clearly: the reward given to the "faithful" (= trustworthy) servants is to control ten or five cities (Luke 19:17, 19).

7.0 Conclusion

The general reader or the reader pressed for time would do well to obtain works that are easily accessible and available, like Heilbroner (1985) for the economy in history or Malina (1993) and Malina and

Rohrbaugh (1992) for economics in the Bible. The last two books also orient the reader to cultural issues involved in reading the Bible. For readers interested in the broader historical-economic contexts of the Bible, Finley (1973) and Gottwald (1985) are especially helpful, though more difficult. Readers intrigued by the social-theoretical questions should turn first to Childe (1964), Carney (1975), and Lenski (1984).

There is more to be explored than one can adequately cover in the scope of a short chapter, but the reader will begin to see how economic issues are everywhere in the pages of the Bible, embedded within political, family, or religious contexts. Our economic assumptions and experiences do not help us to read the Bible and its concerns with economy sensibly or reliably. Barton's "man nobody knows" is truly a figment of modern liberal imagination, though Barton was right that Jesus had something to do with economic life. A different kind of "common sense" about the ancient economy needs to be acquired. For this task, a world of reading and fascinating exploration awaits the courageous.

8.0 Works Cited

Dates followed by "!" indicate additional relevant bibliography.

Applebaum, Shimon
    1976   "Economic Life in Palestine." In *The Jewish People in the First Century*. 2:631–700. Ed. S. Safrai and M. Stern. CRINT. Philadelphia: Fortress; Amsterdam: Van Gorcum.
Austin, M. M., and P. Vidal-Naquet
    1977!   *Economic and Social History of Ancient Greece: An Introduction*. Trans. and rev. by M. M. Austin. Berkeley: University of California Press.
Barton, B.
    1925   *The Man Nobody Knows*. New York: Grosset & Dunlap.
Carney, T. F.
    1975!   *The Shape of the Past: Models and Antiquity*. Lawrence, Kans.: Coronado.
Childe, V. Gordon.
    1964   *What Happened in History*. New York: Penguin.
Clark, C., and M. Haswell
    1970   *The Economics of Subsistence Agriculture*. 4th ed. New York: St. Martin's.
Duncan-Jones, R.
    1982   *The Economy of the Roman Empire: Quantitative Studies*. 2d ed. Cambridge: Cambridge University Press.

Finley, M.
    1975!   *The Ancient Economy*. 2d ed. London: Hogarth Press.
Foster, George M.
    1967   "Peasant Society and the Image of Limited Good." In
             Peasant Society: A Reader. Ed. J. Potter, M. Diaz, and G. Fos-
             ter. Pages 300–323. Boston: Little, Brown, and Company.
Frank, T., gen. ed.
    1933–40 *An Economic Survey of Ancient Rome*. 6 vols. Baltimore:
             Johns Hopkins University Press.
Gottwald, N.
    1979!   *The Tribes of Yahweh: A Sociology of the Religion of
             Liberated Israel, 1250–1050 B.C.E.* Maryknoll, N.Y.: Orbis.
    1985   *The Hebrew Bible: A Socio-Literary Introduction.*
             Philadelphia: Fortress.
Heichelheim, F.
    1938   "Roman Syria." In *An Economic Survey of Ancient Rome.*
             Ed. T. Frank. 4:121–258. Baltimore: Johns Hopkins
             University Press.
Heilbroner, R.
    1993   *The Making of Economic Society*. 9th ed. Englewood
             Cliffs, N.J.: Prentice-Hall.
Herskovits, M.
    1952!   *Economic Anthropology: The Economic Life of Primitive
             Peoples.* 2d ed. rev. and enlarged. New York: Knopf.
Hoselitz, B.
    1959!   *A Reader's Guide to the Social Sciences.* New York: Free
             Press.
Jeremias, J.
    1969   *Jerusalem in the Time of Jesus.* Trans. F. H. Cave and C. H.
             Cave. Philadelphia: Fortress.
Kautsky, J. H.
    1982   *The Politics of Aristocratic Empires.* Chapel Hill:
             University of North Carolina Press.
Klausner, J.
    1925   *Jesus of Nazareth: His Life, Times, and Teaching.* Trans.
             H. Danby. New York: Macmillan.
Lenski, G.
    1984   *Power and Privilege.* 1966. Reprint, Chapel Hill:
             University of North Carolina Press.
Malina, B.
    1993!   *The New Testament World: Insights from Cultural
             Anthropology.* 2d ed. Louisville: Westminster/John Knox.
Malina, B., and R. Rohrbaugh
    1992!   *Social Science Commentary on the Synoptic Gospels.*
             Philadelphia: Fortress.

Malinowski, B.
    1961   *Argonauts of the Western Pacific.* 1922. Reprint, New
            York: E. P. Dutton.
Marcuse, H.
    1964   *One-Dimensional Man.* Boston: Beacon.
Moxnes, H.
    1988   *The Economy of the Kingdom: Social Conflict and Economic
            Relations in Luke's Gospel.* OBT. Philadelphia: Fortress.
Nash, M.
    1968!   "Economic Anthropology." *International Encyclopedia of
            the Social Sciences.* 4:359–65. New York: Macmillan.
Oakman, D.
    1986!   *Jesus and the Economic Questions of His Day.* Lewiston,
            N.Y.: Mellen.
Plattner, S., ed.
    1989!   *Economic Anthropology.* Stanford: Stanford University
            Press.
Polanyi, K.
    1944!   *The Great Transformation.* Boston: Beacon.
    1977!   *The Livelihood of Man.* Ed. H. W. Pearson. New York:
            Academic Press.
Polanyi, K., C. M. Arensberg, and H. W. Pearson, eds.
    1957!   *Trade and Market in the Early Empires.* Glencoe, Ill.: Free
            Press.
Potter, J., M. Diaz, and G. Foster, eds.
    1967!   *Peasant Society: A Reader.* Boston: Little, Brown and Co.
Redfield, R.
    1956   *Peasant Society and Culture.* Chicago: University of
            Chicago Press.
Rostovtzeff, M.
    1941!   *The Social and Economic History of the Hellenistic World.* 3
            vols. Oxford: Clarendon.
    1957!   *The Social and Economic History of the Roman Empire.* 2d
            ed. 2 vols. Oxford: Clarendon.
Safrai, S., and M. Stern, eds.
    1976!   *The Jewish People in the First Century.* 2 vols. CRINT.
            Philadelphia: Fortress; Amsterdam: Van Gorcum.
Ste. Croix, G. E. M. de
    1981!   *The Class Struggle in the Ancient Greek World from the
            Archaic Age to the Arab Conquests.* Ithaca: Cornell
            University Press.
Thorner, D.
    1968!   "Peasantry." *International Encyclopedia of the Social
            Sciences.* 11:503–11. New York: Macmillan.

Thurnwald, R.
  1932   *Economics in Primitive Communities.* London: Oxford
            University Press.
Warriner, D.
  1965   *The Economics of Peasant Farming.* 2d ed. New York:
            Barnes and Noble.
Weber, M.
  1950   *General Economic History.* Glencoe, Ill.: Free Press.
  1952   *Ancient Judaism.* Trans. and ed. H. H. Gerth and D.
            Martindale. Glencoe, Ill.: Free Press.
  1976   *The Agrarian Sociology of Ancient Civilizations.* Trans. R. I.
            Frank. Atlantic Highlands: Humanities Press.
  1978   *Economy and Society.* 2 vols. Trans. E. Fischoff, et al. Ed.
            G. Roth and C. Wittich. Berkeley: University of
            California Press.
Wittvogel, K. A.
  1957   *Oriental Despotism.* New Haven: Yale University Press.
Wolf, E.
  1966!   *Peasants.* Foundations of Modern Anthropology Series.
            Englewood Cliffs, N.J.: Prentice-Hall.

7

Patronage and Clientage

John H. Elliott
University of San Francisco

1.0 Introduction: Subject, Sources, and Issues

The literary and epigraphic evidence from the Greco-Roman period abundantly attests the existence of a Roman social institution known as *clientela*, or, in modern terms, patronage and clientage. This fundamental and pervasive form of dependency relations, involving the reciprocal exchange of goods and services between socially superior "patrons" and their socially inferior "clients," shaped both the public and private sectors of ancient life as well as the political and religious symbolizations of power and dependency.

The following representative evidence may serve to illustrate our subject at the outset: (1) an early second-century CE letter from the Roman senator Pliny the Younger to his patron, the emperor Trajan; (2) a third-century CE bronze tablet inscription from Rome; and (3) two passages from the NT writing of Luke–Acts.

1. A Request of Pliny to Trajan the Emperor
Gaius Pliny to the Emperor Trajan. Valerius Paulinus, sir, has left a will which passes over his son Paulinus and names me a patron of his Latin freedmen. On this occasion I pray you to grant full Roman citizenship to three of them only; it would be unreasonable, I fear, to petition you to favor all alike, and I must be all the more careful not to abuse your generosity when I have enjoyed it on so many previous occasions (Pliny, *Epistles* 10.104).

2. Public Praise of a Patron
In the consulship of Imperator Caesar Marcus Aurelius Severus Alexander, 13 April: the council of the community of the people of Clunia co-opted Gaius Marius Pudens Cornelianus, legionary legate, a man

of the highest distinction, as its patron for itself, its offspring and posterity, because of his many outstanding services to them as individuals and collectively; the envoy used was Valerius Marcellus of Clunia (*ILS* 6109).

3. A Patron of the Jews in the Time of Jesus
Now a centurion had a slave who was dear to him; he was sick and at the point of death. When he heard of Jesus, he sent to him elders of the Jews asking him to come and heal his slave. And when they came to Jesus, they besought him earnestly, saying, "He is worthy to have you do this for him, for he loves our nation, and he built us our synagogue" (Luke 7:2–5).

4. Jesus as Patron and Benefactor
Benefactor/patron that he was, Jesus went about healing all who were tyrannized by the devil, for God was with him (Acts 10:38).

In the first example, Pliny indicates that, in accord with the will of the deceased Valerius Paulinus, he has been designated the patron of his friend's Latin freedmen. Acting in accord with his role as patron, he now petitions the emperor Trajan to grant three of these former slaves full Roman citizenship. In this negotiation Pliny serves as the freedmen's personal go-between with the emperor and makes a request that, in turn, is predicated on the close personal relationship of Pliny and Trajan as client and patron. The request itself is couched in the conventional language of restraint, gratitude for favor regularly received, and praise of the emperor's acclaimed generosity. All this language is typical of patron-client interactions.

In the second case, the council of an entire civic community, the people of Clunia, publicly declares a Roman legionary legate to be its Roman patron and, as his clients, publicly extols the honor of this generous benefactor.

Third, the evangelist Luke also records an instance of patronage involving Jesus and his Palestinian compatriots. In the town of Capernaum, a Roman centurion had generously assisted the local Jewish populace in constructing a synagogue. With this benefactor's beloved slave on the point of death, the Jewish elders of the grateful community serve as a personal intermediary between their benefactor and Jesus, their fellow countryman, and negotiate a meeting of the two. Again a benefactor is praised by his client-beneficiaries, and again a petitioner, the centurion, expresses his request in humble and deferential terms: "Worthy sir, do not trouble yourself to come to me. . . . I did not presume to come to you. Just speak a healing word and my servant will be healed." Finally, the negotiation has a successful outcome: the trust of the petitioning centurion is praised and his servant is healed. The centurion himself becomes a client of

Jesus who in turn provides him access to the healing power and favor of God.

Our final example, from the second part of Luke's work, the book of Acts, expressly describes Jesus with the language of patronage. Here in a summary of Jesus' activity offered by Peter in the presence of another Roman centurion (10:34–44), Jesus' healing actions are specifically recounted and he is celebrated as patron and "benefactor." "Anointed with the Holy Spirit and the power of God," he "did good" (εὐεργετῶν, *euergetōn*) and healed and thereby served as the mediator or broker for all who sought God's power and favor.

Though a widespread and enduring feature of ancient social relations, this institution of patronage and clientage has received less attention than it deserves, particularly on the part of students of early Christianity. Among the several reasons for this state of affairs is that although patronage in modern industrial democratic societies still operates *covertly*—from "old boy networks" to political patronage to the Sicilian mafiosi—*overtly and ideally* it is seen to conflict with and undermine the principle of equality fundamental to modern democratic theory. Consequently, modern analysts of ancient society, tending to assume for the ancient world political and social structures akin to their own, have failed to note, or have dismissed as insignificant, the prevalence and meaning of a pattern of social relations so alien to their own social experience and democratic values.

Nevertheless, the abundant literary and epigraphic witnesses to this ancient institution, together with the possibility of cross-cultural comparison with traces of its existence and operation today, provide the incentive for a systematic and less culturally biased analysis. Such an analysis, in turn, holds the promise of clarifying more precisely key features of the social contours and cultural scripts that shaped the world and literature of early Christianity.

The ancient evidence covers the full range of social relations, including both private and public life. It includes the protection as well as the financial and legal assistance that republican patricians provided their plebian clients and the enduring bonds and obligations between slave owners and their former freedmen and freedwomen. It also involves the influence powerful senators wielded on behalf of the public careers of their protégés, the patronal power assumed by the emperor in governmental adminstration, and Rome's relation to its so-called client states.

The sources attesting this institution are both literary and epigraphic. These include the hundreds of *commendationes* or personal recommendations of clients or "friends" contained in the epistles of Cicero and the similarly numerous recommendations or requests contained in the epistles of the younger Pliny or the correspondence of Cornelius Fronto, the well-connected tutor of Emperor Marcus Aurelius. We also see frequent references to patron-client relations in the epigrams of the satirist Martial as well as in the philosophical discourses (e.g., of Dio of Prusa and Plutarch) on the obligations of politicians and kings or emperors to advance the careers and fortunes of their clients and "friends." Further evidence is provided by imperial decrees and letters of appointment and, particularly in the east, in addition to the body of official and personal correspondence, by the mass of monuments and inscriptions publicly acknowledging and expressing gratitude for the benefits conferred by municipal and imperial "saviors" and "benefactors." In addition to the sources already cited, illustrative samples of this evidence in English translation are contained in such works as that of A. R. Hands (1968) and in the sources collected by Barbara Levick (1985), Frederick Danker (1982), and John L. White (1986).

These sources show that a system of patronage and clientage was in place in the Roman period, identify some of the key actors, and indicate several of the social processes and cultural values at work. What these primary sources do not explicitly deal with are features of the institution one must know in order to understand how and why it worked: the social, economic, and political conditions that generated and fostered a patronage system; the history of its development and change over time; its essential characteristics as a social institution and the nature and extent of its role in the operation of the social system as a whole; the persons or classes who benefited from this arrangement and how diverse interests were served; the symbols of belief by which the institution was ideologically legitimated; the possible contradictions it involved and consequently the societal competition and conflict it may have fostered; and, finally, its social consequences, both manifest and latent, both short-term and long-range.

These broader issues require consideration if we are to move beyond the stage of social description of patronage and clientage to an explanation of the factors and forces that made it a viable and acceptable form of social relations in antiquity and later. Put another way, to detect and understand the "what, how, and why" of possible patron-client relations in the NT and early Christianity requires a comprehension of the total social system and the interrelation of its working parts. To understand the workings of a carburetor in a Chevy or Ford requires some comprehension of the workings of the motor in general and its function within the car's structure and operation as a whole. At the moment, such a comprehensive frame of reference and the interdisciplinary method this entails is still in its early stage of development (see Elliott 1993 for an introduction to the method of social-scientific criticism in current biblical study).

For the most part, research on patronage has been undertaken in three traditionally unrelated fields: (1) the work of the ancient historians on Roman patronage; (2) the study of anthropologists, sociologists, and political scientists on structures and operations of patronage in industrial and preindustrial societies; (3) and some relatively minimal attention afforded the subject by exegetes and students of the social world of early Christianity. The following literature survey highlights important works from each of these three fields as well as areas of possible complementarity.

2.0 Patron-Client Relations: A Description

Before proceeding to this survey, let us first be clear about the phenomenon under discussion. Because of its complexity and variability, the phenomenon of patronage and clientage is difficult to capture in a single definition. The institution involves issues of unequal power relations, pyramids of power, power brokers, protection, privilege, prestige, payoffs and tradeoffs, influence, "juice," "clout," "connections," *Beziehungen, raccomendazioni,* "networks," reciprocal grants and obligations, values associated with friendship, loyalty, and generosity, and the various strands that link this institution to the social system at large.

Basic features of the patron-client institution in the ancient world are outlined in Ste. Croix 1954, Badian 1958, Gelzer 1969, Momigliano 1970, Carney 1975, Saller 1982, Roniger 1983, Malina 1988, and Wallace-Hadrill 1990. Cross-cultural overviews include Landé 1977, Gellner and Waterbury 1977, and Eisenstadt and Roniger 1980, 1984. The first set of historical studies discuss specific instances of this institution in the world of the Bible. The second set of sociologically oriented studies describes the social and political circumstances under which patron-client relations are established, the principles and expectations informing patron-client interactions, and the social aims and consequences of such relations.

Such research indicates that the patron-client relationship has several salient characteristics. In general, the relation is one of personal loyalty and commitment *(fides)* of some duration entered into voluntarily by two or more individuals of unequal status. It is based on differences in social roles and access to power, and involves the reciprocal exchange of different kinds of goods and services of value to each partner. In this relationship of binding and long-range character designed to advance the interests of both partners, a "patron" *(patronus, patrona)* is one who uses his or her influence to protect and assist some other person who becomes the patron's "client" *(cliens).*

In return, this client provides to the patron certain valued services. The influence of the patron could be enlisted to secure for the client a diversity of "goods" including food, financial aid, physical protection, career advancement and administrative posts, manumission, citizenship, equality in or freedom from taxation, the inviolability of person and property, support in legal cases, immunity from expenses of public service, help from the gods, and, in the case of provincials, the status of *socius* or friend of Rome (προξενία, *proxenia*).

The client in this relationship remains under the power *(potestas)* and within the *familia* of the patron for life (as in the case of manumitted slaves). He or she owes the patron a variety of services *(obsequium)* and is obligated to enhance the prestige, reputation, and honor of his or her patron in public and private life. For example, the client favors the patron with daily early-morning salutations, supports his political campaigns, pays his fines, furnishes his ransom, supplies him information, does not testify against him in the courts, and gives constant public attestation and memorials of the patron's benefactions, generosity, and virtue.

In this reciprocal relationship a strong element of solidarity linked to personal honor and obligations is informed by the values of friendship, loyalty, and fidelity. A paradoxical combination of elements of inequality in power with expressions of mutual solidarity in terms of interpersonal sentiment and obligation makes the relationship an unstable one. Voluntary relations and mutual obligations are frequently inadequate protection against possible coercion and exploitation.

3.0 Historians on Roman Patronage

Modern historians of antiquity have devoted varying degrees of attention to the topic, primarily in relation to earlier and later phases of the imperial period, and differ as to its continuing role in imperial politics. The important monograph of classicist Richard Saller (1982) reviews the history of this research and argues persuasively for the influence of this institution throughout the imperial period, along the lines suggested by Syme (1939), Alföldy (1985), and Ste. Croix (1954). Further seminal observations on patronage are included in the works of Badian (1958) and Gelzer (1969). A more recent collection of eleven essays edited by Andrew Wallace-Hadrill (1990) traces aspects of patron-client relations from classical Athens to late antiquity.

Saller's study analyzes the language, features, workings, and consequences of imperial patronage, imperial manipulation of patronage as a mechanism of government administration, the types of benefactions and those who had access to them, patronage among senators and provincials, and the reciprocity ethic that made patronage a viable institution. The methodological advance marked by this work is the manner in which Saller, like Carney (1975), complements historical and social description with attention to the perspectives and relevant research of the social sciences. Saller's sixteen-page bibliography provides a good point of orientation for future research.

Saller's study focuses on one important area of ancient Roman patronage and brings the reader up-to-date in this field. Neither he nor any of the historical research he reviews (with the exception of Carney), however, attempts to see the Roman system of patronage in broader, cross-cultural scope, or its possible relevance for the early Christian scene.

4.0 Social-Scientific Study on Patronage and Clientage

The second of the three fields cited earlier, that of the social sciences, however, has produced a large body of research on the matter of patronage and clientage in cross-cultural and political-science perspective. In this arena many of the issues cited above are examined: the social characteristics of different articulations of patronage; the conditions fostering its emergence, development, and change; its place within and impact on social systems at large; and its social consequences. In this field the subject has received its fullest attention and thus the literature is extensive. Important essay collections (including theoretical analyses and bibliographies) have been edited by Gellner and Waterbury (1977), Boissevain and Mitchell (1973), Schmidt, et al. (1977), Eisenstadt and Lemarchand (1981), and Roniger (1983). An informative and comprehensive survey of research together with examples of theoretical model analysis are contained in Eisenstadt and Roniger 1980 and in the introductory essay of Landé in Schmidt et al. 1977. These offer a good place for the reader to begin. Several additional articles and monographs on patronage in Mediterranean societies are of particular interest to scholars trying to situate and interpret the Mediterranean writings of the NT: D. D. Gilmore (1982:192–94), Gellner and Waterbury (1977), Boissevain (1974), and Campbell (1964).

In this research, empirical field study is used to develop theory, conceptual models, and methods appropriate for analyzing and explaining the phenomenon of patronage as a means for ordering social relations and social exchange in accord with the structures, values, and norms of the society at large. Thus this research provides the analyst of the social world of early Christianity with both a method of analysis and a means of theoretical integration and interpretation necessary for the interpretation of the texts and contexts of the early Christian period.

5.0 Biblical Exegesis and Social-World Analysis

Finally, in the field of biblical exegesis and social-world analysis, the subject of patronage and clientage has received far less attention. No entries on it are contained in the standard reference works, few articles have patronage as their central focus, nor is any systematic study yet at hand. Occasional references to the institution in current studies of the early Christian social world (e.g., Meeks 1983; Stambaugh and Balch 1986) describe the phenomenon but fail to explain it comprehensively.

There are, however, a few notable exceptions to this situation. Bruce Malina (1980) and John Pilch (1980) use the patron-client relation to explain the nature and activity of religious prayer. Malina points out how in the early and later church the presumed relationship of prayerful devotees to God (and later, also to the saints) replicates on the symbolic level of religious belief the social relationship of client and patron. Pilch illustrates the pattern with reference to the Gospel of Luke.

In the area of textual interpretation, one should consult Halvor Moxnes (1988) on the Gospel of Luke. He employs social-scientific research, including work on patronage, to investigate features of social conflict and economic interaction reflected in the Third Gospel, and especially in Jesus' critique of the patronal "lovers of money." Moxnes argues that Luke's portrait of Jesus and the kingdom of God opposes the unequal dependency relations of the patron-client system represented by the Pharisees. In its place, the Lukan Jesus calls for a general reciprocity among equals who have God as their sole benefactor and patron. See also Moxnes 1991.

Although it offers no analysis of patronage as such, Frederick Danker's collection of inscriptional data on the role of the benefactor in the Greco-Roman age (1982) also deserves mention. The specific terminology of Roman patronage and clientage (*patronus, cliens, clientela, officium, beneficium, meritum, favor, gratia,* etc.) is generally absent in the East. Likewise there is a question about the degree to which the specifically Roman form of patronage was adopted in eastern areas of the Mediterranean, though some impact is surely beyond question. However, Danker's evidence on public saviors and benefactors and the dependency relations typical of the eastern Mediterranean, together with his analysis of the ethos and values these relations reflect, suggests several points of convergence with patronage and clientage. This work, as well as his study on Luke (1987), includes extensive commentary on NT texts and the manner in which benefactor/patron conventions have provided a metaphor for the early Christian conceptualization of God and Jesus as consummate Benefactors and models for Christian emulation.

In a study emanating from The Context Group, Bruce Malina (1988) expands on this notion of divine patronage and the mediating role of Jesus as "broker," describing it as a dominant analogy behind synoptic theology in general. He shows how this theological concept was rooted in actual mundane experiences of Mediterranean peasant society and the relations of superior "haves" and inferior "have nots." Then after clarifying the biblical patronal language of "favor/ grace" (χάρις, charis; χαρίζομαι, charizomai; χάρισμα, charisma) and the functions of God-as-patron and Jesus-as-broker, he explains the part that patronage played in the organization, program, and theology/ ideology of the early Jesus movement. The splendid social-science commentary on the Synoptic Gospels by Malina and R. L. Rohrbaugh likewise illuminates numerous Gospel texts that reflect the influence of the patron-client institution (1992:74–76, 235–37, 326–29).

Such studies of early Christian and Greco-Roman texts have begun to reveal a broad semantic field of terms whose relevance to this social institution merits closer analysis. The following list of terms is illustrative but certainly not exhaustive: χάρις, charis, "favor, grace"; εὐεργέτης, euergetēs, "benefactor"; ἀγαθωσύνη, agathōsynē, "goodness, generosity"; εὐποιία, eupoiïa, "doing of good"; ἀρετη/, aretē, "magnanimous acts, virtue"; τιμή, timē, "honor"; ἔντιμος, entimos, "honorable"; προστάτις, prostatis, "helper, good friend, patron." Also important are terms for giving and receiving aid: λαμβάνω, lambanō, "to take or receive"; δίδωμι, didōmi, "to give or grant"; δέχομαι, dechomai, "to receive or accept," and paronyms; βοηθέω, boētheō, "to help"; χορηγέω, chorēgeō, "to supply or provide"; ὠφελέω, ōpheleō, "to help or aid"; ὀνίνημι, oninēmi, "to benefit or profit"; παράκλητος, paraklētos, "helper, intercessor"; ἐπισκέπτομαι, episkeptomai, "to care for, look out for." Any terms for generosity or magnanimity or terms for showing or receiving honor, respect, gratitude, and praise merit further study.

Although these few studies mark only the beginning of serious attention to the issue of patronage on the part of biblical scholars, they nevertheless provide an important stimulus and guide for further exploration of early Christian theology and social life. In particular, such studies help to clarify two key items. The first is the role that patron-client relations played in the social organization (Daley 1993), networking, and expansion of the early Christian movement (Chow 1992; L. M. White 1993). The second is to show how patronage and clientage provided early Christians the model for conceptualizing and describing their relation to Jesus Christ as mediator and to God as heavenly patron and benefactor.

6.0 Conclusion

In sum, patron-client relations played a key role in Roman public and private life. With Roman expansion eastward and the emperor's adoption of patronage as a mode of political administration, the institution assumed ever increasing significance as a model for ordering social relations of dependency. Within this scene of Roman dominion and its dominating social institutions, Christianity emerged and expanded. This rapid expansion was due in no small part to the social networks that its members "worked" for personal advantage as well as for the good of the movement: protection, material support, legal aid, hospitality, opportunities for employment and trade, places for assembly and worship. It remains a task for future scholarship to determine to what extent these social networks and the accompanying theological conceptualizations of their communities were influenced by the patron-client relationship.

The literature reviewed in this chapter introduces the student of the NT and its social world to the relevant primary sources on patronage and clientage in the ancient world and its characteristic features as a dominant form of dependency relations. Also here are the theory and models useful for a comprehension of its history, its significance in social relations, and its social consequences. Thus the reader is equipped with both a theoretical framework and a body of data for a more sensitive cultural reading of the NT, including a more accurate historical and social comprehension of the social relations described there. To the extent that these social relations are reflected in and legitimated by symbolic beliefs about the human-divine relationship, the study of this topic will lead to a greater comprehension not only of the social context of early Christianity but also the experiences that shaped its organization, values, and symbols of faith.

7.0 Works Cited

Alföldy, Geza
    1985   *The Social History of Rome.* London: Croom Helm.
Badian, Ernst
    1958   *Foreign Clientelae (264–70 B.C.).* Oxford: Clarendon.

Boissevain, Jeremy
    1974   *Friends of Friends: Networks, Manipulators and Coalitions.*
            New York: St. Martin's.
Boissevain, Jeremy, and J. Clyde Mitchell, eds.
    1973   *Network Analysis: Studies in Human Interaction.* The
            Hague: Mouton.
Campbell, John K.
    1964   *Honour, Family, and Patronage: A Study of Institutions and
            Moral Values in a Greek Mountain Community.* Oxford:
            Clarendon.
Carney, Thomas F.
    1975   *The Shape of the Past: Models and Antiquity.* Lawrence,
            Kans.: Coronado.
Chow, John K.
    1992   *Patronage and Power: A Study of Social Networks in
            Corinth.* JSNTSup 75. Sheffield: Sheffield Academic Press.
Daley, Brian E.
    1993   "Position and Patronage in the Early Church." *JTS*
            44:529–53.
Danker, Frederick W.
    1982   *Benefactor: Epigraphic Study of a Graeco-Roman and New
            Testament Semantic Field.* St. Louis: Clayton.
    1987   *Luke.* 2d ed. Proclamation Commentaries. Philadelphia:
            Fortress.
Eisenstadt, S. N., and Rene Lemarchand, eds.
    1981   *Political Clientelism, Patronage, and Development.*
            Contemporary Political Sociology 3. Beverly Hills: Sage.
Eisenstadt, S. N., and Louis Roniger
    1980   "Patron-Client Relations as a Model of Structuring
            Social Exchange." *Comparative Studies in Society and
            History* 22:42–77.
Eisenstadt, S. N., and L. Roniger, eds.
    1984   *Patrons, Clients, and Friends: Interpersonal Relations and
            the Structure of Trust in Society.* New York: Cambridge
            University Press.
Elliott, John H.
    1993   *What Is Social-Scientific Criticism?* Guides to Biblical
            Scholarship, New Testament Series. Minneapolis:
            Fortress.
Gellner, Ernest, and John Waterbury, eds.
    1977   *Patrons and Clients in Mediterranean Societies.* London:
            Duckworth.
Gelzer, Matthias
    1969   *The Roman Nobility.* Trans. R. Seager. New York: Barnes
            and Noble.

Gilmore, David D.
1982   "Anthropology of the Mediterranean Area." *ARA* 11:175–205.

Hands, A. R.
1968   *Charities and Social Aid in Greece and Rome.* London: Thames and Hudson.

Landé, Carl H.
1977   "The Dyadic Basis of Clientelism." In *Friends, Followers, and Factions: A Reader in Political Clientelism.* Ed. S. W. Schmidt, et al. Pages xiii–xxxvii. Berkeley: University of California Press.

Levick, Barbara
1985   *The Government of the Roman Empire: A Sourcebook.* London: Croom Helm.

Malina, Bruce J.
1980   "What Is Prayer?" *TBT* 18:214–20.
1988   "Patron and Client: The Analogy behind Synoptic Theology." *Forum* 4(1):2–32.

Malina, Bruce J., and Richard L. Rohrbaugh
1992   *Social Science Commentary on the Synoptic Gospels.* Minneapolis: Fortress.

Meeks, Wayne A.
1983   *The First Urban Christians: The Social World of the Apostle Paul.* New Haven: Yale University Press.

Momigliano, Arnaldo
1970   "Cliens" and "Patronus." *Oxford Classical Dictionary.* 2d ed. Pages 252, 791. Oxford: Clarendon.

Moxnes, Halvor
1988   *The Economy of the Kingdom: Social Conflict and Economic Interaction in Luke's Gospel.* OBT. Philadelphia: Fortress.
1991   "Patron-Client Relations and the New Community in Luke-Acts." In *The Social World of Luke-Acts: Models for Interpretation.* Ed. Jerome H. Neyrey. Pages 241–68. Peabody, Mass.: Hendrickson.

Pilch, John J.
1980   "Praying with Luke." *TBT* 18:221–25.

Roniger, Louis
1983   "Modern Patron-Client Relations and Historical Clientelism: Some Clues from Ancient Republican Rome." *Archives Européennes de Sociologie* 24:63–95.

Ste. Croix, G. E. M. de
1954   "Suffragium: From Vote to Patronage." *British Journal of Sociology* 5:33–48.

Saller, Richard
    1982   *Personal Patronage under the Empire.* New York:
                Cambridge University Press.
Schmidt, Steffen W., et al., eds.
    1977   *Friends, Followers, and Factions: A Reader in Political
                Clientelism.* Berkeley: University of California Press.
Stambaugh, John E., and David L. Balch
    1986   *The New Testament in Its Social Environment.*
                Philadelphia: Westminster.
Syme, Ronald
    1939   *The Roman Revolution.* Oxford: Clarendon.
Wallace-Hadrill, Andrew, ed.
    1990   *Patronage in Ancient Society.* Leicester-Nottingham
                Studies in Ancient History 1. London and New York:
                Routledge.
White, John L.
    1986   *Light from Ancient Letters.* Philadelphia: Fortress.
White, L. Michael, ed.
    1993   *Social Networks in the Early Christian Environment: Issues
                and Methods for Social History. Semeia* 56. Atlanta:
                Scholars Press.

Part Three:

Social Dynamics

8

Meals, Food, and Table Fellowship

Jerome H. Neyrey
University of Notre Dame

1.0 The Importance of Meals, Food, Fellowship, and Commensality

> Nor do we take our food from the same table as Gentiles, inasmuch as we cannot eat along with them, because they live impurely. But when we have persuaded them to have true thoughts, and to follow a right course of action, and have baptized them with a thrice blessed invocation, then we dwell with them. For not even if it were our father, or mother, or wife, or child, or brother, or any other one having a claim by nature on our affection, can we venture to take our meals with him; for our religion compels us to make a distinction. Do not, therefore, regard it as an insult if your son does not take his food along with you, until you come to have the same opinions and adopt the same course of conduct as he follows (*Clementine Homilies* 13.4, ANF).

Meals, food, table etiquette, and commensality remained a constant problem in the traditions ascribed to Jesus and in the history of the early church. The quotation from the *Clementine Homilies* indicates the potential of commensality to symbolize group boundaries as well as social conflict. In regard to foods, one of the three customs that characterized Judeans, a kosher diet, was abrogated first by Jesus (Mark 7:19) and then by the early church (Acts 10:14–16; 1 Cor 10:23–27). In Acts, Peter's vision of unclean foods descending from heaven (10:9–15) functions as a cipher for a further discussion of impartial membership in the church (10:28–29, 34). Thus the change from a restricted to an open diet symbolizes for the disciples of Jesus a change in membership, from an exclusively Jewish group to one that included Gentiles as well (10:28; 15:23–29). The longest piece of exhortation in Paul's first letter to Corinth deals with diet, namely, the eating of meat sacrificed to idols (1 Cor 8, 10). This issue and the foods of participants at the Lord's Supper (1 Cor 11:17–34) have major social repercussions in the community. Diet, or what one eats, can serve as an identifying mark (e.g., pasta, egg rolls, goulash), and so functions as an important social clue.

As regards Jesus' own eating customs, his choice of table companions, his disregard for washing rites preceding meals, and his unconcern for tithed bread all provoke controversy with other religious reformers. According to Luke 14, Jesus gives instructions for table etiquette and fellowship that fly in the face of custom. Paul, too, has much to say about the eating habits of the Corinthian community (1 Cor 8:7–13; 10:14–11:1; 11:17–34). He speaks to a different kind of problem in Rom 14–15, but one that also has to do with food, commensality, and group identity and unity. Paul criticizes Peter's eating practices in the celebrated confrontation at Antioch (Gal 2:11–14). Conflicts between Paul and Judaizers over kosher food play a major role in the struggles noted in Phil 3:19. The issue of commensality is formally addressed in the instruction to Gentiles that they observe the Noachic dietary regulations (Acts 15:20, 29). Thus meals, table etiquette, and commensality were major social concerns for Jesus, Paul, and the early churches.

How can readers understand the particular ceremony of meals and table fellowship? Why are meals so important as symbols of broader social relationships? How can we peer beneath the surface and grasp the social dynamics encoded in meals and commensality—what anthropologists call "the language of meals"? This chapter surveys writings on the various ways in which meals, diet, etiquette, and commensality may be profitably understood. Although strictly historical studies of Jewish and Greco-Roman meals are vital to our understanding, and we take a brief look at them first, cultural and social analysis of the function and dynamics of meals is our major focus.

2.0 Historical Studies of Meals

General books on the daily life of Greeks and Romans regularly provide a detailed report of when they ate, what they consumed, and how they partook of it. Judeans typically ate two meals a day, whereas Greeks and Romans ate three meals a day. The dissertation of Dennis Smith (1980) may be the most thorough source of this material in English. Moreover, it contains a splendid collection of ancient documents pertaining to meals that give depth and life to the generalizations made about eating habits. Unfortunately, this dissertation has not been published and so remains inaccessible to most readers; but Smith has excerpted and digested parts of it in a series of articles (1981, 1987, 1989).

The main daily meal for Greeks and Romans (δεῖπνον, *deipnon*, *cena*) was eaten in the evening and was generally rather formally structured with rules of etiquette and tradition. From Roman satire (Petronius, *Satyricon*) we have the description of a famous meal presented by a former slave, Trimalchio, to his nouveau riche acquaintances (see also Philo, *On the Contemplative Life* 48–60). This document is an excellent repository of cultural facts about Greco-Roman meals and offers a suggestive comparison with Christian meals. The article of Richard Pervo (1985) presents the reader not only with a clever analysis of Trimalchio's banquet, but also with an incipient social analysis of meals in general. He begins his analysis with a noteworthy observation:

> Food is a social substance and currency. What one is able (and chooses) to serve expresses one's own position and helps define one's relationship to others. What you, the guest, are offered is a measure of your standing in the eyes of society and your host (1985:311).

Although Pervo's title suggests that he will do a social analysis of meals, his approach is really that of the history of religions (this comment is not meant to denigrate his fine descriptive eye). He is beginning to ask important social questions about who eats what and with whom, about gluttony, decorum, places at table, social status, and the symposium form. But there is no conceptual model here to organize his insights or to lead him to ask questions about the meaning of food and what commensality communicates.

The literature on meals in antiquity has also attended to several specific types of meals that we briefly describe here: the symposium, the Passover meal, and funerary meals. As we shall see, all such meals tend to have a regular structure.

2.1 Symposium

This meal was distinguished not so much for its banquet as for the extended colloquium and drinking that followed. Plutarch dedicates his *Table Talk* to Senecio with a plea that he not forget the great tradition of the symposium in antiquity:

> Since you too, Senecio, believe that forgetfulness of folly is in truth "wise," as Euripides says, yet to consign to utter oblivion all that occurs at a drinking-party is not only opposed to what we call the friend-making character of the dining-table, but also has the most famous of the philosophers to bear witness against it,— Plato, Xenophon, Aristotle, Speusippus, Epicurus, Prytanis, Hieronymus, and Dio

of the Academy, who all considered the recording of conversations held at table a task worth some effort (1. pref. 612D–E, LCL).

The symposium was a formal banquet that was highly structured both in terms of specific roles for the participants (a host, chief guest, other guests) and specific courses of foods (hors d'oeuvres, main course, and dessert; postprandial conversation and drinking). The procedure was punctuated by periodic washing of the hands (see Plato, *Symposium* 175A). Walter Burkert (1991:7) explains its form and function:

> The symposium is an organization of all-male groups, aristocratic and egalitarian at the same time, which affirm their identity through ceremonialized drinking. Prolonged drinking is separate from the meal proper; there is wine mixed in a krater for equal distribution; the partici- pants, adorned with wreaths, lie on couches. The symposium has private, political, and cultural dimensions: it is the place of *euphrosyne*, of music, poetry, and other forms of entertainment; it is bound up with sexual- ity, especially homosexuality; it guarantees the social control of the *polis* by the aristocrats. It is a dominating social form in Greek civilization from Homer onward, and well beyond the Hellenistic period.

Two recent books, both of which are the results of symposia on the "symposium," contain highly informative studies of various aspects of the classical meal. William Slater's volume (1991) contains articles on the betrothal symposium, foreigners at this meal, the age at which persons were allowed to recline, the Roman triclinium, and other studies dealing with Roman aspects of the symposium. The second collection, by Oswyn Murray (1991), is more systematic in its topics: space, furniture, social forms, entertainment, and discussion materials in relationship to the symposium. Both of these books are advanced reading material on the symposium and presume more basic knowledge of the topic.

Some scholars have argued that the symposium form influ- enced the Lukan presentation of some meals of Jesus (Luke 14 and 22:14–38; see Smith 1987). It has influenced the shape of the Passover meal as well. S. Stein (1957) has shown that the shape of the seder depends as much on the Hellenistic symposium as it does on the biblical traditions in Exodus. He notes this in regard to some techni- cal terms describing aspects of the ritual, foods eaten, reclining posture, but especially talk at the meal. In a general article that presents many of the insights of his dissertation, Smith (1981) exam- ines the symposium form under two rubrics: (1) its history, its im- portance for philosophical groups, and the social expectations of behavior at such gatherings; and (2) the disputes at the meal described in 1 Cor 11:17–34. Early on the article informs us of the social implications of deviant behavior at meals. The importance of

the symposium for us lies in the formal sense that there were prescribed courses of both food and talk. Thus the mouth was regulated
in terms of what and when specific things were eaten and drunk, as
well as what was said. The symposium communicated "order," not
chaos (Plutarch, *Table Talk* 1.2 616A–B), and so involved explicit and
implicit rules of decorum.

2.2 Passover

The Passover was clearly an influential type of meal that colored
the way Judeans and Christians perceived and structured other eating
and liturgical events. One of the most important studies of the Passover
is the classic work of Joachim Jeremias (1968). He examines the rich
traditions of Passover with a specific eye to historical questions, seeking
to determine (1) whether Jesus' Last Supper was a Passover meal, and
(2) what the shape of that meal was in the first century. From a
careful reading of the first half of this book, readers gain a clear sense
of the formal shape of that famous ceremony and how various items
in the Gospel accounts of the Last Supper parallel the structure of
the Passover meal. While the thrust of Jeremias's book is another
quest for the historical Jesus and his original words, it also supplies
the reader with a wealth of information about the Passover meal.

Moreover, the reader may wish to consult two ancient texts
concerning the Passover. The most complete text describing the sequence of events at the passover is *t. Ber.* 4.8–9 (see also Philo, *On the
Special Laws* 2.145–75 and *Questions and Answers on Exodus* 1.1–23). It
is an especially important text for gaining a clear sense of a fixed
sequence of courses and events, a characteristic of most ancient
meals. Although nothing is said there about the prescribed conversation at the Passover (i.e., the Passover haggadah), we know that the
mouth was regulated both as to what was eaten and what was said.
A second Passover text, *m.Pesaḥ.* 10.1–9, indicates that at least three
cups were drunk; that the specific foods consumed were unleavened
bread, lamb, and bitter herbs; and that the youngest son asked four
specific questions of his father. We may presume that seating at this
meal was also a matter of formal arrangement.

2.3 Funerary Meals

Meals accompanying a funeral and meals commemorating the
dead are another important type that historians and interpreters of
biblical texts should attend to. At the burial rites for Patroclus, Achil-
les slaughtered a host of bulls, lambs, goats, and pigs, which were
then roasted and eaten by those participating in the funeral rites
(*Iliad* 23.111; see *b. Ketub.* 8b). Even in the Hebrew scriptures we read

of controversy over food offerings left on the tombs of the dead (Isa 65:4). In Amos 6:1–7 and Jer 16:1–9, as well as in Ugaritic and Phoenician texts, we know of a funeral meal called the *marzēaḥ*, at which guests reclined to eat a banquet. We have only fragmentary information about this meal, but two articles can quickly inform a reader on the state of research. On a popular level, Philip King (1988) examines the reference in Amos 6:4–7 and offers a detailed description of the various elements mentioned there. His interpretation of the term "banquet" contains a summary of what scholars argue constitutes a *marzēaḥ* meal: it was a meal at which one (a) reclined, (b) was anointed with oil, (c) and consumed a meat meal; (d) it was accompanied by singing or other music, and (e) climaxed in excessive drinking of wine. Marvin Pope's study (1981) leads a reader through Ugaritic texts relative to this meal, which he deftly interprets in terms of its relationship to elements of the cult of the dead—one of the major occasions for a *marzēaḥ*. We gather tidbits of information about the funerary meal, rather than a full description, simply because the data are fragmentary. But it is important for the reader to appreciate that from ancient down to Roman times, Israelites and Judeans engaged in funerary meals.

Of special significance to students of the NT is the study by Charles A. Kennedy of commemorative meals consumed at funeral sites (1987). Investigating the term εἰδωλόθυτος, *eidōlothytos*, "food offered to idols," Kennedy argues that εἴδωλον, *eidōlon*, may be correctly translated as "image" or "likeness," especially that of a person who has died. And -θυτος, *-thytos*, while it contains the notion of sacrifice, applies equally to dinner parties (Herodotus 8.99), since all animals cooked and consumed at a meal would have first been ritually slaughtered and offered to the gods. Kennedy supports his translation by a study of commemorative meals consumed at the site of burial. Such meals were eaten at a tomb by family and freedpersons at specified days in the mild months of the year. Even if Kennedy is not correct in offering this as the appropriate scenario for the prohibition of eating idol meat in 1 Cor 8 and 10, he has called attention to this type of meal, which surely played a large part in the funeral rituals of the ancients and so deserves our attention.

3.0 Foods and Diet

3.1 Foods Available/Cultivated for Consumption

What did people eat? What did they not eat? What does this tell us? John Pilch (1993:231) organizes his study of diet around a citation from Sirach: "The basic necessities of human life are water, fire, iron, and salt, flour, honey, and milk, the juice of the grape, oil, and clothing" (Sir 39:26). He then describes what people drank (water, goat's milk, honey, wine, oil) and what they ate (various types of grain). His description is crisp, filled with historical and cultural information, readable, and quite accessible.

Another Jewish text, a mishnaic passage (*Ketub.* 5.8–9), has served as the basis for several studies of the diet in Roman Palestine (Broshi 1986; Malina and Rohrbaugh 1992:339–40):

> He who maintains his wife by a third party may not provide for her less than two *qabs* of wheat or four *qabs* of barley [per week]. . . . And one pays over to her a half *qab* of pulse, a half *log* of oil, and a *qab* of dried figs or a *maneh* of fig cake. And if he does not have it, he provides instead fruit of some other type (*m. Ketub.* 5.8).

Malina and Rohrbaugh fill out these terse remarks, which concern the support a man owes to his divorced wife. They observe that the amounts specified suggest an intake of about eighteen hundred calories per day, slightly above the minimum recommended by the United Nations Food and Agriculture Organization.

Grain, oil, and wine were the most important commodities, especially grain and the products made from it. One-half of the caloric intake of much of the ancient Mediterranean region came from bread. Since wheat was much superior to barley, the husband who provided an estranged wife with barley bread was required to provide her twice the ration of wheat. Vegetables (lentils, beans, peas, chickpeas, lupines, cabbage, and turnips) were common, but of much inferior status. An estranged husband was also required to provide olive oil and fruit, principally the dried fig. Another quarter of the caloric intake came from wine, usually for males and wealthy women. It is estimated that an adult male in ancient Rome consumed a liter of wine daily.

Meat and poultry were expensive and rarely eaten by peasants. Most people ate it only on feast days or holidays, though temple priests ate it in abundance. Livestock kept solely to provide meat was unknown in Roman Palestine and was later prohibited by the talmudic sages. Fish was a typical sabbath dish. Milk products were usually consumed as cheese and butter. Eggs, especially chicken eggs, were also an important food. Honey was the primary sweetener (figs met some needs) and was widely used in the Roman period. Salt served not only as a spice but also as a preservative of meat and fish; pepper, ginger, and other spices were imported and expensive.

Examining the "bread basket" of Palestine, Broshi takes the reader through the same food groups mentioned above, but with a more scientific concern for the caloric value of each item and a comparison of their consumption patterns in contemporary nations. He also cites valuable comparative materials from ethnoarchaeological research and from mishnaic and talmudic texts. In this study we learn in detail about various types of bread and how they were made. We also learn about olive oil and about other oils made from seeds and nuts. Broshi also notes the full array of fruits and vegetables (thirty kinds each) available. He introduces us to the cattle economy of the Roman period, when the raising of animals for meat was actually prohibited. Fish, especially in fish sauces, formed a regular part of the diet. Broshi also mentions the raising and consumption of nonkosher items such as boars and rabbits. The article is also valuable for its excellent bibliography.

A third convenient study of this material was done by Gildas Hamel (1990). He documents in considerable detail from ancient authors the various food groups consumed in Roman Palestine (fruits, grains, legumes, vegetables, meat and animal products, spices, and drinks). His recounting includes important information on the amount of a given item from a typical tree or field, food preparation of various items, popularity of specific foods, and accessibility of specific foods to rich and poor. His treatment of bread is especially worthwhile. He concurs with R. J. Forbes's judgment that "roughly speaking, classical diet consisted mainly of bread and porridge made from wheat or barley supplemented by vegetables, fish, and spices and not much else" (22).

Furthermore, ancient writers describe the luxurious banquets of aristocrats. These authors delight in enumerating all the exotic and rare foods found in the Roman Empire. Among the many texts available, readers will find profit in Philo's brief description in his *Contemplative Life* 48–57 and Petronius's elaborate satire of such meals in his *Satyricon*. Other classical authors mention in great detail the variety of foods available for consumption, in particular Pliny, *Natural History* 17–19, and Athenaeus, *Deipnosophists* 1–2.

3.2 Dietary Restrictions

Of particular interest to Bible readers is the diet of Judeans in the second temple period. It was a kosher diet that prohibited "unclean" foods. Anthropologist Mary Douglas refocuses critical analysis of the biblical diet by offering valuable clues on the cultural significance of the classification of foods, in particular "the abominations of Leviticus" (1966:41–57). After discussing the ancient tradition of allegorizing the distinction between clean and unclean foods in terms of virtue and vice, Douglas interprets the abominations of Leviticus in terms of symbolic anthropology, specifically in terms of God's holiness and separateness. Holiness is related to wholeness;

Leviticus focuses attention on the necessary physical perfection of things that may be offered in sacrifice and eaten. Correspondingly, hybrids and imperfect things are an abomination because they do not conform to the class to which they presumably belong. She points to a cultural understanding of what constitutes a "clean" sky, land, and sea animal, an understanding that is not fully spelled out in the Bible but that can be teased out with careful reading. Foods are clean that completely fulfill their definition in terms of diet, locomotion, and place. Perfect sky animals (birds) should not dive into the sea, nor should they eat fish in place of grain, nor should they hop on the ground. Complete land animals should walk on legs and eat grass or grain (i.e., chew the cud). Likewise, clean sea animals should not crawl out of the sea; they must swim as fish do, and thus have scales.

Douglas's taxonomy of clean and unclean animals has enjoyed a healthy scholarly conversation and issued in a richer version of her analysis of the diet of the Israelites (1975:261–73). In examining the classification of birds, fish, and animals, she now adds that concern must be had for the multiple dimensions of Hebrew thought and culture. She notes three rules for meat: (a) rejection of some animal kinds as unfit for table (Lev 11; Deut 14); (b) of those admitted as edible, the separation of the meat from blood before cooking (Lev 17:10; Deut 12:23–27); and (c) the total separation of milk from meat, which involves the minute specialization of utensils (Exod 23:19; 34:26; Deut 14:21). Analyzing dietary restrictions, Douglas can then identify what makes an animal an abomination, a classification that now includes notions of suitability for temple sacrifice and consumption as food.

Douglas then argues that the three rules noted above have close social and cultural correlations with other aspects of the world of the Hebrews. Animals fit for temple sacrifice (and so consumption) must be bodily whole or unblemished. This accords with the rule that Levites who are selected for sacred temple duties must be of pure descent and unblemished (Lev 21:18–23). In regard to the second rule, specific birds, for example, may neither be offered nor eaten (m. Ḥul. 3.6), because they eat carrion and do not separate the meat from the blood before eating. The third rule, which prohibits meat cooked in milk, replicates procreative functions, thus reflecting sexual rules concerning who may marry whom. Thus dietary restrictions replicate values, structures, and patterns found in other areas of Hebrew culture. In examining dietary concerns, then, readers of ancient documents should be aware of the way these rules replicate other aspects of the social world of the peoples they represent.

Douglas's insights are refined in Jean Soler's excellent article (1979). He brings an anthropologist's eye not only to Leviticus but also to the Priestly material in the early parts of Genesis that serves as the appropriate lens for reading Lev 11 and Deut 14. He offers confirmation and expansion of Douglas's observations, especially the replication of the cultural understanding of wholeness and purity in relation to the physical body. The importance of his contribution lies in the careful analysis of the creation story (Gen 1) and its symbolic replication in the ideology of the Israelite and Judean peoples.

The symbolic meaning of dietary restrictions for Judeans and Christians is based on the old adage, "You are what you eat." Holy people eat holy (or whole) foods, hence Peter objects to God concerning the unclean foods he is commanded to eat; as a "holy" person, he has kept a holy diet (Acts 10:13–14). Part of the conflict with Jesus' disciples over eating grain plucked on the sabbath lies in the issue of whether the grain was properly tithed. Untithed food is not clean, hence those who ate it could be considered unclean themselves. The social importance of the abolition of the Judean kosher diet for Christians is noted in the actions of Jesus and Paul, who declare all foods clean (Mark 7:19; 1 Cor 10:25–30; see Acts 10:15). The residual problem of dietary restrictions is surely behind the crisis over eating at Antioch. Peter, who should keep a kosher diet because he is the "apostle to the circumcised," starts to eat with the uncircumcised. Paul then accuses him of hypocrisy when he returns to his kosher diet (Gal 2:11–14). Thus analysis of the symbolic importance of dietary restrictions has much to say about who belongs to the group and who is welcome. After all, "you are what you eat" (i.e., group identity confirmed by specific diet). Moreover, "likes eat with likes" (i.e., group identity confirmed by commensality).

We have concentrated on the diet and dietary customs of Judeans because these impinge directly on biblical texts. But a reader might profitably consult the fine survey article of Don Brothwell (1988) for materials on the Greco-Roman world. He relies heavily on Pliny the Elder for his information, and favors the Roman over the Greek world, which makes this article of particular importance to students of second temple Judaism and early Christianity. Brothwell describes in detail the various foods eaten and their percentage and importance in the diet of the ancients. He focuses on the basic elements of diet, but includes the more unusual foods available and their sources of origin. The article includes an excellent, if brief, bibliography.

4.0 Social and Anthropological Interpretations of Meals

What the cross is to Jesus, the meal is to the early church: its primary symbol. Yet meals are never easy to read, for much more communication is put forth than is apparent in the passing of plates and the eating of foods.

4.1 Social Aspects of Meals

In recent years there has been increasing interest in the "social" dimensions of meals. For example, Gerd Theissen (1982) analyzes the conflict described in 1 Cor 11:17–34 in terms of the social strata of the persons present at the group's meal. His study is "social" in that it asks questions about groups. What were the different groupings at the meal? What were the various points at which the meal began? What different quantities of food were consumed and by whom? Were the meals consumed by various groupings qualitatively different? This valuable study greatly advances our understanding of the conflict Paul describes. Theissen shows that at least two groups were at the meal, one of which was wealthy enough to eat meat and drink well, and another poor and deprived of abundant food and beverage. His study is not really "sociological," however, since he relies exclusively on Greco-Roman parallels to interpret the text and advances no abstract or social-scientific model of meals.

Also recommended is the study by Philip Esler (1987) of table fellowship between Jews and Gentiles as this reflects social relations in Luke–Acts. Taking a clue from Mary Douglas, Esler situates his interpretation of meals in terms of anthropological notions of external threat and purity laws; thus he focuses directly on meals and group identity and boundaries. He then presents a wealth of primary data from antiquity on the unlikelihood of Jews eating with Gentiles. Turning to other NT documents, he examines the importance commensality plays in group identity in Galatians, Mark, and Matthew. Finally, Esler deals with the new social practice of Jesus' Jewish disciples in eating with Gentile converts, first in the case of Cornelius (Acts 10–11), then in regard to the apostolic council (Acts 15), and finally in the meal described in Acts 27:33–38. This substantial study contains more history of eating traditions than social analysis, but it thereby fills a reader's need to know what the prevailing customs were for Jews dining with Gentiles. It employs only one aspect of anthropology in its analysis, albeit a major one (external threat and purity laws) that touches on the very theme that Luke is arguing.

4.2 Anthropological Aspects of Meals

Gillian Feeley-Harnik (1981) offers a more anthropological interpretation of Jewish and Christian meals, as she draws on formal cultural studies of diet, commensality, and cultural values. Dealing

first with Jewish sectarianism in the Greco-Roman period, she indicates that commensality or its absence should be interpreted in terms
of group membership: "Likes eat with likes." Hence the meals of
Judeans indicate either their distinctive group affiliation, if eaten
with other Judeans, or their separation, if commensality was refused.
Moreover, food functioned as a metaphor for the word of God.
Hence concern for doctrinal and ethnic purity are replicated in the
dietary and commensality practices of the Judeans. Her basic thesis
can be succinctly summarized: "Food, articulated in terms of who
eats what with whom under which circumstances, had long been
one of the most important languages in which Jews conceived and
conducted social relations among human beings and between human beings and God. Food was a way of talking about the law and
lawlessness" (1981:72). She then states her hypotheses about the
symbolic nature of food and eating in the Hebrew scriptures:

1. The Lord's power is manifested in his ability to control food: to feed
is to bless, to confer life; to feed bad food or to starve is to judge or
punish, to confer death.

2. Acceptance of the power and authority of the Lord is symbolized by
acceptance of his food.

3. Rejection of the power and authority of the Lord is symbolized by
seeking after food he has forbidden.

4. People "limit" or "tempt" the Lord—that is, question the extent of
his power or authority—by questioning his ability to feed them.

5. The Lord's word is equated with food.

6. Eating joins people with the Lord or separates them (1981:72).

Feeley-Harnik then studies the Christian custom of eating Christ's
body and blood, examining how Jesus' Last Supper differed from the
Passover meal. She concludes, "In contrast to the passover that
brings the family together, Jesus' sacrifice breaks it apart to create
new bonds" (1981:144).

A reader looking for a succinct entrance into the "language of
food" will find Feeley-Harnik's fourth chapter a most useful tool ("Food
Symbolism in the Judaic Tradition," 71–106). The approach is that of
cultural anthropology, which aims to offer a model that one can apply
to a cross-cultural analysis of meals in various geographical regions
and at different times. The chapter is deftly organized around the key
question of "who eats what with whom under which circumstances,"
which links food consumption with group identity and values.

Another highly recommended work is a brief study of meals
and their social dynamics in Luke by Halvor Moxnes (1987). While

focusing on Luke's Gospel, Moxnes reads the document through the lens of a multidimensional model of meals drawn from cultural anthropology. The delight of this piece lies in its easy but solid presentation of a series of critical perspectives on meals. Meals function as boundary markers between groups (i.e., Jesus and the Pharisees), as starting mechanisms for new groups (i.e., Jesus' feedings), as indicators of hierarchy and internal social stratification (i.e., seating), and as occasions for reciprocity. When applicable, Moxnes contrasts the traditional social expectations encoded in meals with the strategy of Jesus and the new portrait of God developed by Luke. Because of its brevity, depth, and application of social-science models to a biblical text, Moxnes's article is an excellent place to start a critical study of meals.

Mary Douglas (1982a) analyzes British meals as "a system of communications." Although her focus is on specific issues such as the introduction of new foods into the British diet, she argues that food preparation and consumption are more than issues of nutrition, for they are social events and constitute a medium of social relationships. This point allows her to ask questions about the implicit rules concerning time, place, and sequence of actions and objects that structure the preparation and consumption of foods. This important insight alerts readers of ancient texts to ask questions about the typical times for eating, the amount and quality of the food consumed, the sequence of foods served, and particular customs regulating what, where, and how it is eaten. This study provides an excellent introduction to the fact that meals and foods are not merely material objects to be studied in terms of nutrition, but social events that occur in regular patterns rich in meaning and communication.

In an earlier article (1975:249–75), Douglas also examines food as a code. As is typical of most anthropological investigations, she discusses the theory of meals and commensality as "communication" or "language" or "code":

> If food is treated as a code, the messages it encodes will be found in the pattern of social relations being expressed. The message is about different degrees of hierarchy, inclusion and exclusion, boundaries and transactions across boundaries. Like sex, the taking of food has a social component, as well as a biological one. Food categories therefore encode social events (1975:249).

Douglas examines the various patterns that occur in meals: (a) temporal schemes of meals: meals that climax the week (i.e., the Sunday midday meal), seasonal meals occurring on regular holidays, and meals related to the life cycle (birth, wedding, and funeral meals); and (b) the patterned activity of meals (from soup to nuts). This examination leads her to appreciate how the meaning of a meal is found in a system of repeated analogies. "Each meal carries something of the meaning of the other meals; each meal is a structured social event which structures others in its own image." This is a most useful insight for our study. As we observed earlier, the symposium influenced the shape of the Passover as well as the presentation of many of Jesus' meals, including the Last Supper. Solemn meals such as Passover for Judeans, the Eucharist for Christians, or symposia for Greeks and Romans might be expected to encode values and structures of the general culture. And the patterns of these meals can be expected to embody social categories such as "hierarchy, inclusion and exclusion, boundaries and transactions across boundaries."

These two articles of Douglas are quite abstract and are not recommended for beginning readers. Their value lies in the theoretical underpinnings for a more detailed analysis of meals vis-à-vis social behavior. Thus Douglas's key insight that food consumption is a "code" or "communication" has served as a charter for other scholars who have absorbed this perspective and who examine how "the message it encodes will be found in the pattern of social relations being expressed. . . . Food categories encode social events" (1975:249). Among those who have adapted the materials of Douglas and other anthropologists for biblical interpretation is Jerome Neyrey (1991; see §4.3).

Of particular importance to readers is the work of Jack Goody (1982). His opening chapter should be required reading, because Goody takes us through the history of sociological and anthropological analysis of cooking, meals, and food consumption. Through a crisp survey of the major works on the topic, he explains the ideology encoded in functionalist and structuralist approaches to meals. He offers a critical perspective on Lévi-Strauss's classic distinction between the raw and the cooked, as well as on the work of Douglas. Finally, he lays out his own systematic agenda for studying the topic (1982:37–38; see fig. 8.1).

Process	Phase	Locus
Growing	Production	Farm
Allocating/storing	Distribution	Granary/market
Cooking	Preparation	Kitchen
Eating	Consumption	Table
Clearing up	Disposal	Scullery

Figure 8.1: Goody's Agenda for Studying Meals

Economic issues dominate the production phase, which has to do with organization of resources and the technology of producing and storing food. Political issues are central to the distribution phase, where rents, tributes, and taxes must be paid. With the preparation phase, attention shifts from fields and granaries to the kitchen. Here women rather than men and servants rather than mistresses take over the process; systems of division and stratification of labor are made explicit. Finally, in the consumption phase, attention must be paid to the identity and differentiation of those who eat, the practice of eating together or separately, the importance of feasts and fasts, food prohibitions and preferences, table manners and modes of serving. Goody, therefore, has laid out a practical agenda of the kinds of questions a careful researcher should have in mind when considering meals. The remainder of his book fleshes out these basic approaches and provides data and modeling for students.

4.3 Practical Models for Interpreting Meals

How should a reader of the Bible think about meals? Neyrey first offers a practical, multilayered model for interpreting meals in a study of Mark 7, and then later develops a more complete one in an investigation of meals in Luke–Acts. He begins his analysis of Mark 7 (1988) by noting two textual emphases in that part of the Gospel: (a) frequent mention of bread (6:38–44, 52; 7:2–5, 27–28; 8:4–10, 16–21), and (b) the association of Pharisees with hands, lips, and bodily surfaces and of Jesus with heart and bodily interior (7:1–23).

Neyrey then employs two practical models to examine the symbolic issues of bread/kosher diet and hands/lips versus heart in Mark 7: (a) a model of purity advanced by Douglas (1966:41–57) and developed by Malina (1981:122–52); and (b) a model of body symbolism, also derived from Douglas (1966:114–28; 1982b:65–81) and developed further by Neyrey himself (1986a).

In regards to "purity systems," Neyrey notes how the elaborate purity system of first-century Judeans served to classify as much of the world and as many of its objects as possible in terms consonant with the dominant cultural value of "holiness" or "separateness." This classification system then told them what could be eaten, whom they could marry, where objects and persons should be positioned, and the like. What fit this system was holy; what violated it was unclean.

Moreover, this cultural tendency to build a fence around the Torah in all aspects of life (m. ʾAbot 3.14) helps us understand the Pharisaic custom of washing hands (and vessels) before eating. The holy interior must be guarded from anything unclean; and so washing rituals serve as "fences" to separate clean from unclean (the same applies to tithes on foods, which transform them into "holy" foods fit for consumption). The rules for foods and eating thus replicate the more dominant cultural norm of a "holy" people, separate from the Gentiles and consecrated to God. By attacking these rules Jesus also attacks the Judean social values of ethnic and religious separateness.

Neyrey further developed these social science models for understanding meals and table fellowship in a study of Luke–Acts (1991:361–87). Here he builds on his earlier efforts to crack the code of food as communication, addressing five distinct areas that are important for the student of meals in the NT. First he develops an understanding of meals as ceremonies rather than rituals. Second, he relates meal practices to the larger purity system or symbolic universe (see the discussion of Douglas [1966:41–57, 114–28] above). Third, he offers a discussion of meals and body symbolism in Luke–Acts (cf. Neyrey 1986a, 1988), especially the way that control of the social body is replicated in control of the physical body.

In a fourth level of analysis Neyrey provides models for understanding meals as a form of social and economic reciprocity. In antiquity inviting people to a meal inevitably carried with it the expectation of an invitation in return. Thus theories of exchange relations appropriate to the first century are used to describe the forms of social and economic reciprocity applicable to the study of meals.

The fifth and final layer of Neyrey's study of Luke–Acts discusses the role of meals in patron-client relations. People in the NT world were constantly seeking patrons and clients in the standard game of securing a safe and steady supply of the limited and scarce goods of life. Patrons often distributed food to clients and expected public praise in return. Like other biblical writers, Luke also considers God as the patron of Israel and the well-to-do in God's covenant community as patrons to the poor.

5.0 Jesus' Meals and Table Companions: Current New Testament Issues

New Testament scholarship on the Gospels currently gives considerable attention to both the significance of Jesus' eating habits and to the presence or absence of females at the meals portrayed.

5.1 Gospel Accounts of Jesus' Eating

In his book on themes in Luke, Robert Karris (1985) writes on "The Theme of Food." The approach is basically that of redaction criticism, and the first part of the study contains a useful listing of all the passages and terms concerned with food and meals in Luke. By way of interpretation, Karris classifies his materials into three related themes. First, God's impartial generosity is manifested in the adequate food provided, especially for the needy. Second, Jesus, "glutton and drunkard," ate with tax collectors and sinners, which constitutes an "acted parable" of God's particular care for outcasts. Finally, Jesus' Last Supper is foremost a symposium at which he delivers a farewell address that contains major material about new social relationships. This comprehensive and readable survey of the specifically Lukan material is an excellent orientation to the basic issues concerning Jesus' table fellowship and its significance for Christology and church.

In a similar vein, Scott Bartchy (1992) invites the reader to examine the same materials, but from a much richer perspective. Bartchy takes formal cognizance of the symbolic nature of meals, foods, and table fellowship; he introduces his materials in terms of relevant and productive concepts from cultural anthropology. Thus he calls attention to (a) the importance of purity rules concerning diet and meals, and (b) the breaking of social boundaries by Jesus' deviant table habits. He offers good insights into the way Jesus' praxis in both Mark and Luke functions as social indoctrination: "serving" of others in Mark and "open table fellowship" in Luke. Bartchy's article is pithy and pregnant, and can serve as an excellent orientation to the issue of the symbolism of meals in the Gospels.

Although Dennis Smith (1989) debates whether the portrait of Jesus' eating habits reflects the historical Jesus or a later idealization of him, his article contains a fine survey of the major motifs in the Gospels concerned with meals. After a brief review of scholarship, Smith defines meals in antiquity, offering a terse historical description of ancient meals and an acknowledgment of anthropological perspectives on the social meaning of meals. He abandons the latter perspective to do more strictly historical reporting, namely, description of Jesus' meals with disciples, his concern with dietary regulations, and his commensality with outcasts. Recognizing that Jesus' table customs should be construed as parabolic actions, Smith's own analysis leads him to the historical judgment that the portrait of Jesus at table reflects the "idealized, historic Jesus of the tradition."

5.2 Jesus' Table Companions

The Gospel accounts of Jesus' eating habits have also sparked studies of the presence or absence of women at the meals described in the NT. Given the place of feminist scholars in the biblical guild it

is not surprising that such efforts are emerging. Kathleen Corley, first
in a summary article (1989) and then in a book (1993), examines the
topic from the perspective of history and social description.

Corley (1989) deftly takes a reader through the important ancient data about the presence and absence of women at meals. She
interprets her valuable collection of classical texts in the light of
social questions, especially the status of women. She builds on the
insight that table fellowship is the most important generative matrix
of the social formation of the Jesus movement groups. Acknowledging the classical cultural expectation of a gender-divided world
(males in public space, females in private space), she argues that the
presence or absence of women at meals may be shown either to
conform to this cultural code or to engage it.

Corley's own collection of classical texts and her digest of the
critical literature allow her to make important historical distinctions. In classical Greece women were generally absent from meals,
even within the household; but in Rome during the end of the
Republic, women might be present at public meals in the household, if only for the first part of the meal. The participation of
women at meals where nonrelated males are present almost always reflects the customs of aristocrats. The "flamboyant behavior"
of aristocratic Roman women is balanced by philosophical criticism
of this new practice and by the celebration of the more traditional
virtues urged for females.

Thus Corley's method is basically a historical description of
changing patterns. Her data and interpretation tend to confirm that
women who appear in public at meals would be considered a social
anomaly, and thus bear the stigma of a "public" woman, most likely
labeled a courtesan or prostitute. This study acquaints readers with
basic historical and cultural materials pertaining to Greco-Roman
meals. It is sensitive to the social implications of eating patterns,
although it does not itself engage in anthropological explanations of
meals. It is highly recommended for its completeness and balance.

Corley's article seems to be a digest of her dissertation, which
was later published as a book (1993). The book has the great advantage of presenting much fuller collections of material about Greco-
Roman meal patterns, as well as detailed investigations of the
presence of women at meals in the Synoptic Gospels. Of particular
interest for students of meals is Corley's excellent second chapter
(1993:24–79), in which she succinctly but persuasively describes the
social expectations about women at table and the historical realization of those expectations. She notes, as she did in her article, the
changing social patterns in Greece and Rome. She shows how traditional social directives in the Greek cultural world concerning
women at meals were modified by Romans at the end of the Repub-

lic, and how social criticism of this Roman relaxation of custom led to a reaction which restored and strengthened traditional expectations about women. Moreover, Corley's book takes readers through each of the synoptic meal scenes at which women are said to be or might be present, how this would be perceived by the ancients, and how the evangelists conform to traditional cultural expectations concerning women at meals. This study easily puts an inquiring reader in touch with the latest secondary literature on the relevant social, historical, and exegetical discussions of women at table in antiquity. Like the earlier article, the focus is historical, but it provides valuable data that might be processed using more formal models of cultural analyses of meals.

5.3 Jesus' Refusal to Fast

There were five fast days in the liturgical calendar of second temple Judeans; Pharisees are said to have fasted twice a week (Luke 18:12; *Did.* 8.1). Along with prayer and almsgiving, fasting was considered the core of piety (Tob 12:8; see Acts 10:30- 31), especially after the destruction of the temple. Fasting, then, denotes religious observance and characterizes holy persons (Philo, *On the Contemplative Life* 34; Luke 2:27; 1 Tim 5:5). But what if one refuses to fast, such as Jesus apparently did according to Mark 2:18–22? If consumption of food is "communication," then is nonconsumption (i.e., "fasting") also communication? It is not enough to examine the reasons given by Judeans for fasting: (a) atonement (Lev 16:29), (b) participation in funeral rites (2 Sam 1:12), or (c) preparation for revelatory experiences (2 Esd 5:13). What does a refusal to fast communicate?

Bruce Malina (1986) offers an anthropological interpretation of fasting (and refusal to fast) that deals precisely with the symbolic messages communicated. He focuses on the culturally specific meaning of fasting, namely, why first-century Mediterraneans fasted and why this behavior would have meaning for their contemporaries. He identifies three perspectives on fasting: (a) a functionalist approach (fasting occurred especially when food supplies were limited), (b) a conflict approach (nonconsumption as boundary marking and conflict resolution), and (c) a symbolic approach (meanings of consumption and nonconsumption depend on the features of a given social system and its core values).

Malina distinguishes abstinence, fasting, and avoidance. Abstinence, such as dieting and asceticism, affects the nonconsumer; one might abstain to purge, to purify, to lose weight, to cause visions, and the like. In contrast, fasting is intended to have an effect on someone other than the nonconsumer; it is practiced as a form of social interaction or communication. Avoidance of specific foods, such as Jewish prohibitions of nonkosher animals, falls beyond the control of the nonconsumer, for it is socially commanded by the group.

As communication, fasting can operate on both a vertical and a horizontal level, depending on whether the nonconsumer wishes to have an effect on persons higher in rank than him- or herself (God, the king, etc.) or on persons of his or her own status (kin and clan). In addition, Malina employs the notion of four symbolic media of communication (power, commitment, influence, and inducement). Fasting is the refusal to interact with others in those media, and so communicates a rejection of the institution in which they are rooted.

He describes the sort of messages conveyed by nonconsumption or fasting. It communicates a negation of reciprocities that make up social interaction. Thus it puts the person fasting "out of bounds" or apart from the normal patterns of exchange; in terms of ritual analysis this new state is called the "liminal state," that is, a state of transition. Hence one who fasts is essentially seeking to change his or her status, and the fast is directed toward those who can effect this transition. Fasting, then, is a form of "self-humiliation" by those of low status to persuade those in higher status to reverse their low status. This goes a long way toward our understanding of fasting in contexts of mourning, national calamity, group sense of impurity, or some estimate of the negative state of the group. Some evil is present, and fasting petitions hierarchically superior persons to deal with this evil and hence reverse the current status of the petitioners.

Finally Malina addresses the issue of nonfasting, such as is reported of Jesus in Mark 2:18–20. Jesus' refusal to fast communicates two things. First, he did not concern himself with the boundary maintenance of his contemporary Judeans, that is, he did not perceive either himself or his group as polluted and so in need of status reversal. Second, he thought that the needed status reversal ("Repent, believe in the gospel!") had already come with his own mission.

Malina's chapter asks questions and offers perspectives that are generally not found in standard discussions of fasting. His treatment of fasting and refusal to fast is the last chapter in a rich, practical book that examines the cultural meaning of behavior, especially food consumption and nonconsumption.

6.0 Conclusions: Specific Issues and Specific Readings

What, then, should a reader read and in which order? The answer lies in the questions readers ask and the orientation they bring to this topic. The issues that galvanize readers are generally either historical studies of meals or interpretation of them in the light of anthropological and social models. This dichotomy probably reflects the past training of readers as well as their intellectual aesthetics.

If readers' interests lie in matters historical or literary, then Karris (1985) is an excellent orientation to the topic in the Jesus materials. This descriptive study should be supplemented with any or all of Smith's articles (1981, 1987, 1989). There is a some repetition in them, but they nonetheless feed readers with materials from the Hellenistic world and make understandable some aspects of meals described in the Christian scriptures, especially their symposiac structure.

This chapter, however, has been oriented from the beginning toward issues of meaning and symbolism in regard to meals. The dominant orientation here is the interpretation of meals as a form of language, a communication, a code, or a symbol. In this line of inquiry, the works of formal anthropologists such as Feeley-Harnik (1981) and Douglas (1966, 1975, 1982a, 1982b) are highly important, even if difficult to follow. Feeley-Harnik's book should be read; its clear exposition of social questions to ask about meals has greatly influenced the literature of biblical interpreters. But it does not spell out in depth a model to use or a rationale for its observations, so readers cannot stop there.

The studies by Bartchy (1992) and Moxnes (1987) are ideal for beginning readers. They are deep and worth digesting, though brief in their exposition. Readers will come back again and again to these accessible studies for orientation and insight. Those wanting to see a survey of social science models applied to NT meal stories, including those having to do with economics and social relations, will want to consult the studies of Jerome Neyrey.

7.0 Works Cited

Bartchy, Scott
   1992   "Table Fellowship." *Dictionary of Jesus and the Gospels.*
           Pages 796–800. Downers Grove, Ill.: InterVarsity Press.
Broshi, Magen
   1986   "The Diet of Palestine in the Roman Period—
           Introductory Notes." *Israel Museum Journal* 5:1–56.
Brothwell, Don R.
   1988   "Foodstuffs, Cooking, and Drugs." In *Civilization of the
           Ancient Mediterranean: Greece and Rome.* 3 vols. Ed.

Michael Grant and Rachel Kitzinger. New York: Charles Scribner's Sons. 1.247–61.

Burkert, Walter
    1991   "Oriental Symposia: Contrasts and Parallels." In *Dining in a Classical Context*. Ed. William J. Slater. Pages 7–24. Ann Arbor: University of Michigan Press.

Corley, Kathleen
    1989   "Were the Women around Jesus Really Prostitutes? Women in the Context of Greco-Roman Meals." SBLSP 1989:487–521.
    1993   *Private Women, Public Meals: Social Conflict in the Synoptic Tradition*. Peabody, Mass.: Hendrickson.

Douglas, Mary
    1966   *Purity and Danger*. London: Routledge & Kegan Paul.
    1975   "Deciphering a Meal." In *Implicit Meanings*. Pages 249–75. London: Routledge & Kegan Paul.
    1982a   "Food as a System of Communication." In *In the Active Voice*. Pages 82–124. London: Routledge & Kegan Paul.
    1982b   *Natural Symbols*. New York: Pantheon.

Esler, Philip Francis
    1987   "Table-fellowship." In *Community and Gospel in Luke–Acts*. Pages 71–109. Cambridge: Cambridge University Press.

Feeley-Harnik, Gillian
    1981   *The Lord's Table: Eucharist and Passover in Early Christianity*. Philadelphia: University of Pennsylvania Press.

Goody, Jack
    1982   *Cooking, Cuisine, and Class: A Study in Comparative Sociology*. Cambridge: Cambridge University Press.

Hamel, Gildas
    1990   "Daily Bread." In *Poverty and Charity in Roman Palestine, First Three Centuries C.E.* Pages 8–56. Berkeley: University of California Press.

Jeremias, Joachim
    1968   *The Eucharistic Words of Jesus*. 3d ed. Philadelphia: Fortress.

Karris, Robert J.
    1985   "The Theme of Food." In *Luke: Artist and Theologian*. Pages 47–78. New York: Paulist.

Kennedy, Charles A.
    1987   "The Cult of the Dead in Corinth." In *Love and Death in the Ancient Near East: Essays in Honor of Marvin H. Pope*. Ed. John Marks and Robert Good. Pages 227–37. Guilford, Conn.: Four Quarters Publishing Company.

King, Philip
1988   "Using Archaeology to Interpret a Biblical Text: The
        Marzeaḥ Amos Denounces." *BAR* 14(4): 34–44.
Malina, Bruce
1986   "Testing the Models: The Case of Fasting." In *Christian
        Origins and Cultural Anthropology.* Pages 185–204.
        Atlanta: John Knox.
1993   *The New Testament World: Insights from Cultural
        Anthropology.* 2d rev. ed. Louisville: Westminster/John
        Knox.
Malina, Bruce, and Richard Rohrbaugh
1992   *Social Science Commentary on the Synoptic Gospels.*
        Minneapolis: Fortress.
Moxnes, Halvor
1987   "Meals and the New Community in Luke." *SEÅ*
        51:158–67.
Murray, Oswyn
1991   *Sympotica: A Symposium on the Symposium.* Oxford:
        Clarendon.
Neyrey, Jerome H.
1986a   "Body Language in 1 Corinthians: The Use of
        Anthropological Models for Understanding Paul and
        His Opponents." In *Social-Scientific Criticism of the New
        Testament and Its Social World.* Ed. John H. Elliott. Pages
        129–70. *Semeia* 35. Decatur, Ga.: Scholars Press.
1986b   "The Idea of Purity in Mark." In *Social-Scientific
        Criticism of the New Testament and Its Social World.* Ed.
        John H. Elliott. Pages 91–128. *Semeia* 35. Decatur, Ga.:
        Scholars Press.
1988   "Symbolism in Mark 7." *Forum* 4(3):63–92.
1991   "Ceremonies in Luke-Acts: The Case of Meals and Table
        Fellowship." In *The Social World of Luke–Acts: Models for
        Interpretation.* Ed. Jerome H. Neyrey. Pages 361–87.
        Peabody, Mass.: Hendrickson.
Pervo, Richard I.
1985   "Wisdom and Power: Petronius' *Satyricon* and the
        Social World of Early Christianity." *ATR* 67:307–28.
Pilch, John
1993   "The Necessities of Life: Drinking and Eating." *TBT*
        31:231–37.
Pope, Marvin
1981   "The Cult of the Dead at Ugarit." In *Ugarit in
        Retrospect.* Ed. Gordon D. Young. Pages 159–79. Winona
        Lake, Ind.: Eisenbrauns.

Slater, William J.
1991   *Dining in a Classical Context.* Ann Arbor: University of
          Michigan Press.
Smith, Dennis
1980   "Social Obligation in the Context of Communal Meals."
          Unpublished Th.D. thesis. Harvard University.
1981   "Meals and Morality in Paul and His World." SBLSP
          1981:319–39.
1987   "Table Fellowship as a Literary Motif in the Gospel of
          Luke." *JBL* 106:613–38.
1989   "The Historical Jesus at Table." SBLSP 1989:466–86.
Soler, Jean
1979   "The Dietary Prohibitions of the Hebrews." *New York
          Review of Books* June 14:24–30. Reprinted in *Food and
          Drink in History.* Ed. Robert Forster and Orest Ranum.
          Pages 126–38. Baltimore: Johns Hopkins University
          Press, 1979.
Stein, S.
1957   "The Influence of Symposia Literature on the Literary
          Form of the Pesah Haggadah." *JJS* 8:13–44.
Theissen, Gerd
1982   "Social Integration and Sacramental Activity: An
          Analysis of 1 Cor. 11:17–34." In *The Social Setting of
          Pauline Christianity: Essays on Corinth.* Ed. and trans.
          John H. Schütz. Pages 145–74. Philadelphia: Fortress.

9

Millennialism

Dennis C. Duling
Canisius College

The purpose of this essay is to describe a phenomenon that social scientists and social historians call "millennialism," and then to review the relevant literaturefor those interested in pursuing the topic. In discussing the literature we stress the potential value of millennialism for the study of ancient Judaism and early Christianity.

1.0 A Definition of Millennialism

Millennialism describes a social movement of people whose central belief is that the present oppressive world is in crisis and will soon end, usually by some cataclysmic event, and that this world will be replaced by a new, perfect, blissful, and trouble-free world, often believed to be a restoration of some perfect time and place of old. So intense is this hope that those who accept it engage in preparing for the coming new age, or even try to bring it about, especially by some political activity.

2.0 Four Well-Known Illustrations of Millennialism

There are many movements from different times and places that social scientists and historians influenced by the social sciences describe with the word "millennialism." Here are four well-known illustrations.

2.1 First-Century Visionary Christianity

In Revelation, the last book of the Christian NT, several passages indicate that a small group of early Christians believed that
they were being persecuted. It was written in Asia Minor (western
Turkey) during the late first century, and in it John of Patmos, the
book's author, emphasized that their oppression was religious and
political. He said that some Christians had been executed because
they had refused to worship the Roman emperor as a god (2:1; 6:9,
16–18). Like Jesus, they were martyrs. According to John, the heavenly
Jesus, symbolized as a sacrificial lamb, would return as conquering
Warrior-Messiah. He would bind and imprison his evil archenemy,
Satan, in a pit sealed for a thousand years. As part of one of his last
visions, he wrote:

> Then I saw thrones [in heaven], and seated on them were those to
> whom judgment was committed. Also I saw the souls of those who
> had been beheaded for their testimony to Jesus and for the word of
> God, and who had not worshipped the beast [probably the Roman
> emperor (Rev 14:16–17)] or its image and had not received its mark on
> their foreheads or their hands. They came to life, and reigned with
> Christ a thousand years. The rest of the dead did not come to life until
> the thousand years were ended. This is the first resurrection. Blessed
> and holy is he who shares in the first resurrection! Over such the
> second death has no power, but they shall be priests of God and of
> Christ, and they shall reign with him a thousand years. And when the
> thousand years are ended, Satan will be loosed from his prison, and
> will come out to deceive the nations (Rev 20:4–8a).

After telling of the final defeat of Satan by a fire from heaven, the
seer concluded his work with visions about a new heaven, a new
earth, and a new Jerusalem prepared for God's persecuted elect,
with the promise that the Messiah would soon return (Rev 21).

2.2 The Extreme "Left Wing" of the Protestant Reformation: Thomas Müntzer

In the early sixteenth century, the Protestant reformers Luther,
Zwingli, and Calvin faced opposition from other "left wing," or
radical, reformers who believed that the Reformation had not gone
far enough. Among the more extreme of these reformers was
Thomas Müntzer (St. Clair 1992:153–90). Educated as a priest,
then influenced by Luther's views, Müntzer broke with the Catho-
lic Church. In Zwickau, Germany, he experienced a religious conversion. After that, he affirmed that it was necessary to despair of
this world, abandon worldly pleasures, and be reborn through the

Holy Spirit. He continually sought to organize a new "covenanted" church of the elect. An inspired preacher, he argued that the experience of spiritual baptism made external water baptism unnecessary. Drawing on Revelation, he preached that the Turks were the evil antichrist (Rev 20:7–10; see also 2 Cor 2:10), and that the elect must prepare for the second coming of Christ by taking up arms. Müntzer believed that a new, perfect social order of justice and love would be established, by bloody revolution if necessary.

Driven out of Zwickau in 1521, he migrated to Prague, where he was also banished. He returned to Germany, wandered about in poverty, settled at Allstedt, and married a former nun. He gained a following among the peasants and in 1524 organized bands of revolutionary Christians into "the Christian league." His famous *Sermon to the Saxon Princes* said that the end of the world was near and challenged the princes to protect the revolutionary elect; otherwise, God would transfer power to the people.

In 1525 the peasants of southern Germany, suffering under heavy taxes and rents, revolted. Müntzer became their leader and his theology became their ideology. After their defeat at Frankenhausen, Müntzer was captured, tortured, forced to recant, and beheaded, and his head was displayed on a pole (St. Clair 1992:153–68).

2.3 The Native American Ghost Dance Movement

The proud warrior culture of the Plains Indians of North America stressed fighting and the wild buffalo hunt, enhanced by the Spaniards' introduction of the horse. These Native Americans achieved honor by success in battle, hunting buffalo, and providing for their kin. Bands of Plains Indians gathered periodically for the Sun Dance celebration.

Between 1870 and 1890, the westward march of whites, who usually viewed the Native Americans as savages, destroyed this culture. The whites decimated the great buffalo herds, and after defeating the Native Americans in battle, located them on reservations. Then, on January 1, 1889, an eclipse of the sun occurred and at this time a Paiute sheepherder in Nevada called Wovoka saw a vision. Some years later Black Elk, second cousin of Crazy Horse, recalled these events.

> Out yonder in the west at a place near where the great mountains (the Sierras) stand before you come to the big water, there was a sacred man among the Paiutes who had talked to the Great Spirit in a vision, and the Great Spirit had told him how to save the Indian peoples and make the Wasichus [the whites] disappear and bring back all the bison and the people who were dead and how there would be a new earth. . . .

Wasichus called him Jack Wilson, but his name was Wovoka. He . . . [said] that there was another world coming, just like a cloud. It would come in a whirlwind out of the west and would crush out everything on this world, which was old and dying. In that other world there was plenty of meat, just like old times; and in that world all the dead Indians were alive, and all the bison that had ever been killed were roaming around again (Neihardt 1932:196–98).

Wovoka's visionary hope, which included the resurrection of the dead ("Ghosts"), spread rapidly among the Plains Indians. Eventually this Ghost Dance fervor reached the warlike Dakota Sioux, whose living conditions on the reservation had become desperate. The frightened whites sent troops to keep peace. When reservation police killed Sitting Bull, some Indians fled to the hills. After they surrendered and gave up most of their arms, a scuffle followed at their camp at Wounded Knee, South Dakota. The soldiers massacred a band of about 150 to 200 Indian men, women, and children. Many of the martyred were wearing "ghost shirts" as a sign that they followed Wovoka; they believed that the shirts made them bullet-proof (La Barre 1970:229–32).

2.4 Melanesian Cargo Cults

Imagine a lonely jungle airstrip deep in the highlands of New Guinea in the South Pacific. Beside it are a radio shack, a thatched hangar, and a bamboo beacon tower. Natives with ornaments in their noses and bands on their arms staff the airstrip twenty-four hours a day, lighting the runway at night by bonfires. They are eagerly expecting the arrival of cargo planes full of canned goods, clothing, watches, radios, and motorcycles. The planes will be piloted by their ancestors who have returned from the dead. Suddenly the natives hear a plane overhead. Their ancestors certainly must be looking for the airstrip, but the whites in the towns below are also sending messages. The ancestors must be confused because they land at the wrong airport. So the natives continue to wait. They hope for the removal of the dominance of the white man, a unification with venerable ancestors, a new and better life. Europeans tell the natives that material cargo is the result of hard work and industrialization. However, the natives, who see officials keep the goods for themselves, and who are led by visionary prophets, know otherwise: these material goods come from distant places and are created by supernatural means. Thus the movement, or some version of it, spreads from village to village (Harris 1974:133–52).

This New Guinea example is characteristic of religious movements of the Pacific islands of Melanesia. The natives hold that the arrival of Western-style goods (cargo), usually believed to have come from the gods, ancestors, or culture heroes, will usher in the new age of salvation. In preparation the natives sometimes destroy their crops or slaughter their livestock, symbolizing the end of the old age. They build symbolic docks or airstrips related to the arrival of European material goods for colonial officials. Ecstatic religious phenomena and rituals, sometimes initiated by a prophet, often occur. Anthropologists call these movements "Cargo Cults" (Worsley 1968; Burridge 1969; Trompf 1990, 1991).

In summary, early Christians hoped for a new, better world, like the original paradise; German Christian peasants rebelled against a dominant elite; Native Americans resisted whites and longed for a return to the ways of former times; and native islanders defied colonial powers while at the same time hoping for Western cargo. Many social scientists see common themes in these movements and understand them as examples of millennialism. Before we look at some common themes, an examination of terms will be helpful.

3.0 Millennialism and Apocalypticism

The term "millennialism" comes from the NT book called Revelation. Latin eventually succeeded Greek as the language of the church and its Bible, and the Latin word for the thousand-year reign of Christ and the martyrs in the passage from Revelation quoted above is *millennium* (Latin *mille*: "1,000"). Several other equivalent names used by social scientists are "millenarism," "millenarianism," "chiliasm" (Greek χιλιάς, *chilias* = Latin *millennium*), "nativistic movements" (referring to uprisings of native peoples against oppressive colonial outsiders), "revitalization movements" (from the hope that the "golden age" of the past will be reestablished and "revitalize" people in the future), "messianic movements" (from the fact that many such movements often have a charismatic "messianic" leader), and "crisis cults" (from the observation that such movements often arise in a period of cultural crisis). Note that all these terms stress groups or social movements.

The counterpart to these terms in the language of biblical scholars is "apocalypticism." Apocalypticism comes from two Greek terms: ἀποκαλύπτειν, *apokalyptein*, and ἀποκάλυψις, *apokalypsis*. The first term is a verb, "to uncover," "to reveal (a secret)." The second term is a noun, "revelation," or, as taken directly from the Greek, an "apocalypse." The book of Revelation also goes by the name "Apocalypse." Moreover, biblical scholars call any book or part of a book like Revelation an "apocalypse." An apocalypse is a literary work that records a vision, usually to a human being, usually represented as a "seer" in an altered state of consciousness, about another, perfect, supernatural world (space) that will finally replace this evil world (time) (modified from J. Collins 1979:9; Duling 1994:75–88).

Because most apocalypses contain thinking about the end of the world, many scholars call this sort of thinking "eschatological" (Greek ἔσχατον, eschaton = "end"). Using "apocalyptic" as an adjective, they refer to apocalyptic eschatology, or revelations concerning the end. Apocalyptic eschatology dominates apocalypses, but such thinking about the end is not limited to them; it is also found in other types of literature, for example, Gospels (esp. Mark, Matthew) or letters (esp. 1, 2 Thessalonians). Many scholars have interpreted Jesus' sayings as a mild form of apocalyptic eschatology.

"Apocalypticism," the third term, and the one of most concern here, is, like the adjective "apocalyptic," an English word derived from ἀποκάλυψις, apokalypsis (Hanson ["The Genre"] in Hanson et al. 1992:279–80). It refers to a social movement that lives by apocalyptic ideas. This term corresponds roughly to what social scientists call millennialism. Indeed, some scholars of the Bible prefer the term "millennialism" to "apocalypticism" (e.g., Isenberg 1974:35; Davies 1989:253; Horsley 1987:121–47; Crossan 1991:158–67).

Finally, many biblical scholars use the adjective "apocalyptic" as a noun. So used, it usually sums up all three of the above: written apocalypses, apocalyptic eschatological thought, and apocalyptic movements (Hanson ["The Genre"] in Hanson, et al. 1992:280). Earliest Christianity was permeated with apocalyptic (apocalyptic books, thought, and movements). Indeed, Ernst Käsemann once stated: "apocalyptic . . . was the mother of all Christian theology" (Käsemann 1969:40).

In sum, then, we have two terms that are roughly equivalent: millennialism and apocalyptic. Most social scientists prefer the term "millennialism," or one of its equivalents, while NT scholars usually prefer the term apocalypticism.

4.0 Millennialism: A Social-Scientific Synthesis

Ted Daniels's annotated bibliographical survey of studies and reviews of millennialism (1992) contains 3,762 entries. It is obviously impossible to discuss all of these studies; this sketch will resort to a superficial, but hopefully useful, synthesis of four of the classic, most important, and influential studies of millennialism: Anthony F. C. Wallace's "Revitalization Movements" (1956); Yonina Talmon's surveys of millennialism (1962, 1966, 1968); Kenelm Burridge's social-anthropological studies of colonial situations (1969); and Weston La Barre's "crisis cults" (1971).

4.1 The Accepted Social Order

Most people take for granted some mental picture of their society and the way it works (Wallace: a "mazeway"), especially if it is traditional and functioning relatively smoothly (Wallace: "steady state"). (The social-scientific theoretical perspective that societies are like biological organisms that try to maintain homeostasis, or harmonious equilibrium, is called "functionalism.") The political context may be relatively permissive (Burridge).

4.2 Crisis

However, something happens to disturb this order (Wallace: "mazeway" disintegration). For La Barre, there is a "crisis," a "culture shock," a deeply felt frustration or basic problem, and routine methods, secular or sacred, cannot cope with it, producing a massive helplessness (1971:11). Examples are: a natural disaster; a military conquest and occupation that disrupts the normal way of life; a group within the society that dominates another; or an outside, more powerful, seemingly more "complex" group, often perceived as "superior," that dominates a simpler society, as in the case of colonialism.

4.3 The Experience of Deprivation

Such factors lead the group in crisis to perceive a discrepancy between what they want and what they actually receive, to feel "relatively deprived." The group becomes frustrated about being able to share in the political power, material gain (money is of decisive significance; cf. Burridge 1969:106, 146), or social participation and aspiration to which they are traditionally accustomed. The deprived group experiences a conflict between alien and traditional cultural values, and becomes confused about right and wrong. It also experiences social isolation when traditional group ties (relatives, friends, etc.) are disrupted. The group may be "prepolitical," that is, it may have either as yet no developed political institutions, as in simpler societies, or no access to political power, such as peasants in feudal societies.

In such stressful conditions adaptable persons may try to change their perception of the world by "regressive" behavior (passivity, dependency, alcoholism, etc.), which produces guilt, conflict, misunderstanding, and more stress, resulting in loss of meaning, disillusionment, and apathy (Wallace).

4.4 The Millennial Movement

A possible alternative response, however, is a millennial movement. For Talmon, these movements are "religious movements that expect imminent, total, ultimate, this-worldly collective salvation" (Talmon 1962:125). Wallace refers to "revitalization movements," in which revitalization is a "deliberate, organized, conscious effort by members of a society to construct a more satisfying culture" (Wallace 1956:265).

The following are some common features of such millennial movements:

1. *Ideology* (Talmon 1962:406–7; 1968:352–53).

a. *Time.* Time is usually viewed as linear, moving toward a final, future consummation. The past is ambiguous. It is evil; yet it is also a mythical golden age. The future will be good and thus the golden age will return; yet, paradoxically, history will end. In contexts where duration and change are vague, time can be cyclical.

b. *Space.* The belief is that the "more-than-historical" and "historical" worlds will converge; "heaven" will appear on earth. A new social order will appear.

2. *Group orientation.* The emphasis is on establishing the new order for the repressed group ("the elect"), not saving individual souls. The group believes that it will be liberated from sin and pain and be happy (Talmon 1968:353). It tries initially to tap and rechannel traditional sources of authority; at this point the group lacks certainty and direction (Burridge).

3. *Leaders and followers.*

a. *The Prophet.* Usually a prophet or "messianic" figure, either a mythical hero/heroine or an actual (often martyred) person, sometimes preceded by a precursor, mediates between the other world and this world. She or he receives a revelation, that is, a dream, vision, or ecstatic experience. Prophets are expected to have such revelations, though occasionally they are caused by some severe physical stress. In the revelation a supernatural being explains why the society is in trouble and what the solution is (Wallace: "mazeway reformulation"). This results in a "conversion."

b. *Communication of message; leader and followers.* The prophet preaches that supernatural beings will care for the people who will benefit from the newly formed society. The prophet attracts followers. Her or his personal power leads to disciple-converts. Most millennial groups are loosely organized with strong leaders and ardent disciples, plus a larger circle of followers. Leaders emphasize old cultural themes or incorporate new cultural ideas derived from contact with outsiders.

4. *Emotionalism.* Highly emotional elements often accompany millennial movements. Examples are hysteria, paranoia, trance states, fantasies, mass possession, sexual excesses, and asceticism. Altered states of consciousness are sometimes accompanied by strange motor phenomena, for example, twitching, shaking, and convulsions.

5. *Group action.* It is uncertain how the new order will be established. Many say it will happen by divine intervention. Yet the most radical movements believe that the millennium is near and they set about preparing for it. Opposition by dominant powers within or outside the society sometimes leads such groups to political and diplomatic maneuvers. Some movements believe that they can hasten or retard salvation and they become quite active. Occasionally, a group may become revolutionary and even resort to violence. The more real the belief, the more active the group becomes. Such responses normally produce counterhostility by the dominant powers. A major crisis can occur if the appointed time does not happen, but disintegration need not necessarily follow (see Festinger, Riecken, and Schachter 1956:12, 208); indeed, millennialism can recur over and over again within the same culture (Hobsbawm 1965).

6. *Organization.* Only a few millennial groups become quickly organized with hierarchical leaders; most, as noted above, are loosely organized. Eventually, however, some stronger form of organization must take place. Transfer of power within an institutional structure is necessary if the movement is to survive. Multiple forms of leadership can emerge. Maintenance of authority within the group may become a problem, especially within radical, but comparatively nonactive, groups. Splintering may result.

7. *Cultural change: the new social order.* If successful at reducing stress, the whole or a controlling part of the population accepts the new program as normative. Cultural change takes place (Wallace: revitalization). A social program, sometimes successful, sometimes not, gradually replaces emotionalism. The leadership becomes responsible forc preserving doctrine and the performance of ritual. Charismatic authority becomes "routine," but its character is endangered. A social system may emerge (Wallace refers to a "new steady state").

5.0 Social-Scientific Explanations of Millennialism

Social scientists have several common theories that try to explain why millennialism occurs (La Barre 1971:14–26). These can be outlined as follows:

Political: group members protest internal cultural domination or colonial imperialism, or both ("liberation movements").

Military: such movements are rationales for rebellion and war, which break down the normal political processes.

Economic: the economically deprived try to gain their legitimate share of goods.

Messianism: groups of this type result from cultural contacts with Christianity.

The "great man" theory: sacred charismatic and organizational leaders trigger the movement.

"Acculturation": millennialism provides a synthesis derived from culture's clash with, and adaptation to, a new culture.

Psychological stress: when needs are not met, disintegration of personalities results; millennialist groups become an outlet for collective paranoid fantasies that come from irrational fears and expectations, or from competing cultural traditions.

There are critiques of each of these theories, especially when one is used to the exclusion of others ("reductionism"). La Barre stresses that no single theory adequately explains millennialism (1971:26).

6.0 Millennialism in Historical Perspective

Most historians have sought the origins of millennialism in ancient Jewish and Christian apocalypticism. There are three competing theories about the time of origin:

1. From the ninth to the sixth century BCE, when the first Israelite prophets protested economic, political, and social oppression by their own kings and hoped for a coming "Messiah" to usher in a new, better society.

2. From the late sixth to late fourth century BCE, the period of the later Jewish prophetic writings, when the Jews were dominated by the Persians, whose religion, Zoroastrianism, contained characteristically apocalyptic themes.

3. From the late fourth century BCE to the fourth century CE when, as a result of conquests by Greeks and Romans, Jews and other conquered native peoples experienced a nostalgia for the past golden age of national independence, alienation about the present,

and hope for the future; this was the period of the earliest full-blown Jewish apocalypse, namely, Dan 7–12 (165 BCE), and the flourishing of written apocalypses.

Judaism spawned Christianity. Both religions produced documents riddled with apocalyptic thought, as well as some apocalypses. Later, both Judaism and Christianity contributed to Islamic millennialism (Mahdism). Many scholars have documented similar ideas and movements throughout Western history. A special case is the United States. In this country there has been much discussion of millennialism from the perspective of conservative Christian theology.

7.0 Controversial Issues

Three of the most important controversial questions related to millennialism in the study of early Christianity are the following.

7.1 Is Millennialism Cross-Cultural or Based on Cultural Contact with Christianity?

If millenarian movements in Euro-American religious history are renewals of ancient millennialism, what about the Ghost Dance movement of the Plains Indians? Is Native American religion really a "distant comparison"? After all, Wovoka had come into cultural contact with Presbyterians, Mormons, and Indian "Shakers." Some anthropologists raise similar questions about Cargo Cults. The natives in the South Pacific often develop their views in connection with contact with Westerners, for example, colonialism, or occupation during World War II. Yet other anthropologists argue that the most important elements of the Cargo Cults, especially their ritual focus on material goods, are native to the islands (Burridge 1969:62; La Barre 1971:8). Many social-scientific interpreters are receptive to this approach, in part because millenarian motifs can be documented apart from Jewish, Christian, or Islamic influence, for example, in pre-Ch'in China (before 221 BCE; Shek 1987), among the Suarani of South America, the Karen of Burma, the Lakalai of the island of New Britain (Schwartz 1987:528b), and the Tiv of central Nigeria (Bohannan 1958).

7.2 Can Ancient Social Movements Be Postulated Behind Ancient Historical Religious Documents?

It is difficult to determine the actual social conditions in which an ancient piece of literature was written; it is especially difficult with symbolic apocalypses. Were the oppressive conditions portrayed in the book of Revelation "real," imagined, anticipated, based on John's private visionary world, or elaborated from his knowledge of other apocalypses such as Dan 7–12, to which he frequently alludes? Traditional historians are reluctant to generalize about social settings or groups unless the text explicitly mentions such groups (J. Collins 1987:10).

Social scientists, however, would argue that literature does not arise in a vacuum; it must therefore reflect some concrete social situation. Thus Hellholm contends that the definition of apocalypse should include: *"intended for a group in crisis with the purpose of exhortation and/or consolation by means of a divine authority"* (Hellholm 1983:168). Should this social context for the apocalypses be correct, any apocalypse could have been written in and for a millennial movement (Hengel 1974:194–96).

A closely related problem is that not all biblical interpreters agree that apocalypses were composed solely in and for millennial movements (J. Collins 1987:8, 10–11). Some scholars influenced by the social sciences share this point of view. P. R. Davies argues that apocalypses were written by "wise men" in scribal groups who were generally of the educated elite: "what determines the production of apocalyptic literature is not a millenarian posture nor a predicament of persecution, though these may be contributory factors. It is scribal convention" (Davies 1989:263). Because historians must rely on ancient written documents, and millennial movements usually arise among oppressed peoples who do not write, J. Dominic Crossan argues that apocalypticism must be related to two kinds of millennialism, "one literate and one illiterate, one of words and one of deeds, one for the upper and one for the lower classes, one for scribes and one for peasants" (Crossan 1991:158). But then we are left with other questions: Were these millennialisms ever related? If so, how?

7.3 In What Way Should Comparative Methods Be Used to Study Ancient Religion?

Comparative analysts usually recognize two kinds of comparisons. "Close comparisons" compare information (ideas, literary forms, social movements) from about the same time and place, that is, from the same or nearby cultures. "Distant comparisons" compare information from times and places more removed from what is being interpreted; they are "cross-cultural" (Esler 1987:9–12).

Most traditional historians prefer "close comparisons." Thus, John Collins speaks of a "Hellenistic matrix" for ancient apocalyptic; he argues that "there is only limited overlap between the Jewish

apocalyptic literature and the anthropological descriptions of millenarian movements" (1987:205–6). The social historian Richard Horsley is open to cross-cultural comparisons, but he is not certain they
can be found. For example, he thinks that Cargo Cults do not meet
the important criterion that peoples and situations should be
broadly similar to the those in the Bible (1989:7). Christopher Rowland (1985) is willing to use millennial parallels from later Western
Christian history, but is reluctant to make comparisons with other
cultures. Bengt Holmberg poses both methodological and theological objections to distant comparisons (1990:79–81).

Such caution is not limited to biblical scholars. An anthropologist who specializes in Cargo Cults, G. W. Trompf, maintains
that comparing millennialism with Jewish apocalypticism, the left
wing of the Reformation, and the Ghost Dance phenomenon often
reflects Western anthropologists' and sociologists' premature and
simplified attempts at general classification. The specific colonial
context, Trompf argues, must be carefully and specifically diag-
nosed (1991:190–91).

Most social scientists and some social historians, however, are
open to "distant comparisons." They see cross-cultural similarities
and want to know more about the tendency for similar phenomena
to arise in similar social situations. They do not require that every
detail be present; rather, they think of comparable movements.
These scholars suggest interpretations that we otherwise might not
see and raise questions that we otherwise might not ask. While it is
important to proceed with caution, from this perspective millennial
movements can help interpret first-century apocalypticism, especially given the difficulty of knowing about real groups behind
ancient literary sources.

8.0 Sample: The Early Christian Q Community as a Millennial Movement

If, as Käsemann puts it, apocalyptic is "the mother of all Christian
theology" (1969:40), many passages in the NT could be cited to
illustrate millennialism (see below, §9). The Q Community provides
one sample.

According to the widely accepted "Two-Source Theory," the
authors of the Gospels of Matthew and Luke used, modified, and
rearranged the Gospel of Mark. They also shared about 235 of the
same or similar verses *not* found in Mark, plus other sources and
traditions. Since it is unlikely that they knew each other's Gospels,

these 235 or so verses must have come from a second, lost source. Scholars call this source "Q" (from German: *Quelle,* "source"). They use Lukan chapters and verses prefaced by "Q" to refer to its chapters and verses (thus, Matt 3:10 and Luke 3:9 = Q 3:9). Extracting them from Matthew and Luke and putting them together shows that Q consisted mostly of Jesus' sayings. Jesus spoke Aramaic, but Q probably came to the writers of Matthew and Luke as a document in Greek translation (Duling 1994:11–16). The form, or genre, of the whole collection was generally like other ancient sayings collections, notably the *Gospel of Thomas,* 114 sayings attributed to Jesus, discovered in 1945 at Nag Hammadi, Egypt (Kloppenborg, et al. 1990).

The Q source contains a saying condemning three Galilean towns (Q 10:13) but makes no reference to known events in the latter first century CE. These facts, plus its content, lead most scholars to place its origins in Galilee among the first or early second generation of Christians (50–70 CE?). From the perspective of political history, Galilee had been continually subject to outside colonial powers: Assyrians (721 BCE), Babylonians (597 BCE), Persians (539 BCE), Greeks (332 BCE), and Romans (63 BCE). Galilee was a rural farming region and its population appears to have been mostly Jewish. Yet by the first century CE it contained important Hellenistic areas and cities and was surrounded by Hellenistic city-states, a situation producing cultural stress. Other political, economic, and social conditions were also stressful. The Galileans were ruled by Roman governors and the "half-Jewish" Herodians, who were usually supported by wealthy priestly families of Judea and aristocratic lay groups; beneath them were agents ("retainers") of these ruling classes, for example, tax officials and military personnel, as well as wealthy merchants and landowners. The vast majority of Galileans were mainly peasants (freeholders or tenant farmers), but the masses also included artisans, slaves, freedmen and freedwomen, and people so marginal that they were expendable. The oppression of the Palestinian majority population by the Romans and their supporters led to revolt in 66 CE, and Galileans joined in the Roman-Jewish war, 66–70 CE (Duling 1994:35–64).

The Q material probably took shape some years before the revolt and implies a community already under some stress. Q contains two main types of sayings, wisdom and apocalyptic (Kloppenborg, et al. 1990:22; Mack 1993:105–47; Duling 1994:147–54). The *forms* of the wisdom material are dominated by short, pithy sayings (aphorisms), many of which challenge conventional wisdom. In *content,* they imply poverty, for example, "blessed are you who are poor" (Q 6:20b), which probably refers to Galilean peasants. Some sayings emphasize that Jesus is the wandering, homeless "Son of man" who provides a pattern of homelessness, poverty, and lack of family as a "voluntary ideal" for Q's wandering missionary leaders (Q 10:4; 12:13–14, 33–34; 16:13); God will provide for life's essentials (11:3, 9–13; 12:22b–31). Discipleship may include rejection of family (9:59–60; 14:26), homelessness (9:58), and the possibility of martyrdom (e.g., 9:57–58; 12:4–7; 14:27; 17:33; 16:13). There is carelessness about food laws (10:8), yet little sympathy for non-Jews (6:33; 12:30). Another ethical ideal is nonviolence (6:29); as God forgives and extends mercy (6:27–29, 32–38), so should the disciple. Yet, the kingdom of God is dawning (6:20b; 9:62; 10:9; 11:2; 12:2, 29–31; 13:18–21). Again, these Q wisdom sayings are nonconventional wisdom and point to social dislocation.

The second type of material found in Q, apocalyptic sayings, implies a stronger reaction to stressful cultural conditions and suggests increasing opposition from outsiders. It implies a shift toward millennialism. Many Q sayings in this group are in the *form* of authoritative prophetic judgment sayings and apocalyptic words that warn or threaten (Kloppenborg, et al. 1990:22; Mack 1993: 131–32). With regard to *content*, these apocalyptic sayings do not directly oppose the Roman colonial powers, as one might expect from a millennial movement; yet they do condemn "this generation" and its leaders, especially the religiously strict Pharisee party, as hypocrites (Q 7:24–28, 31–35; 11:14–18a, 19–23, 39b–44, 46–52; 13:34–35). "This generation" is blind, stubborn, a "brood of vipers" (3:7); it follows Satan; it is an "evil generation" (7:31–34; 11:29). Many sayings warn or threaten those who do not respond to John the Baptist (the precursor: 3:6b-17; 7:27) and his judgment preaching, to Jesus (the prophet) and his message about the kingdom of God, or to missionaries who follow Jesus' lifestyle and spread Jesus' message from village to village (7:31–35; 11:19–20, 23–26, 29–36, 49–51; 12:39, 54–59; 17:37b). In these apocalyptic sayings, the kingdom will come at the end of time; it will be accompanied by violence (16:16). While no one knows the precise time, judgment will be soon (3:9, 17; 11:51b; 12:51–53, 54–56) and the judge will be God's representative, the Son of man, whose coming will be universal, visible, sudden, and without warning (17:24, 37b; 12:39–40; 17:26–30, 34–35). Insiders will be forgiven (e.g., 17:3b–4) and there will be openness to the Gentile outsiders (7:1–10), all the more proof of judgment on "Israel" (22:28–30). These events will create divisions in families (14:26).

In short, Q apocalyptic sayings point to the development of a millennial movement in Galilean peasant villages. Its sayings imply a "deliberate, [loosely] organized, conscious effort by [certain] members of a society to construct a more satisfying culture" (Wallace 1956:265). The Q collection stresses opposition to "this generation," especially to the Pharisees and their interpretation of the Torah. It hopes for a final, future end, a liberation from sin and pain, and happiness for the oppressed. A precursor, John the Baptist, is remembered as a proclaimer of judgment. A prophet, Jesus, Son of man, is remembered for explaining why the society is in trouble and what the solution is. Jesus mediates God's will for the group, whose missionaries follow in Jesus' steps. Jesus is remembered as condemning social ills, gaining a following of disciple-converts, attracting larger crowds, and promising that God will care for his elect people. His sayings stress ancient prophetic themes, yet incorporate new ideas. The millennium is near. Sayings are preserved that help prepare for it; they warn, yet offer hope. There will be divine intervention when the kingdom is finally established and the Son of man returns for judgment.

As political movements, most millennial movements fail. The millennial movement implied by Q may have failed or at least gradually subsided. Its sayings were not preserved in the form of a collection, but were incorporated into the pacifist, somewhat more sedate, narrative Gospels of Matthew and Luke, which in turn became part of a collection of mostly pacifist Christian books, the NT. Some of Q's apocalyptic was preserved, especially in Matthew, but balanced by other concerns. There is much evidence for other millennialism in early Christianity (see below, §9). Yet Christianity was developing more fixed patterns of leadership and forms of ritual, and eventually it formulated doctrines. Ultimately, the expected new social order had to wait until Christianity became the established religion of the Roman Empire in the fourth century.

9.0 Suggested Reading Sequence for Further Study

Further study of millennialism can profitably proceed by exploring, first, social-scientific discussions of millennialism; second, academic discussions of apocalypticism in Judaism at the time of Christian origins and early Christianity; and, third, NT research that acknowledges a debt to social-scientific studies of millennialism.

Yonina Talmon has written standard surveys of millennialism (1962, 1966, 1968), though some scholars consider her accent on linear time too "Western." One should also consult the introduction to Norman Cohn's work (1961), sometimes criticized for considering the phenomenon as social illness, and the overviews by Hillel Schwartz (1987), Michael St. Clair (1992), and Ted Daniels (1992).

There are several native accounts of millennial movements and some brief, popular discussions of them. One can read about

Thomas Müntzer's Reformation views in St. Clair (1992:153–90). A Native American, Black Elk, describes the Ghost Dance phenomenon (Neihardt 1932:196–98), and other native reports have been compiled by David Miller (1959). For Cargo Cults, one should consult Marvin Harris's lively description (1974:133–52).

Study can proceed to more extensive book-length discussions and scholarly articles. The above sketch mentions some of the most cited authors: A. F. C. Wallace (1956), Norman Cohn (1961), Eric Hobsbawm (1965), Peter Worsley (1968), Bryan Wilson (1973), Kenelm Burridge (1969), and Weston La Barre (1971). An earlier, classic article is Ralph Linton's "Nativistic Movements" (1943). Sylvia Thrupp collects key articles from a 1960 symposium on the subject (1970). Ted Daniels (1992) has compiled the most extensive bibliography; it contains summaries and criticisms of many approaches.

Further study of apocalypticism by biblical scholars might begin with brief surveys of the phenomenon, then turn to representative ancient literary sources, and finally explore more in-depth studies. Quick overviews are the articles by Paul Hanson, A. Kirk Grayson, John J. Collins, and Adela Yarbro Collins (1992). John J. Collins has written an excellent historically oriented survey (1987).

For apocalyptic thought in the NT itself one should read some representative passages: Mark 13 (the "Little Apocalypse"); the sayings source Q reconstructed behind the first three Gospels (Kloppenborg, et al. 1990; see §8 above); 1 Thess 4:13–5:11; and Revelation, especially 20:1–22:7, which focuses on the millennium and the new Jerusalem. Excellent background in Judaism can be found in Dan 7–12, and many other Jewish apocalypses are available in translation with annotations (Charlesworth 1983). One should read these texts with annotations, or better, learned commentaries, for example, J. Massyngberde Ford on Revelation (1975; 2d ed. forthcoming). Webb Mealy has written a technical study of a key Revelation passage (1992). Robert Jewett has published an especially important commentary that relates millennialism to a Pauline church (1986).

In addition to Bible passages and commentaries, some other works on early Judaism and Christianity show direct influences from social-scientific studies of millennialism. Notable is S. R. Isenberg's article (1974), which draws especially on Burridge's anthropological work (1969) in portraying the Teacher of Righteousness (founder of the group behind the Dead Sea Scrolls), Jesus, and Paul as millennial prophets. Horsley and Hanson (1985) offer an overview of political and peasant revolt in Palestinian Judaism. Also important for Judaism are general studies by Stephen Sharot (1982) and Lester Grabbe (1989), and analyses of particular apocalypses by Stephen Reid (1989) and Philip Esler (1994). Similarly, the ideas of David

Hellholm and others in the volume that came out of the international colloquium on apocalypticism (Hellholm 1983) often reflect the social-scientific study of millennialism.

Impressions of the effect of social-scientific millennial research on the study of early Christianity can be gained by reading ch. 3 of Bengt Holmberg's survey (1990), though Holmberg is often critical of social-scientific methods and results. Holmberg claims rightly that John Gager's chapter "Earliest Christianity as a Millenarian Movement" (in Gager 1975) has been an important catalyst. Gager tries to explain early Christian apocalypticism in terms of the social-psychological theory of "cognitive dissonance," that is, the distress that occurs when prophecies fail, which nonetheless often leads a group to intensify its beliefs and to seek new converts (Festinger, et al. 1956; cf. Esler 1994, who applies the concept to Jewish apocalypticism). Holmberg also points to the influential study of Paul by Wayne Meeks (1983), which allows that the millenarian model is useful for describing the churches founded by Paul, though Meeks rejects the view that one can characterize the Pauline communities by social and economic deprivation. Holmberg's third example is Jewett's study of the Thessalonian letters, noted above.

Some scholars describe many early Christian movements that emerged from the life and teachings of Jesus as millennial. Paul Hollenbach summarizes some early discussion (1983). Marcus Borg's readable books (1987, 1994) orient Jesus' life directly to millenarian studies, notably the itinerant prophet as founder of a "revitalization movement" (Wallace 1956). Strong impulses for such study have come from Gerd Theissen's classic work (1977), which stresses Jesus as an itinerant prophet who began a nonviolent reform movement of wandering charismatics supported by local communities in a time of social, political, and economic dominance by colonial powers. Richard Horsley builds on but challenges Theissen's view by shifting the emphasis to the local peasant communities themselves (1987); he looks at Jesus in the context of the spiral of violence in Palestine dominated by peasant unrest with an ideology of apocalypticism (1987, 1989). Neither Theissen's nor Horsley's study is based on cross-cultural millennialism, that is, distant comparisons. In contrast, J. Dominic Crossan draws on Horsley's model of increasing peasant unrest in first-century Judaism but buttresses it with general studies of apocalypticism and millennialism in anthropology (1991:158–61). For Crossan, John the Baptist, not Jesus, looks like the millennial prophet (1991:421). Crossan has also published a popular version of his views (1994).

Research on millennialism has influenced other dimensions of the study of early Christianity. Leonard Thompson analyzes the book of Revelation from this perspective (1986). Howard Kee's study of the Gospel of Mark is indirectly related to the theme (1977). Charles E. Hill discusses chiliasm in the first two centuries of Christianity (1992). Kloppenborg shows that the final version of Q, a source behind the first three Gospels, is apocalyptic (Kloppenborg, et al. 1990), and Mack attempts to develop the social-historical implications of this position (1993). From this perspective Q can also provide a sample for millennial interpretation (§8 above).

10.0 Works Cited

Bohannan, T. J.
 1958 "Extra-Processional Events in Tiv Political Institutions." *American Anthropologist* 60:1–12.
Borg, Marcus
 1987 *Jesus: A New Vision: Spirit, Culture, and the Life of Discipleship.* San Francisco: Harper & Row.
 1994 *Meeting Jesus Again for the First Time.* San Francisco: HarperCollins.
Burridge, Kenelm
 1969 *New Heaven, New Earth: A Study of Millenarian Activities.* New York: Schocken.
Charlesworth, James H., ed.
 1983 *The Old Testament Pseudepigrapha.* Vol. 1, *Apocalyptic Literature and Testaments.* Garden City, N.Y.: Doubleday.
Cohn, Norman
 1961 *The Pursuit of the Millennium: Revolutionary Messianism in Medieval and Reformation Europe and Its Bearing on Modern Totalitarian Movements.* New York: Harper & Row.
Collins, Adela Yarbro, ed.
 1986 *Early Christian Apocalypticism: Genre and Social Setting.* Semeia 36. Decatur, Ga.: Scholars Press.
Collins, John J.
 1979 "Introduction: Towards the Morphology of a Genre." In *Apocalypse: The Morphology of a Genre.* Ed. John J. Collins. Pages 1–20. Semeia 14. Missoula, Mont.: Scholars Press.
 1987 *The Apocalyptic Imagination.* New York: Crossroad.
Crossan, John Dominic
 1991 *The Historical Jesus: The Life of a Mediterranean Jewish Peasant.* San Francisco: Harper.
 1994 *Jesus: A Revolutionary Biography.* San Francisco: HarperCollins.

Daniels, Ted
1992   *Millennialism: An International Bibliography.* New York: Garland.

Davies, Philip R.
1989   "The Social World of Apocalyptic Writings." In *The World of Ancient Israel: Sociological, Anthropological, and Political Perspectives.* Ed. R. E. Clements. Pages 251–71. Cambridge: Cambridge University Press.

Duling, Dennis C.
1994   *The New Testament: Proclamation and Parenesis, Myth and History.* Fort Worth: Harcourt Brace College Publishers.

Esler, Philip
1987   *Community and Gospel in Luke–Acts.* Cambridge: Cambridge University Press.
1994   "Millennialism and Daniel 7" and "The Social Function of 4 Ezra." In *The First Christians in Their Social Worlds: Social-Scientific Approaches to New Testament Interpretation.* Pages 92–109, 110–30. London and New York: Routledge.

Festinger, Leon, Henry W. Riecken, and Stanley Schachter
1956   *When Prophecy Fails: A Social and Psychological Study of a Modern Group that Predicted the Destruction of the World.* Minneapolis: University of Minnesota Press.

Ford, J. Massyngberde
1975   *Revelation.* AB 38. Garden City, N.Y.: Doubleday.

Gager, John
1975   "Earliest Christianity as a Millenarian Movement." Chapter 3 of *Kingdom and Community: The Social World of Early Christianity.* Englewood Cliffs, N.J.: Prentice-Hall.

Grabbe, Lester
1989   "The Social Setting of Early Jewish Apocalypticism." *Journal for the Study of the Pseudepigrapha* 4:24–47.

Hanson, Paul D., A. Kirk Grayson, John J. Collins, and Adela Yarbro Collins
1992   "Apocalypses and Apocalypticism." *ABD.* 1:279–92. New York: Doubleday.

Harris, Marvin
1974   *Cows, Pigs, Wars, and Witches: The Riddles of Culture.* New York: Random House (Vintage Book).

Hellholm, David, ed.
1983   *Apocalypticism in the Mediterranean World and the Near East.* Tübingen: Mohr.

Hengel, Martin
1974   *Judaism and Hellenism.* Trans. John Bowden. 2 vols. Philadelphia: Fortress; London: SCM.

Hill, Charles E.
1992   *Regnum Caelorum: Patterns of Future Hope in Early Christianity.* Oxford: Oxford University Press.

Hobsbawm, Eric
1965   *Primitive Rebels: Studies in Archaic Forms of Social Movements.* 1959. Reprint, New York: Norton.

Hollenbach, Paul W.
1983   "Recent Historical Jesus Studies and the Social Sciences." SBLSP 1983:61–78.

Holmberg, Bengt
1990   *Sociology and the New Testament: An Appraisal.* Minneapolis: Fortress.

Horsley, Richard A.
1987   *Jesus and the Spiral of Violence: Popular Jewish Resistance in Roman Palestine.* San Francisco: Harper and Row.

1989   *Sociology and the Jesus Movement.* New York: Crossroad.

Horsley, Richard A., and John S. Hanson
1985   *Bandits, Prophets, and Messiahs: Popular Movements in the Time of Jesus.* Minneapolis: Winston.

Isenberg, S. R.
1974   "Millenarism in Greco-Roman Palestine." *Religion* 4:26–46.

Jewett, Robert
1986   *The Thessalonian Correspondence: Pauline Rhetoric and Millenarian Piety.* Philadelphia: Fortress.

Käsemann, Ernst
1969   "The Beginnings of Christian Theology." In *Apocalypticism.* Ed. Robert W. Funk. Pages 17–46. *Journal for Theology and the Church 6.* New York: Herder and Herder.

Kee, Howard Clark
1977   *Community of the New Age: Studies in Mark's Gospel.* Philadelphia: Westminster.

Kloppenborg, J. S., M. W. Meyer, S. J. Patterson, and M. G. Steinhauser
1990   *Q-Thomas Reader.* Sonoma, Calif.: Polebridge.

La Barre, Weston
1970   *The Ghost Dance.* New York: Doubleday.

1971   "Materials for a History of Studies of Crisis Cults: A Bibliographic Essay." *Current Anthropology* 12:3–44.

Lanternari, Vittorio
1963   *The Religions of the Oppressed.* New York: Mentor.

Linton, Ralph
1943   "Nativistic Movements." *American Anthropologist* 45:230–40. Reprinted in *Reader in Comparative Religion: An Anthropological Approach.* 4th ed. Ed. William A.

Lessa and Evon Z. Vogt. Pages 415–21. New York: Harper & Row, 1979.

Mack, Burton
1993   *The Lost Gospel: The Book of Q and Christian Origins.* San Francisco: HarperCollins.

Mealy, J. Webb
1992   *After the Thousand Years: Resurrection and Judgment in Revelation 20.* JSNTSup 20. Sheffield: JSOT Press.

Meeks, Wayne A.
1983   *The First Urban Christians: The Social World of the Apostle Paul.* New Haven: Yale University Press.

Miller, David H.
1959   *Ghost Dance.* New York: Duell, Sloan and Pearce.

Neihardt, John G.
1932   *Black Elk Speaks.* New York: William Morrow. Reprint, Lincoln: University of Nebraska Press, 1979.

Reid, Stephen B.
1989   *Enoch and Daniel: A Form Critical and Sociological Study of the Historical Apocalypses.* Berkeley: BIBAL.

Rowland, Christopher
1985   "Reading the New Testament Sociologically: An Introduction." *Theology* 88:358–64.

St. Clair, Michael J.
1992   *Millenarian Movements in Historical Context.* New York: Garland.

Schwartz, Hillel
1987   "Millenarianism: An Overview." *Encyclopedia of Religion.* 9:521–32. New York: Macmillan.
1990   *Century's End: A Cultural History of the Fin de Siècle from the 990s to the 1990s.* New York: Doubleday.

Sharot, Stephen
1982   *Messianism, Mysticism, and Magic: A Sociological Analysis of Jewish Religious Movements.* Chapel Hill: University of North Carolina Press.

Shek, Richard
1987   "Chinese Millenarian Movements." *Encyclopedia of Religion.* 9:532–36. New York: Macmillan.

Talmon, Yonina
1962   "Pursuit of the Millennium: The Relation between Religious and Social Change." *Archives européennes de sociologie* 3:25–48. Reprinted in *Studies in Social Movements: A Social Psychological Perspective.* Ed. Barry McLaughlin. Pages 400–27. London: Free Press.
1966   "Millenarian Movements." *Archives européennes de sociologie* 7:159–200.

1968 "Millenarism." *International Encyclopedia of the Social Sciences.* 10:349–62. New York: Free Press.

Theissen, Gerd
1978 *Sociology of Early Palestinian Christianity.* Trans. John Bowden. Philadelphia: Fortress.

Thompson, Leonard
1986 "A Sociological Analysis of Tribulation in the Apocalypse of John." In *Early Christian Apocalypticism: Genre and Social Setting.* Ed. Adela Yarbro Collins. Pages 147–74. *Semeia* 36. Decatur, Ga.: Scholars Press.

Thrupp, Sylvia L., ed.
1970 *Millennial Dreams in Action: Studies in Revolutionary Religious Movements.* 1962. Reprint, New York: Schocken.

Trompf, Gary, ed.
1990 *Cargo Cults and Millenarian Movements: Transoceanic Comparisons of New Religious Movements.* Berlin and New York: Mouton de Gruyter.

1991 *Melanesian Religion.* Cambridge: Cambridge University Press.

Wallace, Anthony F. C.
1956 "Revitalization Movements." *American Anthropologist* 58:264–81. Reprinted in *Reader in Comparative Religion: An Anthropological Approach.* 4th ed. Ed. William A. Lessa and Evon Z. Vogt. Pages 421–29. New York: Harper & Row, 1979.

Wilson, Bryan R.
1973 *Magic and the Millennium: A Sociological Study of Religious Movements of Protest Among Tribal and Third-World Peoples.* London: Heinemann.

Worsley, Peter
1968 *The Trumpet Shall Sound: A Study of "Cargo Cults" in Melanesia.* 2d ed. New York: Schocken.

10

Ancient Reading

Lucretia B. Yaghjian
Weston Jesuit School of Theology

1.0 Ancient Reading, Modern Readers: Setting the Agenda

> Now there was an Ethiopian eunuch, a court official of the Candace, queen of the Ethiopians, in charge of her entire treasury. He had come to Jerusalem to worship and was returning home; seated in his chariot, he was reading the prophet Isaiah. Then the Spirit said to Philip, "Go over to this chariot and join it." So Philip ran up to it and heard him reading the prophet Isaiah. He asked, "Do you understand what you are reading?" He replied, "How can I, unless someone guides me?" (Acts 8:27–31, NRSV).

An important conversation is going on among NT scholars regarding reading theory, reader-response criticism, and the social environment of biblical texts. As the conversation has developed, however, the difference between ancient and modern understandings of the phenomenon of reading itself has not always been sufficiently recognized. What is needed is cognizance of the way reading actually worked in the original culture of the biblical documents. This chapter provides: (1) a brief introduction to ancient reading in its biblical context, including cultural comparisons between ancient and modern understandings of reading; and (2) a cross-disciplinary survey of relevant literature on ancient reading for the nonspecialist reader of the NT. It includes: orality and literacy studies; historical studies of ancient reading practice, production, and pedagogy; biblical studies of ancient Jewish reading practice and pedagogy; and social-science resources for ancient reading theory and practice.

In our Western, industrialized, and literacy-driven cultural context, reading is a fundamental and inalienable right, along with "life, liberty, and the pursuit of happiness." Our public education system introduces most Americans to reading skills by the time they are six years of age, and learners are taught to read visually, silently, and by themselves. Inexpensive printing costs keep books accessible, plentiful, and portable. Accustomed as we are to reading on trains and airplanes, on stationary bicyles and in bed, we might find nothing unusual about a first-century CE government official reading in his carriage on his way home from a religious pilgrimage. But what did "reading" mean in the ancient world?

2.0 Preliminary Definitions

If we are to "understand" reading in the cultural world of the NT, we must first take off the conceptual lenses through which we habitually read, and begin to read with our ears as well as our eyes. Second, we must change our societal image of reading from a private rendez-vous with the printed page to a public broadcast of oral and/or written communication. Finally, we must revise our culturally biased definitions of "literacy" and "illiteracy," and allow the biblical documents to spell out their own contextual ones.

Both the Hebrew *qārāʾ* ("to call out; to encounter; to read") and the Greek ἀναγινώσκω, *anaginōskō* ("to know again; to recognize"; hence, "to read"), have oral and communal roots. In the Hebrew scriptures, to read is to "call out," or read aloud, in a public "encounter," as in Ezra's reading of the law at Jerusalem's Water Gate to the returned exiles:

> The priest Ezra brought the law before the assembly, both men and women and all who could hear with understanding. . . . He read from it facing the square before the Water Gate from early morning until midday, in the presence of the men and the women and those who could understand; and the ears of all the people were attentive to the book of the law (Neh 8:2–3).

The NT retains this sense of public reading aloud in its use of ἀναγινώσκω, *anaginōskō*, as in Jesus' public reading in the synagogue at Nazareth that inaugurates his ministry in Luke's Gospel (Luke 4:16–22; see §6.2 below). However, while ἀναγινώσκω, *anaginōskō*, always appears in relation to a read or referenced text, it does so in varying oral contexts, as we shall see below. Hence the interaction between oral and literate processes characteristic of ancient communication is built into the biblical usage of ἀναγινώσκω, *anaginōskō*. Moreover, this Greek word is derived from γινώσκω, *ginōskō* ("to know"). In biblical culture, people "knew" what they heard; hence reading was a "knowing again," or "recognizing" the written characters used to transcribe what was originally heard. Accordingly, the verb ἀκούειν, *akouein* ("to hear"), could also mean "to read" in some Hellenistic contexts (Hendrickson 1929; Schenkevald 1992). Although this usage might confuse us, it should not surprise us in a culture for whom virtually all reading was "reading aloud."

Reading, however, is more than its linguistic description. Reading is a cultural activity that is practiced by readers, and readers always read in a context. Because oral and written contexts intersected in Mediterranean antiquity, cultural literacy, or "knowing the tradition," did not depend on technical literacy, or "knowing letters," even though the social practice of reading embraced both of these. In this chapter, we will encounter varying contextual meanings of the words, "reading," "readers," "literacy," and "illiteracy." To help readers distinguish these different meanings, we begin with some contextual definitions that take as their starting point the interaction between oral and literate processes in antiquity:

1. *Auraliterate reading* is the practice of hearing something read, or reading received aurally by "readers' ears" (Polybius 6.38.4.4), as when Paul writes (for oral/aural delivery) in 2 Cor 1:13: "For we write you nothing other than what you can read and also understand." This usage of ἀναγινώσκω, *anaginōskō*, is rare in the NT, but it is used here by Paul and in Eph 3:4 (ἀναγινώσκοντες, *anaginōskontes*) as an inclusive strategy to address a mixed audience of readers and hearers.

2. *Oraliterate reading* is oral recitation or recall of a memorized text (or story from a text) as in the Matthean reading controversies (Matt 12:1–4; see §4.0 below). We call this reading "oraliterate," or reading orally performed but given some textual context. "Oraliterate" readers may not "know letters" (Greek: ἀγράμματος, *agrammatos*), but they know the "sacred writings" by heart (1 Tim 3:14–15) and can recite them with the natural proficiency of people brought up in an oral environment. As we shall see, oraliterate reading is used in the NT as a defensive strategy for maintaining community honor and interpretive authority vis-à-vis other (typically antagonistic) groups.

3. *Oculiterate reading* is linguistic decoding (by eye) from a written text, performed by readers who can decode written letters, exemplified by Jesus' reading in the synagogue at Nazareth (Luke 4:16ff.) and the Ethiopian eunuch's reading of Isaiah (Acts 8:27ff.). In oculiterate reading, both eye and ear participate in the reading process, and a written document is not only referred to but "read from." Oculiterate reading and readers provide cultural legitimation for the marginalized NT communities and their leaders, placing the

Christian movement within the authoritative Jewish reading tradition and within literate Hellenistic culture.

4. *Scribaliterate reading* is reading for technical, professional, or religious purposes on behalf of a particular interpretive community or "school," as exemplified by Philip's interpretation of Isa 53 to the eunuch (Acts 8:32–35). Within the NT context, such interpretive activity was the provenance of professional scribes, identified with the religious elite but by no means limited to them (cf. Matthew's "scribe trained for the kingdom": Matt 13:52). Scribaliterate reading embraces oculiterate, oraliterate, and auraliterate reading in its repertoire, and is exemplified par excellence by Luke (and other NT authors), whose scribal hand claims authoritative status for his reading of the tradition (Luke 1:4).

5. *Illiterate/illiteracy:* Many authors cited here will use the word "illiterate" to refer to "oraliterate" and "auraliterate" ancient readers. Used as technical terms denoting lack of ability to decode written communication, "illiterate" and its cognate "illiteracy" are used correctly. In many contexts, however, they are freighted with an ethnocentric twentieth-century stigma inappropriate to first-century Mediterranean readers, for whom "illiterate" (ἀγράμματος, *agrammatos*) was a technical term used on legal documents, and a socially descriptive epithet, but not a pejorative one (cf. Acts 4:13, where Peter and John are identified as ἀγράμματος, *agrammatos:* their lack of literacy is not a stigma, but a source of amazement, because they speak with the eloquence of educated men). Hence this term should be used with extreme care and cultural consideration.

6. *Literate/literacy:* When the authors cited in this chapter use the terms "literacy" or "literate" in a technical sense to denote the ability to decode written communication, their definition applies to oculiterate and scribaliterate readers only.

3.0 Reading in Context: From Definitions to Questions

However we define reading in a first-century context, it is practiced by readers in a particular social and cultural setting. Therefore we must also ask, Who reads what, where, to whom, for what purpose? And keeping in mind our definitions of biblical reading, we must ask, Who were the oculiterate readers, and who were not? And of those who were not, we must ask, What groups of oraliterate and auraliterate readers typically lacked access to the scarce resources of (technical) literacy, and why? But by far the most intriguing question is, Why concern ourselves with oculiterate reading at all in the cultural context of the New Testament? Such questions will help us to understand reading in biblical antiquity in its larger sociocultural context.

With these questions in mind, let us look at the portrait of a first-century CE reader that Luke gives us in the story of the Ethiopian eunuch. As an educated public servant, or retainer, in the service of his queen, he is an oculiterate male reader. He has the financial resources (from the queen's treasury or from his own income) to purchase (probably in Jerusalem) his own "scroll" of Isaiah (presumably in Greek), which he reads aloud (Acts 8:30). He is recognized as a reader by this act of reading aloud; and remarkably, he is intercepted by a scribaliterate reader—Philip! In a culture for whom literacy rates were never more than 10 percent of the population (Harris 1989; Bar-Ilan 1992), it would have been quite unusual for two such readers to meet on a "desert" road (Acts 8:26). Yet they do, and the private reading scenario becomes a communal act that leads to a public baptism (Acts 8:36–38).

Four things are culturally significant about this Lukan reading scenario. First, the reading is both linguistic decoding (from a scroll) and oral/aural (Acts 8:30), inviting our inquiry into relationships between orality and literacy in the ancient world. Second, reading comprehension requires instruction in a particular reading tradition by an authorized "guide," or pedagogue (Acts 8:31), reflecting the common cultural practice of ancient Jewish, classical, and Hellenistic reading pedagogy. Third, what is read is an ancient Jewish text (Isa 53), and by "beginning with that scripture" (Acts 8:35) Philip invokes not only Hellenistic reading pedagogy but also first-century Jewish reading practice. Fourth, the act of reading is not merely for individual consumption but has social consequences, issuing in the baptism of a traditionally "unclean" foreigner, Gentile, and eunuch (Acts 8:38–39). Yet much of first-century Mediterranean society is missing from this picture (peasants, women, the slave driving the chariot, "ordinary folk"). Thus not only semantic tools but also those of social-science analysis are required of modern readers who wish to understand reading as a social practice in its first-century environment. In the survey of literature on ancient reading that follows, we look at each of these four areas in turn.

4.0 Orality, Literacy, and Reading in the New Testament World

> At that time Jesus went through the grainfields on the sabbath; his disciples were hungry, and they began to pluck heads of grain and to eat. But when the Pharisees saw it, they said to him: "Look, your disciples are doing what is not lawful to do on the sabbath." He said to them: "Have you not read what David did, when he was hungry, and

those who were with him: how he entered the house of God and ate the bread of the Presence, which it was not lawful for him to eat nor for those who were with him, but only for the priests? (Matt 12:1–4, RSV).

This picture of reading painted by Matthew (cf. Mark 2:23–28; Luke 6:1–5) is quite different from Luke's portrait of the Ethiopian eunuch. Reading is portrayed as oral communication, not written comprehension; Jesus is recounting a story (1 Sam 21:1–7) from memory, not decoding script from an unrolled scroll. The reading occasion is not catechetical, but controversial; Jesus is reading to defend his honor and that of his disciples against the Pharisees' accusations. Moreover, the reading takes place on rural (peasant) turf, not on a Roman road connecting two important ancient cities. Reading here is not a means of conversion, but a contest for social control.

In this oral exchange, Jesus refers to reading ("Have you not read [ἀνέγνωτε, *anegnōte*]?" Matt 12:3) in a way that presumes his opponents "have read" the Scripture passage he cites. Although the text does not tell us whether they have previously "heard" the story from 1 Samuel or "read" a written text, "reading" in this context presupposes oral retention and recall of a traditional text by all parties in the conversation. This "oraliterate" reading scenario illustrates how literate reading typically functioned in NT antiquity as "a subset of a basically oral environment" (Botha 1992a:206).

While orality-literacy studies in the humanities have proliferated since the 1970s, biblical scholarship has not kept pace with this trend, perhaps because "print is the medium in which modern biblical scholarship was born and raised, and from which it has acquired its formative methodological habits" (Kelber 1995a:140). Yet the materials collected here include some notable exceptions. For the reader new to this field and confused by its terminology, it may be helpful to classify these works as (1) orality-focused, (2) literacy-focused, and (3) mixed-media studies. We begin with required but reader-friendly selections from each of these categories with the biblical student in mind; we then recommend more specialized reading for those with particular research interests.

1. *Orality-focused studies* take orality and its literary, historical, or social description in particular cultural environments as their point of departure. Paul Achtemeier (1990) offers an indispensable survey of the literature of ancient reading from biblical, classical, Hellenistic, and patristic sources. He argues that "the NT documents . . . are oral to the core, both in their creation and in their performance" (19). In such an environment, "reading" implies hearing, and the authors of the NT writings wrote for "reader's ears" (Polybius 6.38.4.4), not merely for their eyes.

2. *Literacy-focused studies* are no less interested in orality, but their point of departure is literacy and its literary, historical, and social description within particular cultural environments. J. P. P. Botha (1992a) provides an excellent critique of the biblical conversation concerning the extent and uses of Greco-Roman literacy and its implications for NT research. Botha argues that literate people were few in the first century, and that such literacy as existed "remained a kind of imitation talking" (206). Readers daunted by William Harris's definitive work (1989; see below) will find its conclusions summarized here.

3. *Mixed-media studies* take as their point of departure the relationship between orality and literacy within a particular cultural environment. While some studies follow Jack Goody's focus on the interface between the written and the oral (1987), others stress "the great divide" (Ong 1982; see below) between them. In biblical studies, the reigning classic in this category is by Werner Kelber (1983), who documented the shift from orality to writing in Mark's Gospel. More recently Kelber has articulated a mixed-media position (1995). Joanna Dewey (1995a) argues that "early Christianity was an oral phenomenon in a predominantly oral culture," while "the culture of the dominant elite . . . was a manuscript culture" (60). According to Dewey, this oral-literate divide had influenced the transformation of an oral-based, egalitarian Christian movement into an official state religion dominated by the power structure of a literate male elite.

5.0 From Orality to Literacy and Back Again: Backgrounds and Resources

This return to orality in biblical studies is the result of a profound paradigm shift. Birger Gerhardsson (1961) argued for the oral transmission of the Gospel materials in a manner similar to that of the "Oral Torah." Gerhardsson's thesis was challenged (e.g., Kelber 1983), but orality and its consequences for the study of biblical texts were here to stay. The most useful introduction to this conversation is by Walter Ong (1982). In this work Ong not only focuses on the difference between oral cultures and literate ones, tracing the impact of writing, print, and electronic media on human and societal patterns of behavior and cognition, but also develops the implications of the orality-literacy contrast for contemporary scholarly disciplines, including biblical studies. Ong's thesis is that there is a radical and recognizable discontinuity between an oral culture and a written (script, print, or electronic) culture, because "writing restructures consciousness" (78–116).

Not all scholars have been convinced by Ong's "Great Divide Theory" (see Finnegan 1988, discussed below). However, Ong's suggestive catalogue of the "psychodynamics of orality" (31–77) provides the astute biblical reader with templates of the ancient reading experience that can be fruitfully applied to biblical texts. For example, two characteristics of orality that Ong cites are (1) its dependence on memory ("you know what you can recall," 33) and (2) its agonistic nature (while writing "separates the knower from the known," orality presumes a face-to-face encounter that "situates knowledge within a context of struggle," 44). As we have seen, when Matthew's Jesus counters the Pharisees' censure of the disciples' picking grain on the sabbath with, "Have you not *read* what David did . . ." (Matt 12:3), the "reading" is from memory, and it is performed in just such an agonistic context.

However strong the residual orality of biblical culture, reading and writing were strongly connected in antiquity. Jack Goody (1986) explores the function of (written) literacy in religious systems and its relation to institutional authority, power, and control (1–44). His work has been utilized by NT scholars concerned with the shift in early Christianity from oral to textual authority (Dewey 1995b). By contrast, Eric Havelock (1982:39–59) argues for the ability to *read* (not write!) as the major determinant of literacy. He also distinguishes the "pre-literate" and "non-literate" cultures of Greek antiquity from our modern pejorative usage of the term "illiterate."

The only biblical reference to (technical) literacy defines literate persons according to their ability to read:

> The vision of all this has become for you like the words of a sealed document. If it is given to those who can read, with the command, "Read this," they say, "We cannot, for it is sealed." And if it is given to those who cannot read, saying, "Read this," they say, "We cannot read" (Isa 29:11–12, NRSV).

But how many people were technically literate in the Greco-Roman world? If one reads nothing else on this subject, William V. Harris (1989) is essential. While Harris's initial definition of an illiterate person as one "who cannot with understanding both read and write a short simple statement on his everyday life" (UNESCO 1977:12, cited by Harris 1989:3) reflects the rhetoric of UNESCO literacy campaigns more than the contexts in which people in biblical antiquity read and wrote, Harris goes well beyond this definition in his analyses of (a) "Levels of Greek and Roman Literacy" (3–24) and (b) "The Functions of Literacy in the Graeco-Roman World" (25–42). Harris argues decisively that "the classical world, even at its most advanced, was so lacking in the characteristics which produce extensive literacy that we must suppose the majority of people were always illiterate" (13). Citing the expense of writing materials, the lack of public education, and the oral mind-set as factors militating against the spread of literacy, Harris has prompted much reassessment of prevailing assumptions concerning literacy among biblical scholars (e.g., Botha 1992a; see §4.0 above).

To conclude our survey of orality-literacy studies, three "mixed-media" approaches by British cultural anthropologists and one classicist are essential reading for students desiring to sharpen their social-science lenses. Brian Street (1984) critiques "autonomous" models of literacy, in which literacy is treated as a neutral skill whose effects can be predicted and measured irrespective of their cultural contexts. Alternatively, Street proposes an "ideological model" of literacy that "concentrates on the specific social practices of reading and writing," acknowledges their "ideological and therefore culturally embedded nature," and "distinguishes claims for the consequences of literacy from its real significance for specific social groups" (2). From a social-science perspective, then, Street teaches us to define reading as a social practice embedded in a particular cultural context, not merely as a set repertoire of linguistic skills.

Finally, Ruth Finnegan (1988) should be read in concert with Rosalind Thomas (1992) since Thomas, a classical historian, builds on the work of Street and Finnegan to explore and document the interaction of oral and literate processes in Greek antiquity. Finnegan argues (contra Ong; see above) for the interaction of orality and literacy in ancient and contemporary cultures, and cautions the reader against oversimplification in attempts to define either one. Her definition of reading exemplifies this approach and invites us to focus on the practice, production, and pedagogy of ancient reading in the historical studies in our next section:

> Reading is . . . a more problematic term than appears at first. It conceals a number of variants between silent individual reading, reading aloud in private or . . . in public, or basing a full performance on a written text . . . all equally "natural" processes by which written texts can be transmitted, and illustrating well the way written and oral processes can run into each other (172).

6.0 Ancient Reading Practice, Production, and Pedagogy

> Then Paul stood in front of the Areopagus and said, "Athenians, I see how extremely religious you are in every way. For as I went through the city and looked carefully at the objects of your worship, I found

among them an altar with the inscription, 'To an unknown god' " (Acts 17:22–23, NRSV).

Havelock has said, "Of all the activities of mankind which we now take to be ordinary, reading is the one which is most sparsely recorded." The reason for this is that "reading is an activity, not a material artifact, which is why scholarship has paid relatively little attention to the presence or extent of reading in historical cultures" (1982:58, 56). Yet we are not without some clues: we have descriptions of reading and readers in ancient and biblical literature, and we have artifacts (Greek vases, sculpture, and other art objects) depicting people reading. The passage from the Acts of the Apostles above gives yet another Lukan portrait of reading. Paul is portrayed here as reading an altar inscription in the city of Athens, renowned as a center of ancient reading practice and pedagogy. Notice that even in this highly literate environment (cf. Harris 1989:282–84), he reads public inscriptions, not "published" scrolls; and when he quotes "some of your poets" (Acts 17:28), the recitation is oral, not textual. It is from such clues that the historian of ancient reading develops a picture, and the biblical interpreter reconstructs the reading environments of the NT documents.

Our task in this section is to survey historical material on ancient reading that will help us to imagine these varied reading environments and to identify the relevant resources for particular reading communities. While details on the fine points of literate reading may be more pertinent to reading in Luke-Acts than to the "oral media world" of the Pauline communities (and vice versa), readers are encouraged to use this material to develop their own picture of reading in a particular text, and to prioritize selections accordingly.

6.1 Resources for Historical Description of Reading and Readers

Robert Darnton (1992) sets the agenda for this task and is required reading. In this brief but insightful essay, Darnton outlines five historical questions essential to a study of reading in any disciplinary context: (1) How was reading perceived by its culture? (2) How was reading taught and learned, and by whom? (3) How was reading described by contemporary readers and writers? (4) How was the relationship between readers and texts (e.g., reader response) understood? (5) How did the book as a physical object affect the cultural activity of reading?

With these historical questions in mind, the reader should turn next to G. L. Hendrickson (1929), who surveys reading in classical, Hellenistic, and early Christian antiquity. Citing evidence from

Plato, Polybius, Plutarch, Augustine, and Luke–Acts, Hendrickson shows that reading in antiquity was reading aloud, and silent reading (even to oneself) was the rare exception (but see Knox 1968 for another view).

Finally, readers desiring further historical detail should revisit Harris (1989) for his rich collection of historical information on reading in Greco-Roman antiquity, and his exhaustive bibliography. Some earlier monographs worth investigating for those with particular research interests are discussed briefly below.

Who was the ancient reading public and what were their books like? Frederick G. Kenyon (1951) imagines a vigorously literate reading public in Greco-Roman antiquity. While Kenyon's conclusions are based on the reading elite of Greek and Roman high culture and should be read with that caveat in mind, his research on the materials and methods of book production in antiquity (from papyrus and parchment rolls to vellum and the codex) provides a valuable introduction.

For the student of biblical literature, Harry Y. Gamble (1995) has written the only monograph to date that examines the bibliographic history of the early Christian movement. While Gamble focuses on text rather than context, his book provides a broad historical overview of early book production and reading practice that invites further attention to the social implications of his research. For example, his claims for the prominence of books, reading, and writing in the book of Revelation, and his conclusion that "in the Apocalypse . . . we see an intention to publish and a wide readership" (108) reflect an inappropriate tendency to project our print-based culture back upon early Christian antiquity.

Also valuable is the work of Colin H. Roberts and T. C. Skeat (1983) who trace "the most momentous development in the history of the book until the invention of printing . . . the replacement of the roll by the codex" (1), and speculate on the reasons for its preference in early Christian circles. Did Christian readers of the first centuries CE wish to differentiate their "sacred book" from Jewish and pagan books? Was the cost-effective advantage of the codex the compelling factor (Skeat 1982)? While these questions remain tantalizingly open, Skeat and Roberts help modern readers to visualize these ancient books, and provide a valuable survey of extant biblical codices.

Skeat (1956) suggests that books were produced for commercial distribution by simultaneous scribal dictation (described by Cornelius Nepos in his *Life of Atticus* 13.3). Yet dictation and reading aloud went hand in hand in Greco-Roman and biblical sources. Pliny the Elder "kept a secretary at his side with book [for reading aloud] and notebook [for dictation]" when traveling, in order "to give every minute to work" (*Letters of the Younger Pliny* 3.5.89).

Moreover, the careful NT reader will recall Paul's use of dictation. Many Pauline letters conclude with a greeting "in (his) own hand" (1 Cor 16:21; Gal 6:11; 2 Thess 3:17), and Romans concludes with a greeting from "I, Tertius, the writer of this letter" (16:22). In the book of Revelation, the medium of dictation (from the exalted Christ) signals the authority of the message written to the churches (Rev 1:19; 2:1, 8, 12, 18; 3:1, 7, 14). The Pauline communities may have used *lectores* (Starr 1991; Botha 1992), or professional readers among their number, to perform the reading (Col 4:16). Reading community writings aloud was an honorific activity (Rev 1:3), and for Eusebius (*Ecclesiastical History* 3.3.6), frequent reading aloud was "a critical test of canonicity" (Rohrbaugh 1993b:117).

Finally, how were Paul's letters "read" by early Christian communities? Botha (1992b) challenges modern readers to read Paul's letters with the cultural realities of ancient communication in mind. Neither was "Paul's letter written by him as an individual, sitting at a desk and dropping a note to some friends" (32), nor would it have been read "as a little book passing from member to member" of a local house church (25). The letter was created orally, transcribed by a literate member of Paul's local group, delivered by a handpicked Pauline emissary, and performed orally by the deliverer of the letter, using all the tools of the Hellenistic orator's trade.

Ancient reading practice, however, presupposes readers, and readers require pedagogy. Ancient authors were fascinated by the process of learning to read because it reduced a very complex set of operations into something that a child could perform with ease: first recognizing the letters by shape and by sound, then learning to vocalize syllables and words, and finally reading "without hesitation . . . five or seven lines in a breath" (Polybius 10.47.6–10). For an overview of education and reading pedagogy in the Hellenistic world, John Townsend (1992) is a useful introduction. Townsend argues that "in the world of the NT, educational theory and practice were essentially Hellenistic" (312). Yet ancient Jewish reading pedagogy was in some ways distinctive, and we treat it separately below. Readers desiring a more exhaustive treatment of education in the Greco-Roman world should consult Henri I. Marrou (1956).

But who was taught to read in Greco-Roman antiquity? Male citizens, slaves trained as pedagogues for children of the elite, retainers (scribes, secretaries, some government and religious officials) of the elite class, some upper-class Greek and more upper-class Roman women. For material on elite Roman women as literate readers, see Sarah B. Pomeroy (1975:170–76; 1977) and Susan G. Cole (1981). Finally, the collected essays in J. H. Humphrey (1991) provide further epigraphical evidence of Roman literacy (Nicholas Horsfall, Keith

Hopkins) and illiteracy (Ann Ellis Hanson) that will reward the disciplined reader's search for detail.

Some readers may ask if such a detailed search is necessary in regard to literate reading, in the light of all we have learned about the oral environment of the NT. Yet the communities that produced the NT documents were not unaffected by the literate reading explosion of the first and second centuries CE, however oral their message and mind-set. Our most compelling evidence of this is that we are reading those documents twenty centuries later, while what was not written down has been lost to us. By the second century CE, Clement of Alexandria commends Christian authors who "speak through books" above those who speak to "those who are present" (*Stromata* 1.1.301), and the literate reading industry of the privileged few is becoming, for Christian book producers, the technology of the future. While questions concerning power, exploitation, and control of early Christian textuality continue to vex biblical readers, it is through such technology that we become auraliterate readers who hear NT authors "speak through books."

6.2 Ancient Jewish Reading Practice and Pedagogy

When he came to Nazareth, where he had been brought up, he went to the synagogue on the sabbath day, as was his custom. He stood up to read, and the scroll of the prophet Isaiah was given to him. He unrolled the scroll and found the place where it was written:

"The Spirit of the Lord is upon me,
    because he has anointed me
        to bring good news to the poor.
He has sent me to proclaim release to the captives
    and recovery of sight to the blind,
        to let the oppressed go free,
to proclaim the year of the Lord's favor."

And he rolled up the scroll, gave it back to the attendant,
and sat down (Luke 4:16–20, NRSV).

When Luke's Jesus inaugurates his public ministry by reading from the scriptures in the synagogue at Nazareth, he is claiming continuity with a public, oral reading tradition that is written into Israel's scriptures. At strategic moments in the history of ancient Israel, its leaders—beginning with Moses—read from "the book of the law" in public assembly, and this reading ceremony confirmed (and—following disobedience and apostasy—reconfirmed) Israel's covenant with Yahweh (Exod 24; Deut 31; 2 Kgs 22; Neh 8). However, this ancient Jewish reading scenario is crafted by Luke, the

Hellenistic writer, to appeal to his non-Jewish audience as well by placing Jesus "within the social sphere of reading culture" (Robbins 1991:325); no other Gospel writer portrays Jesus reading from a written text. But within the social sphere of first-century CE Jewish culture, how likely is it that Jesus was literate?

There are currently two "schools" of thought regarding the importance and extent of literacy in ancient Judaism. Simply stated, they are (1) the "literacy" school, or those scholars claiming significant and widespread Jewish literacy in the second temple period and thereafter to be a by-product of a scribal "religion of the book"; and (2) the "illiteracy" school, or those questioning these claims in the light of sociohistorical research on the broader cultural conditions required for literacy to flourish. Both of these perspectives can be useful if we correlate the "literacy" school with the reading practice and pedagogy of the elite minority (chief priests, Pharisees, scribes, some wealthy landowners), and the "illiteracy" school with that of the nonelite majority (peasants, artisans, women).

Beginning with the "literacy" school, the standard reference for ancient Jewish reading practice is *Mikra* (Mulder 1988). *"Mikra"* is the technical Hebrew word applied to the reading and reciting of Scripture; as it is used in this volume, it refers primarily to the written text of Scripture and its interpretation. The interested reader should begin with Charles Perrot (1988), who provides a concise introduction to ancient Jewish reading and its historical connection with the synagogue liturgy. A concluding section interprets Jesus' reading in the synagogue (Luke 4:16–20, above) from an ancient Jewish perspective (158–59).

Shmuel Safrai (1976) reviews Jewish reading pedagogy both on the elementary (the *bet sefer*) and more advanced (the *bet midrash*) levels, and argues (contra Bar-Ilan 1992; see below) that Israel was an "education-centered society" by 70 CE (956), and that "as a rule, children did attend school, learned to read the books of the Bible [in Hebrew] and acquired the basic knowledge which enabled them to participate in Jewish life" (949).

While Hebrew reading pedagogy was similar to that of learning to read Greek, there were two important differences. First, Hebrew vowels were not marked in antiquity and had to be supplied by the teacher. Thus "a child or adult who had not received from his teacher the tradition for the reading of a given passage did not know how to read it correctly" (Safrai 1976:950). Second, writing was not typically taught in conjunction with reading, as it was in Greek pedagogy (see Aaron Demsky and Meir Bar-Ilan 1988; Bar-Ilan 1988).

Evidence of women's literacy in Jewish antiquity is based largely on mishnaic and talmudic sources. An important article by Anne Goldfeld (1975) documents talmudic evidence on literate women readers in rabbinic Judaism. Judith Wegner examines the mishnaic and talmudic debate concerning women's eligibility for public reading of the Torah scroll (1988:156–57). Adeline Fehribach (1992) concludes that "the majority decision of the Mishnah was to educate women only to the point where they could function in society without becoming too liberated" (56). Antoinette Clark Wire finds women in Matthew's first-century scribal culture "non-literate" (1991:115).

How many Jewish children of the first century learned Hebrew? The "illiteracy school" draws a very different profile of cultural literacy. Bar-Ilan (1992) defends his projection of 3 percent literacy:

> At first glance this figure looks quite low, and maybe too low. However, in a traditional society, knowing how to read was not a necessity; neither for economic reasons, nor for intellectual ones. . . . Why should a farmer send his son to learn how to read when it entails a waste of working time (= money)? Why should he himself learn how to read if his culture is based on an oral tradition (though with a written Torah)? According to the Torah, there is no need to read or write, except for writing the Mezuzah *Teflin*, and the Torah itself. However, for these purposes there was always a scribe, so a Jew in antiquity could fulfil the commandments of the Torah while being illiterate (55).

If Jesus was a product of an "education-centered society," then it follows that those taking that position would assume that he was literate. Hebrew scholars such as Safrai have argued that Jesus was a scribaliterate Jew, fluent in Hebrew and Greek, and a product of the ancient Jewish reading tradition reflected in the Mishnah and the Talmud. But if the historical Jesus was an uneducated peasant/artisan, this view cannot be correct.

The scholarly issues raised are complex but intriguing. What is certain is that, on the one hand, Luke portrays Jesus as an oculiterate reader, and Matthew portrays him as an oraliterate reader. On the other hand, the opponents of Jesus in the Fourth Gospel consider Jesus' "learning" (γράμματα, *grammata*) deviant because he has "never been taught" (John 7:15). However, at least some members of Hellenistic and Jewish/Christian communities were scribaliterate readers committed to their own reading "schools," and in their hands, such scribal literacy became a means of community formation, legitimation, and apostolic continuity.

Krister Stendahl (1968) imagines the Matthean community as a highly literate scribal "school." Donald Juel (1988) profiles the hermeneutical methods common to first-century Jewish and Christian scribaliterate reading. Vernon Robbins (1992) places Mark's Gospel in the context of the Hellenistic rhetorical "schools." Bruce Chilton (1984) imagines Jesus preaching from Aramaic targums (vernacular translations of the Hebrew scriptures). Read critically, all these authors can contribute to our understanding of the scribaliterate reading practices encountered in the NT.

Finally, a survey of ancient Jewish reading is incomplete without some reference to the community of the Dead Sea Scrolls. Our concern is not so much with who this community was (Essenes? a different sect?) as with how they read, and with the significance of sacred reading for their community. According to their *Manual of Discipline*, "The general members of the community are to keep awake for a third of all the nights of the year reading book(s), studying the Law and worshiping together" (1QS 6:7–8). In other words, literate reading of Torah and other holy books was integral to community formation and self-understanding. While a more detailed review of Qumran literature is beyond the scope of this chapter, a succinct profile of Qumran as a scribaliterate community can be found in Wire (1991:94–98).

7.0 Social-Science Resources for Ancient Reading Theory and Practice

And they brought him a coin. And Jesus said to them, "Whose likeness and inscription is this?" They said, "Caesar's." Then he said to them, "Render therefore to Caesar the things that are Caesar's, and to God the things that are God's" (Matt 22:19–21, RSV).

From the perspective of social-science criticism, ancient reading is embedded in a larger cultural context of ancient communication in which coins were mass-produced texts (Botha 1992a:205), and "money talked." People did not have to be literate to read coins, but coins were designed with a reading audience in mind (Harris 1989:213), employing both iconography (εἰκών, *eikōn*) and writing (ἐπιγραφή, *epigraphē*) to get political messages across to the general populace.

Within this context of ancient communication, the reader should recognize the passage above as another reading controversy between Jesus and his opponents. The question of whether to pay taxes to Caesar was politically dangerous and religiously controversial for Jews under Roman rule. To answer the question, Jesus appeals to the textual authority—not of Torah but of Tiberius (Caesar), inscribed on official Roman coinage. In a culture for whom "writing and money were two powerful agents of communication and control which helped integrate the Roman empire into a single political system" (Hopkins 1991:157), reading coins was no less important than reading Torah scrolls, and much more common. By broadening the context of first-century reading and readers, social-science perspectives can deepen our understanding of how reading worked within the cultural communications system, where it was taking place, and how it was practiced by particular social groups.

This final section provides a profile of available materials most relevant to a social-science analysis of the cultural reading system in biblical antiquity. Given the right conceptual tools, all the selections in this chapter are grist for this mill. While some pertinent materials have already been cited in earlier sections, the sources included here focus on (1) ancient communication studies, (2) cross-cultural reading studies, and (3) social-historical reconstructions of nonelite readers and reading communities.

7.1 Ancient Communication Studies

Botha has written extensively on the subject of ancient communication and the anachronistic understandings that modern readers impose on reading and writing in antiquity. In addition to works we have already cited (Botha 1992a, 1992b), readers might begin with his 1990 article. Here he argues that a literate bias pervades NT scholarship and produces "uncritical and ethnocentrist concepts of NT writings and traditions" (43) that do not take the oral environment of the documents into consideration. Botha's sociocritical analysis of orality-literacy studies gives biblical readers valuable tools for reading ancient authors in terms of their own communication systems. (Selections previously reviewed that also emphasize the social construction of ancient communication include Ong, Goody, Street, Finnegan, and Dewey.)

7.2 Cross-Cultural Reading Studies

Cross-cultural reading studies utilize conceptual models from the social sciences to compare, contrast, or describe reading in different cultural contexts. Bruce J. Malina (1991) offers an excellent introduction to this kind of analysis. While he emphasizes the modern reader's appropriation of an ancient text through apposite "reading scenario models" (15), his description of "low context" (U.S.A.) and "high context" (Mediterranean antiquity) cultures in terms of reading settings is most useful for our understanding of an ancient reading environment where much must be "read between the lines" from a shared cultural context.

Vernon Robbins (1991) provides a social-science model of social location for the Luke–Acts community. Robbins's discussion of "inscribed author" and "inscribed reader" versus "implied author and implied reader" (311) is helpful, as is the profile of the Lukan writing environment (or "technological sphere of writing," 319).

From a social-science perspective, reader-response criticism of ancient biblical reading is a cross-cultural enterprise. Bruce J. Malina and Richard L. Rohrbaugh (1992) provide just such a cross-cultural reader's guide to the Synoptic Gospels, arguing that without adequate cultural background in the reading scenarios common to first-century reader-hearers, "readers socialized in the industrial world are unlikely to complete the text of the NT in ways the ancient authors could have imagined" (14). This commentary helps modern readers reconstruct what Robert Jauss has called the original "horizon of reading" (1982:28) of the Gospel documents, and what Robert Scholes (1989) identifies as cultural "protocols of reading."

Finally, the cross-disciplinary fields of reading anthropology and ethnography have much to offer the student of ancient reading in biblical context. Jesper Svenbro (1993) traces the evolution of reading in Greek antiquity from its oral/aural origins to the development of silent reading. While Svenbro writes for Greek classicists and not for the common reader, his work has important implications for students conversant with the honor-shame cultures of biblical antiquity. Svenbro argues that ancient reading is a cultural strategy for communicating fame (or honor!) through the voice of a reader who "re-sounds" written letters. While he strains perhaps too ingeniously to discover a cultural shift from vocalized reading to silent reading analogous to that of his mentor, Eric Havelock (from an oral to a literate consciousness), Svenbro's is the most comprehensive study of ancient reading to date, and should be consulted by the serious student.

Jonathan Boyarin (1993) offers a valuable cross-disciplinary collection of essays on reading from the fields of anthropology, literature, and cultural studies. While we recommend much in this volume, selections by Daniel Boyarin (10–37) and Susan Noakes (38–57) are essential for the biblical student. Boyarin contrasts modern and biblical connotations of reading to conclude that reading in the ancient biblical texts is a speech act that has societal consequences, while reading in medieval Europe already bears the marks of a more interior, cerebral, and private activity. Noakes contrasts the original Lukan context of Jesus' reading in the synagogue (Luke 4:14–19) with its later cultural appropriations.

7.3 Resources for Reconstruction of Readers and Reading Communities

Social-science criticism can also help reconstitute nonelite, oraliterate, and auraliterate readers who include most of the ancient "reading public." How would a first-century peasant "hear" and hence "read" the parable of the Sower or of the Good Samaritan? Is Mary's recital of the Magnificat in Luke's Gospel an accurate reflection of women's orality, or is a male author putting words in Mary's mouth?

Circum-Mediterranean peasant studies can introduce us to an auraliterate peasant audience's response to hearing Luke's parable of the Good Samaritan (Oakman 1992) or Matthew's parable of the talents (Rohrbaugh 1993a). Lila Abu-Lughod (1986) provides a model of (bedouin) women's oral poetry that combines the secrecy and intimacy of the Mediterranean women's world with a deceptively public expression of what would be "shameful" if spoken in ordinary prose. While Luke's Mary speaks in the Septuagint Greek typically reserved for educated males, she claims the poetic license implicit in the genre of women's oral poetry in her subversive song of cultural reversal (Luke 1:46–56). Malina and Rohrbaugh include male/female oral poetry as a reading scenario (1992:293–94).

Social-historical studies can also be useful to biblical readers for reconstructing the original reading communities and audiences of biblical documents. Two notable examples are Wire (1991), who uses sociological models to determine the status of women's literacy in Matthew's community, and Rohrbaugh (1993b), who utilizes data on ancient literacy and illiteracy to locate Mark's audience on the auraliterate end of the spectrum. Both of these articles provide excellent examples of how biblical scholarship benefits from a culturally contexted study of "the social practices of reading and writing" (Street 1984:1).

8.0 Ancient Reading and Modern Biblical Readers: Concluding Perspectives

In conclusion, how can a knowledge of how reading worked in the cultural world of the NT help us, as modern biblical readers? First, it will help us to understand the process of ancient communication as one of interaction between orality and literacy, and to place ancient reading within that dynamic context. Second, it will sensitize us to ethnocentric constructions of literacy and illiteracy that are inappropriately applied to biblical culture. Third, it should make us more aware of the relationship between oral and written transmission of the biblical documents, and the issues of power and control implied in that relationship. Finally, it invites us to imagine a picture of reading in NT antiquity both culturally specific and complete enough to include all the readers of society in its vision.

"Do you understand what you are reading?" Philip asked the Ethiopian eunuch. "How can I," he replied, "unless someone guide me?" If our first-century eunuch needed a guide into the intricacies of reading a biblical text, how much more do we from so much greater cultural distance. This article has provided a modern reader's guide to ancient reading in the cultural world of the NT. In the words of another ancient biblical reader (Hillel), "The rest is commentary. Go and read!"

9.0 Works Cited

Abu-Lughod, Lila
   1986   *Veiled Sentiments: Honor and Poetry in a Bedouin Society.*
           Berkeley: University of California Press.
Achtemeier, Paul J.
   1990   *"Omne verbum sonat:* The New Testament and the Oral
           Environment of Late Western Antiquity." *JBL* 109:3–27.
Bar-Ilan, Meir
   1988   "Scribes and Books in the Late Second Commonwealth
           and Rabbinic Period." In *Mikra: Text, Translation,
           Reading, and Interpretation of the Hebrew Bible in Ancient
           Judaism and Early Christianity.* Ed. M. J. Mulder. Pages
           21–38. CRINT 2/1. Minneapolis: Fortress; Assen and
           Maastricht: Van Gorcum.
   1992   "Illiteracy in the Land of Israel in the First Centuries
           C.E." In *Essays in the Social Scientific Study of Judaism
           and Jewish Society.* Ed. S. Fishbane and S. Schoenfeld.
           2:46–61. Hoboken, N.J.: Ktav.
Botha, P.J. J.
   1990   "Mute Manuscripts: Analysing a Neglected Aspect of
           Ancient Communication." *Theologia Evangelica*
           23(3):35–47.
   1992a   "Greco-Roman Literacy as Setting for New Testament
           Writings." *Neotestamentica* 26(1):195–215.
   1992b   "Letter Writing and Oral Communication in Antiquity:
           Suggested Implications for the Interpretation of Paul's
           Letter to the Galatians." *Scriptura* 42:17–34.
Boyarin, Daniel
   1993   "Placing Reading: Ancient Israel and Medieval
           Europe." In *The Ethnography of Reading.* Ed. J. Boyarin.
           Pages 10–37. Berkeley: University of California Press.
Boyarin, Jonathan
   1993   *The Ethnography of Reading.* Berkeley: University of
           California Press.

Chilton, Bruce D.
    1984   *A Galilean Rabbi and His Bible: Jesus' Use of the Interpreted Scripture of His Time.* Wilmington, Del.: Glazier.
Cole, Susan G.
    1981   "Could Greek Women Read and Write?" In *Reflections of Women in Antiquity.* Ed. H. P. Foley. Pages 219–45. New York: Gordon & Breach.
Darnton, Robert
    1992   "History of Reading." In *New Perspectives on Historical Writing.* Ed. Peter Burke. Pages 140–67. University Park: University of Pennsylvania Press.
Demsky, Aaron, and Meir Bar-Ilan
    1988   "Writing in Ancient Israel and Early Judaism." In *Mikra: Text, Translation, Reading, and Interpretation of the Hebrew Bible in Ancient Judaism and Early Christianity.* Ed. M. J. Mulder. Pages 1–38. CRINT 2/1. Philadelphia: Fortress; Assen and Maastricht: Van Gorcum.
Dewey, Joanna
    1995a   "Textuality in an Oral Culture: A Survey of the Pauline Traditions." In *Orality and Textuality in Early Christian Literature.* Ed. Joanna Dewey. Pages 37–66. *Semeia* 65. Atlanta: Scholars Press.
    _____ , ed.
    1995b   *Orality and Textuality in Early Christian Literature. Semeia* 65. Atlanta: Scholars Press.
Fehribach, Adeline
    1992   "Between Text and Context: Scripture, Society and the Role of Women in Formative Judaism." In *Recovering the Role of Women: Power and Authority in Rabbinic Jewish Society.* Ed. P. J. Haas. Pages 39–60. South Florida Studies in the History of Judaism 59. Atlanta: Scholars Press.
Finnegan, Ruth
    1988   *Literacy and Orality: Studies in the Technology of Communication.* Oxford: Basil Blackwell.
Gamble, Harry Y.
    1995   *Books and Readers in the Early Church: A History of Early Christian Texts.* New Haven: Yale University Press.
Gerhardsson, Birger
    1961   *Memory and Manuscript: Oral Tradition and Written Transmission in Rabbinic Judaism and Early Christianity.* Lund: Gleerup.
Goldfeld, Anne
    1975   "Women as Sources of Torah in the Rabbinic Tradition." *Judaism* 94:245–56.

Goody, Jack
    1968   *Literacy in Traditional Societies.* Cambridge: Cambridge
            University Press.
    1986   *The Logic of Writing and the Organization of Society.*
            Cambridge: Cambridge University Press.
    1987   *The Interface Between the Written and the Oral.*
            Cambridge: Cambridge University Press.
Hanson, Anne E.
    1991   "Ancient Illiteracy." In *Literacy in the Roman World.* Ed.
            J. H. Humphrey. Pages 159–98. Journal of Roman
            Archaeology Supplement 3. Ann Arbor: Journal of
            Roman Archaeology Supplementary Series.
Harris, William V.
    1989   *Ancient Literacy.* Cambridge: Harvard University Press.
Havelock, Eric A.
    1982   *The Literate Revolution in Greece and Its Cultural
            Consequences.* Princeton: Princeton University Press.
Hendrickson, G. L.
    1929   "Ancient Reading." *CJ* 25:182–96.
Hopkins, Keith
    1991   "Conquest by Book." In *Literacy in the Roman World.* Ed.
            J. H. Humphrey. Pages 13–58. Journal of Roman
            Archaeology Supplement 3. Ann Arbor: Journal of
            Roman Archaeology Supplementary Series.
Horsfall, Nicholas
    1991   "Statistics or States of Mind?" In *Literacy in the Roman
            World.* Ed. J. H. Humphrey. Pages 59–76. Journal of
            Roman Archaeology Supplement 3. Ann Arbor: Journal
            of Roman Archaeology Supplementary Series.
Humphrey, J. H., ed.
    1991   *Literacy in the Roman World.* Journal of Roman
            Archaeology Supplement 3. Ann Arbor: Journal of
            Roman Archaeology Supplementary Series.
Jauss, Hans Robert
    1982   *Toward an Aesthetic of Reception.* Trans. Timothy Bahti.
            Minneapolis: University of Minnesota Press.
Juel, Donald
    1988   *Messianic Exegesis: Christological Interpretation of the Old
            Testament in Early Christianity.* Philadelphia: Fortress.
Kelber, Werner H.
    1983   *The Oral and the Written Gospel: The Hermeneutics of
            Speaking and Writing in the Synoptic Tradition, Mark, Paul
            and Q.* Philadelphia: Fortress.
    1995a   "Jesus and Tradition: Words in Time and Words in
            Space." In *Orality and Textuality in Early Christian*

Literature. Ed. Joanna Dewey. Pages 139–67. *Semeia* 65. Atlanta: Scholars Press.

1995b   "Modalities of Communication, Cognition, and Physiology of Perception: Orality, Rhetoric, Scribality." In *Orality and Textuality in Early Christian Literature*. Ed. Joanna Dewey. Pages 193–216. *Semeia* 65. Atlanta: Scholars Press.

Kenyon, Frederick G.
1951   *Books and Readers in Ancient Greece and Rome*. Oxford: Clarendon.

Knox, Bernard M. W.
1968   "Silent Reading in Antiquity." *GRBS* 9:421–35.

Malina, Bruce J.
1991   "Reading Theory Perspective: Reading Luke-Acts." In *The Social World of Luke–Acts: Models for Interpretation*. Ed. Jerome H. Neyrey. Pages 3–24. Peabody, Mass.: Hendrickson.

Malina, Bruce J., and Richard L. Rohrbaugh
1992   *Social Science Commentary on the Synoptic Gospels*. Minneapolis: Fortress.

Marrou, Henri I.
1956   *A History of Education in Antiquity*. Trans. George Lamb. New York: Sheed and Ward. (Reprint, Madison: University of Wisconsin, 1982.)

Mulder, M. J., ed.
1988   *Mikra: Text, Translation, Reading, and Interpretation of the Hebrew Bible in Ancient Judaism and Early Christianity*. CRINT 2/1. Philadelphia: Fortress; Assen and Maastricht: Van Gorcum.

Neyrey, Jerome H., ed.
1990   *The Social World of Luke–Acts: Models for Interpretation*. Peabody, Mass.: Hendrickson.

Noakes, Susan
1993   "Gracious Words: Luke's Jesus and the Reading of Sacred Poetry at the Beginning of the Christian Era." In *The Ethnography of Reading*. Ed. J. Boyarin. Pages 38–57. Berkeley: University of California Press.

Oakman, Douglas E.
1992   "Was Jesus a Peasant? Implications for Reading the Samaritan Story (Luke 10:30–35)." *BTB* 22:117–25.

Ong, Walter J.
1982   *Orality and Literacy: The Technologizing of the Word*. London: Methuen.

Perrot, Charles
1988   "The Reading of the Bible in the Ancient Synagogue." In *Mikra: Text, Translation, Reading, and Interpretation of*

the Hebrew Bible in Ancient Judaism and Early Christianity.
Ed. M. J. Mulder. Pages 137–59. CRINT 2/1.
Minneapolis: Fortress; Assen and Maastricht: Van
Gorcum.

Pomeroy, Sarah B.
1975   *Goddesses, Whores, Wives, and Slaves: Women in Classical
Antiquity.* New York: Schocken.
1977   *"Technikai kai mousikai:* The Education of Women in the
Fourth Century and in the Hellenistic Period." *AJAH*
2:51–68.

Robbins, Vernon K.
1991   "The Social Location of the Implied Author of
Luke-Acts." In *The Social World of Luke–Acts: Models for
Interpretation.* Ed. Jerome H. Neyrey. Pages 305–32.
Peabody, Mass.: Hendrickson.
1992   *Jesus the Teacher: A Socio-Rhetorical Interpretation of Mark.*
2d ed. Minneapolis: Fortress.

Roberts, Colin H., and T. C. Skeat
1983   *The Birth of the Codex.* London: Oxford University Press.

Rohrbaugh, Richard L.
1993a   "A Peasant Reading of the Parable of the
Talents/Pounds: A Text of Terror?" *BTB* 23:32–39.
1993b   "The Social Location of the Marcan Audience." *BTB*
23:114–27.

Safrai, Shmuel
1976   "Education and the Study of Torah." In *The Jewish
People in the First Century: Historical Geography, Political
History, Social, Cultural and Religious Life and
Institutions.* Ed. S. Safrai and M. Stern. Pages 945–70.
CRINT 1/2. Philadelphia: Fortress; Assen and
Amsterdam: Van Gorcum.

Schenkevald, Dirk M.
1992   "Prose Usage of *AKOYEIN* 'To Read.' " *Classical
Quarterly* 42:129–41.

Scholes, Robert
1989   *Protocols of Reading.* New Haven: Yale University Press.

Skeat, T. C.
1956   "The Use of Dictation in Ancient Book-Production."
Proceedings of the British Academy 42:179–208.
1982   "The Length of the Standard Papyrus Roll and the
Cost-Advantage of the Codex." *ZPE* 45:169–75.

Starr, Raymond J.
1991   "Reading Aloud: *Lectores* and Roman Reading." *CJ*
86:337–43.

Stendahl, Krister
  1968   *The School of St. Matthew.* Philadelphia: Fortress.
Street, Brian V.
  1984   *Literacy in Theory and in Practice.* Cambridge:
          Cambridge University Press.
Svenbro, Jesper
  1993   *Phrasikleia: An Anthropology of Reading in Ancient Greece.*
          Trans. Janet Lloyd. Ithaca: Cornell University Press.
Thomas, Rosalind
  1992   *Literacy and Orality in Ancient Greece.* Cambridge:
          Cambridge University Press.
Townsend, John T.
  1992   "Education: Greco-Roman Period." In *ABD.* 2:312–17.
          New York: Doubleday.
UNESCO
  1977   *Statistics of Educational Attainment and Illiteracy,*
          1945–1974. UNESCO Statistical Reports and Studies 22.
          Paris, UNESCO.
Wegner, Judith Romney
  1988   *Chattel or Person? The Status of Women in the Mishnah.*
          New York: Oxford University Press.
Wire, Antoinette Clark
  1991   "Gender Roles in a Scribal Community." In *Social
          History of the Matthean Community: Cross-Disciplinary
          Approaches.* Ed. David L. Balch. Pages 87–121.
          Minneapolis: Fortress.

Index of Modern Authors

Index of Ancient Sources